S0-BRI-806

WITHDRAWN

WITHDRAWN

MOTION
PICTURES

MOTION
PICTURES

The Development of an Art
from Silent Films
to the Age of Television

By A. R. Fulton

NORMAN

UNIVERSITY OF OKLAHOMA PRESS

139344

By A. R. Fulton

Motion Pictures: The Development of an Art from Silent Films to the Age of Television (Norman, 1960)

Drama and Theatre Illustrated by Seven Modern Plays (New York, 1946)

The publication of this work has been aided by a grant from the Ford Foundation.

PN
1994
F83
1960

Library of Congress Catalog Card Number: 60–13471

Copyright 1960 by the University of Oklahoma Press, Publishing Division of the University. Composed and printed at Norman, Oklahoma, U.S.A., by the University of Oklahoma Press. First edition.

Comm.

5.00 - 3.50

1-16-61 McClurg

To Barbara

Preface

O_f all the cultural phenomena of the first half of the twentieth century, the most characteristic of the age and the most spectacular are the origin and rise of the motion pictures. No other art emerged from a machine, and no other art is so dependent upon it. No other became established so rapidly, and no other can claim—for the first half century of its existence—such meritorious work. No other has ever become so popular, and no other is so little understood.

The explanation of the paradox lies not so much in the newness of the motion pictures as in their popularity. Consider the motion-picture audience. The most nearly comparable was the London audience that attended plays in the time of the first Queen Elizabeth. All classes of Londoners filled the Bankside playhouses, from apprentices and other illiterates to courtiers of one of the most cultivated courts the world has known. If Elizabethan playwrights made concessions to spectators for the most part capable of nothing but inexplicable dumb shows and noise, motion-picture directors reckon no less with popcorn-munching groundlings capable of little more. But even the judicious may be so fascinated by the effects which a director has obtained as not to appreciate how he has obtained them. Disparity between enjoyment and appreciation is greater for the motion pictures than for any of the other arts.

Scientific accomplishments of the age made the motion-picture machine possible, and the invention of the machine came about almost as if it had been waiting only for those accomplishments. Although the motion pictures remained for a while primarily only a machine, the art was not long in emerging. The difference between the art and the machine is clarified by an understanding of how the art emerged and how it developed, at first on the silent screen and then on the screen embellished with sound. And an understanding of the difference between the art and the machine will help to resolve some of the questions about television, in particular: Will television make the motion pictures obsolete?

The province of the motion pictures is appreciated through comparison and contrast of the cinematic way of story-telling with the dramatic and the epic ways. Even after the principle of motion-picture editing was discovered, there was a chance that the motion pictures would be modeled after the drama. The Famous Players Company was established in 1912 to produce plays on the screen instead of on the stage—"Famous Players in Famous Plays"—and the project was inaugurated with the photoplay *Queen Elizabeth,* starring Sarah Bernhardt. Had the course of motion-picture history not somehow changed, acting would have become of greater importance to the motion pictures than it has. The difference between the art of the motion pictures and that of the theatre explains, for example, why Charlie Chaplin, one of the greatest of all motion-picture artists, has contributed little to motion-picture art. The tendency to associate stage and screen, however, persists, even among film reviewers, most of whom review films as though they were plays.

Although plays can be studied by their texts alone, there is no comparable way of studying films. It is true that scenarios are occasionally published, and an examination of a scenario is illuminating. But because a scenario is only a *description* of a film, it is different from the script of a play, which *is* the play. If there is any comparison, it is between the film and the production of the play on the stage. But since a film can be preserved and the production of a play cannot—cannot, in fact, be identically reproduced even in consecutive performances—the study of the motion pictures presents an advantage.

An impetus to the study of the motion pictures has been the institution of 16 mm. film. By virtue of this small-size film, motion pictures originally printed on 35 mm., or commercial, film can be reprinted and exhibited comparatively inexpensively. The Museum of Modern Art established its Film Library in 1935, one of its purposes being the rental of films to colleges, film societies, community study groups, and similar organizations. Other agencies for the distribution of 16 mm. films have since been established. The impetus has been furthered by the announcement that, as the result of a new process, the paper prints of motion pictures made between 1894 and 1912 and deposited for copyright in the Library of Congress can be reproduced on 16 mm. film.

Although, for the most part, the films chosen for this study are discussed chronologically, the book is a history only in that these films represent the origin of the motion pictures as a machine and the emergence of the art dependent upon it. Because, unlike a play, a film must be seen to be appreciated, the films used for illustration are among those available in 16 mm. The films have been chosen, not because they are the greatest in the history of motion pictures—although indeed some of them are—but because an appreciation of them clarifies the difference between the art and the machine and thus increases appreciation of the art itself—its province, its accomplishments, and its possibilities.

This book, representing my own long-term effort to interpret motion pictures as an artistic medium, would not be complete without an expression from me of my indebtedness to the Purdue Research Foundation for the generous aid it has contributed to publication.

I am grateful to Mrs. Ila Carroll and W. S. Hastings for corrections of proofs.

A. R. FULTON

West Lafayette, Indiana
July 1, 1960

Acknowledgments

Permissions have been granted to quote from the following copyrighted material: W. H. Auden, "Night Mail"—poem reprinted by permission of Her Britannic Majesty's Postmaster General and John Grierson, producer of the film *Night Mail;* J. M. Barrie, "Alice Sit-by-the-Fire," *The Plays of J. M. Barrie* (New York: Charles Scribner's Sons, 1945); Stephen Vincent Benét, "The Devil and Daniel Webster," *The Selected Works of Stephen Vincent Benét* (New York: Rinehart and Co., Inc., 1937)—quotations reprinted by permission of the publishers and Brandt and Brandt, agents for the estate of Stephen Vincent Benét; Maurice Bessy and Lo Duca, *Georges Méliès, Mage; et "Mes Mémoires" par Méliès* (Paris: Éditions Prisma, 1945); Willa Cather, *Not Under Forty* (New York: Alfred A. Knopf, Inc., 1936) ; Sergei Eisenstein, *Film Form,* ed. and trans. by Jay Leyda (New York: Harcourt, Brace and Co., Inc., 1949; A. R. Fulton, "It's Exactly Like the Play," *Theatre Arts,* Vol. XXXVII (March, 1953)—quotations reprinted by permission of *Theatre Arts* magazine; A. R. Fulton, "Stroheim's 'Greed,'" *Films in Review,* Vol. VI (June–July, 1955)—quotations reprinted by permission of *Films in Review;* Lillian Gish, "The Birth of an Era," *Stage,* Vol. XIV (January, 1937)—quotations reprinted by permission of Lillian Gish; St. John Hankin, "A Note on Happy Endings," *The Dramatic Works of St. John Hankin* (3 vols., New York: Richards Press Ltd., 1912); Theodore Huff, Script for *The Birth of a Nation*—quotations reprinted by permission of the Museum of Modern Art Film Library; David Lean, "Brief Encounter," *Penguin Film Review,* No. 4 (London and New York, 1947)—quotations reprinted by permission of Penguin Books Ltd., publishers; David Lean, "Extract from the Post-Production Script of *Great Expectations*: Pip Steals the Food," *The Cinema 1952*—quotations reprinted by permission of Penguin Books Ltd., publishers; Pare Lorentz, *The River* (New York, 1938)—quotations reprinted by permission of Pare Lorentz, author and director of the motion picture; W. Somerset Maugham and R. C. Sherriff, "The Facts of Life," *Quartet* (Garden City: Doubleday and Co., Inc., 1950); Liam O'Flaherty, *The Informer* (New York: Harcourt, Brace and Co., Inc., 1925) ; Eugene O'Neill, *Anna Christie: A Play in Four Acts* (New York: Random House, Inc., 1922); Karel Reisz, *The Technique of Film Editing*, 3rd ed. (London and New York: Focal Press Ltd., in co-operation with the British Film Academy, 1955); Robert Emmet Sherwood, *Abe Lincoln in Illinois* (New York: Charles Scribner's Sons, 1939); Seymour Stern, "An Index to the Creative Work of David Wark Griffith," Special Supplement to *Sight and Sound*, Index Series No. 8, Part II (September, 1946)—quotations reprinted by permission of the British Film Institute; Seymour Stern, "The Birth of a Nation," Special Supplement to *Sight and Sound*, Index Series No. 4 (July, 1945)—quotations reprinted by permission of the British Film Institute.

For the illustrations used in this volume I am indebted to the Museum of Modern Art Film Library. My thanks to the Library for allowing me to reproduce these photographs.

A. R. FULTON

Contents

Illustrations

MOTION
PICTURES

1. The Machine

Although the attempt to represent the illusion of motion by pictures is older than civilization, the art of the motion pictures began only half a century ago. From that prehistoric day when an artist drew a many-legged boar on the wall of a cave in Altamira, Spain, down through the centuries, during which time various other devices were originated to depict motion, man had to wait until modern times before the motion pictures could be born. This waiting was necessary because the motion pictures depend, to a greater extent than any other art, upon machinery. The motion pictures, the newest of the arts, the only art to originate in the twentieth century, are a product of the Machine Age.

The motion pictures did not originate as art but as a machine. They were invented. That is, the machinery that makes the pictures, and that makes them motion pictures, was invented. Thus the term *motion pictures* means the device as well as the art.

If one were to hold a piece of motion-picture film up to the light, he would see that it is a series of little pictures arranged crosswise to the length of the film. Each picture, or frame, is approximately four-fifths of an inch wide and three-fifths of an inch high. Examining the frames in relation to one another, one notices that, although each frame may be a picture of the same scene, the position of the objects in each frame is slightly different. When the film, which contains sixteen frames to each foot of film, is run through the motion-picture projector at the rate of twenty-four frames per second, enlarged images of the frames are cast in corresponding succession onto the screen.

The projector operates on the principle of that old toy the

3

magic lantern (and of its modern counterpart, the slide projector). When a glass slide was inserted in the lantern, an image of the slide was cast upon the screen by means of a light directed through the slide and, to enlarge the image, through a magnifying lens. The frames in the film are comparable to the slides in the magic lantern. The images of the frames as they are cast upon the screen do not move any more than the images of the magic-lantern slides moved. The term *motion pictures* is therefore misleading. The pictures do not move but only seem to.

The illusion of motion is caused partly by persistence of vision, the optical fact—said to have been discovered by the astronomer Ptolemy in the second century—that it takes the eye a fraction of a second to record the impression of an image and transmit it to the brain and that, having received the impression, the eye retains it one-twentieth to one-tenth of one second after the image itself has disappeared. Accordingly, the motion-picture projector includes a mechanism which draws the film between the light and the lens in a stop-and-go motion, the film pausing long enough at each frame to allow the eye to take in the picture; then, as a shutter closes and the eye retains the image, the mechanism propels the film ahead to the next frame. The perforations along the edge of the film enable the teeth of the driving mechanism to engage the film and not only to move it along from one frame to the next but also to hold it steady. The stop-and-go motion gives the illusion of a continuous picture. If the film did not pause at each frame, the impression that the eye receives would be blurred.

The illusion that motion pictures move depends also on the imagination of the spectator. Watching a succession of pictures, each one representing a change in the position of the image from that of the preceding one, the spectator imagines that the image is moving because he associates it with a corresponding object that he has seen actually moving. Furthermore, he imagines that he sees more of the picture than he does, for the camera has recorded on the film only a fraction of what happened. A film moves through the camera with a stop-and-go motion similar to that in the projector but with this difference: whereas in the projector the film pauses longer at each frame than the time it takes to move to the next frame, in the camera the film pauses only briefly at each frame, the longer time being that between frames. The reason for this difference is that it takes the eye longer to receive the image and transmit it to the brain than it does for the camera to receive the image and record it on the film. A film moves through the camera at the rate of twenty-four frames per second. Every second, then, the camera takes twenty-four individual snapshots. Suppose that each exposure is 1/500 of one second. The camera would then record 24/500 of what happens in that second, or about 5 per cent. But when the film is projected onto the screen, the spectator has the illusion not only that the pictures are moving but also that he is seeing 95 per cent more than he is. In a film that is one and one-half hours long, the spectator would see only four and one-half minutes of pictures.

Principles of vision and the manufacture of film, camera, and projector—these matters of optics, chemistry, and machinery are inherent in the motion pictures as a device. The art of the motion pictures, depending on the instrument, had to wait for the invention of the device. The machine, however, was not invented to make the art possible. It was originated merely as a device—a device to record and depict motion.

Some of the principles of motion-picture machinery were understood long before the device was perfected, and crude variations of the machinery were devised. As early as 1640, Athanasius Kirchener demonstrated his *Magia Catoptrica* ("magic lantern") in Rome. Almost two centuries later, in 1832, Simon Ritter von Stampfer, of Vienna, made a device he called the stroboscope, whereby drawings on the rim of a disc viewed through slits in a second disc simulated motion. Then, in 1853, another Viennese, Franz von Uchatius, used a magic lantern to project the stroboscope pictures onto a wall. One of the most popular early versions of the motion-picture machine was the zoetrope, or wheel of life. Devised in 1833 by an Englishman, William George Horner, as the Daedalum, or wheel of the devil —because its first pictures were of the devil—it consisted of a shallow cylinder about one foot in diameter with vertical slots in the edge and, on the inside, a series of pictures which, seen through the slots, seemed to move when the wheel was turned. Another kind of wheel machine, patented in 1861 by Coleman Sellers, a Philadelphia machinist, was an arrangement whereby photographs were mounted on paddles. Sellers called his paddle-wheel machine the kinematoscope. Such were the early gropings toward the motion pictures. They were, however, gropings primarily in the direction of motion-picture projection. The motion-picture camera had to wait for the invention not only of photography but also of photographic film.

Photography came first. The date of its origin is usually given as 1839, the year in which the Frenchman Louis Daguerre invented a process whereby a photograph could be exposed on a chemically coated plate. Although the sitter for a daguerreotype had to remain motionless for the several minutes it took the plate to become exposed, refinements in the process decreased the length of this time. In 1872, it occurred to Governor Leland Stanford of California that photography might be the means whereby he could prove his contention—and win a bet of $25,000 —that a running horse takes all four feet off the ground simultaneously. Accordingly, he employed a San Francisco photographer, Eadweard Muybridge, to take pictures at the Stanford race track at Sacramento. The result was unsatisfactory: the pictures were too much blurred to settle the question. Five years later, however, Muybridge tried again. Advised and assisted by a young engineer, John D. Isaacs, Muybridge arranged a battery of twenty-four cameras—their lenses one foot apart—along the race track at Palo Alto and, by an electric device which set the cameras in successive operation as the horse went by, got some pictures that were clear enough to prove the Governor right. In 1879, Muybridge was granted a patent on "a method and apparatus for photographing objects in motion." Three years later, in Paris, Muybridge's photographs were projected in the praxinoscope, a machine devised by Émile Reynard to project pictures from behind a screen.

Another step toward motion-picture photography was the

6

photographic gun, which Étienne Jules Marey invented, in 1882, to photograph the flight of birds. Marey devised his gun on the principle of the revolver, the chambers containing photographic plates which recorded pictures when the trigger was released.

Thomas Edison has been given credit for inventing the motion pictures. It would be more nearly accurate to say that Edison, co-ordinating the ideas of other inventors, promoted in his laboratory the building of both a motion-picture camera and a motion-picture projector. Edison was an inventor aware of the importance of patents on devices that could be manufactured for profit. Since he saw no commercial value in the motion pictures, it is remarkable that he concerned himself with them at all. But he was trying to perfect his phonograph, and he said that in 1887 the idea occurred to him that "it was possible to devise an instrument which should do for the eye what the phonograph does for the ear, and that by a combination of the two, all motion and sound could be recorded and reproduced simultaneously." However, he investigated the idea so desultorily that nine years elapsed before the projection of motion pictures onto a screen became a practical reality. He assigned one of his assistants, William Kennedy Dickson, to the project.

Edison said years later that he had only one fact to guide him, "the principle of optics technically called the persistence of vision." But he and Dickson were also familiar with the zoetrope, and they knew about Muybridge's horse pictures and Marey's photographic gun. In fact, Edison said that the germ of his idea came from the zoetrope and the work of Muybridge, Marey, and others. Dickson started with the zoetrope. Since Edison had already invented a phonograph record and since the purpose was to give eyes to the phonograph, Dickson built a device that seemed to incorporate both zoetrope and record. It was a cylinder corresponding in size to the phonograph cylinder and containing microscopic photographs. Dickson placed it and a phonograph cylinder side by side on a shaft and recorded sound on the phonograph cylinder as synchronously as possible with the photographs. But the pictures were less satisfactory than the sound, and Dickson tried something different.

7

Incorporating in his camera a stop-motion device, he took pictures on sheets of sensitized Celluloid—pictures so small that he recorded about two hundred of them in a spiral arrangement around a single cylinder. After developing and fixing the Celluloid, he placed it on a transparent drum. When the drum was turned, a device lighted up each image from the inside. Here, gropingly but unerringly, he had established an important principle—that the motion pictures depend on light passing through the frame, whether the frame is projected onto a screen or viewed directly. But the curvature of the cylinder brought only the center of each picture into focus. Dickson took another step.

Abandoning the idea of a cylinder, he cemented together sheets of emulsion-covered Celluloid to form a strip half an inch wide. Then, because this area proved too narrow, he substituted a one-and-one-half-inch strip, which allowed for one-inch pictures and additional space for perforations along the edge. The perforations enabled the teeth of a locking device to hold the strip of sheets steady as it moved, by a stop-motion device, through the camera. The year was 1889; Dickson had discovered motion-picture film and recorded a motion picture on it.

From the negative Dickson made a positive print which he placed in a boxlike structure, about four feet high and two feet square, containing a battery-run motor. Propelled by the motor, the strip ran on a loop between an electric lamp and a shutter. The pictures were visible by flashes under a magnifying lens as the viewer looked through a slit in the top of the box.

It happened that 1889 was also the year in which George Eastman, the manufacturer of photographic equipment, applied for a patent on a thin flexible film for his Kodak. Dickson knew of Eastman's invention, and the Eastman film, an improvement over Dickson's stiff, easily broken Celluloid strip, was soon in use in the Edison camera, which was called the kinetograph. The little viewing machine was called the kinetoscope.

Like the original phonograph—an apparatus equipped with earphones—the kinetoscope was a device for the individual—not the group—although there is evidence that at the time Dickson was experimenting with the kinetoscope he succeeded in projecting pictures onto a screen. Keeping Edison's purpose in mind, Dickson had designed the kinetograph and the kinetoscope so that pictures and sound could be recorded simultaneously and, by a simple mechanism, could also be reproduced simultaneously. But the pictures, which were to have been only an adjunct to the phonograph, now took precedence, and it was years before pictures and sound were linked again.

Dickson demonstrated the kinetoscope to Edison in the fall of 1899 upon the latter's return from a trip abroad, but not until more than four years later did the machine have its first public showing. In 1891, Edison applied for patents on his camera and on "an appartus for exhibiting photographs of moving objects." The patents were granted in the spring of 1893, and Edison contracted to manufacture kinetoscopes for Raff & Gammon, a firm organized expressly to sell them. Raff & Gammon would pay Edison $200 apiece for the kinetoscopes and retail them for $300 to $350. Thus on April 14, 1894, Andrew M. Holland, a Canadian, opened a kinetoscope parlor at 1155 Broadway in New York City. The scene was a shoe store which Holland had converted for the purpose and in which he had set up ten kinetoscopes. Each of the machines contained a fifty-foot film made with the kinetograph at the Edison plant at West Orange, New Jersey.

The year before, Edison had put up a building in which to take motion pictures. About thirty feet long and twenty-five wide, it was constructed so that a section of the roof, about midway, could be opened—shutter-like—to admit light. Any desired angle to the rays of the sun could be obtained, for the whole building was swung on a graphited center in the manner of a swinging bridge, the ends being supported by iron rods extending from center posts. The structure was covered with tar paper on the outside and painted black inside, to bring the actors into sharp relief. Dickson called it the kinetographic theatre, but it was familiarly known as the Black Maria. This was the first motion-picture studio in the world.

Dickson was cameraman and director. His first actor was Fred Ott, one of Edison's mechanics. Ott, who had a reputation about the laboratories for loud sneezing, was persuaded by Dickson to sneeze for the camera. Ott had already been the subject for motion pictures of a kind, having appeared before the camera when Dickson was experimenting with photographs on discs. But his sneeze—a close-up now dignified by the title *Fred Ott's Sneeze*—is recognized as the first motion picture.

Dickson was soon filming bits of current variety-show acts —dancers, acrobats, contortionists, trained animals—and each act was abridged to be photographed on not more than fifty feet of film. Sandow the Strong Man appeared before the kinetograph, as did Annie Oakley, Buffalo Bill, and Ruth St. Denis. One film represented part of a scene from a popular farce of the day, Charles Hoyt's *A Milk White Flag.* The repertoire included re-enacted scenes such as *The Execution of Mary Queen of Scots,* which, however, was not filmed in the Black Maria but outdoors. This little film was one of the first to incorporate trick photography; in it the beheading of the unfortunate lady leaves nothing to the imagination.

Not long after the kinetoscope parlor opened, it attracted the attention of Otway and Gray Latham, two young southerners visiting in New York. It occurred to the Latham brothers that this new toy might be a means of making money if it were used to present pictures of prize fights. Accordingly, with Samuel J. Tilden, Jr., and Enoch Rector they formed the Kinetoscope Exhibition Company, and in August of 1894, they opened a parlor at 83 Nassau Street, in New York. The films they offered the public for the occasion were of a six-round fight between Michael Leonard and Jack Cushing, photographed in a ten-foot ring in the Black Maria. The capacity of the kinetoscope had been increased for the occasion from 50 to 150 feet of film, and each of the six enlarged kinetoscopes presented a short round of the fight. About 950 feet in length, this was the longest motion picture that had yet been made. Shortly thereafter, when Colonel Woodville Latham, the father of Otway and Gray, visited the parlor, Otway asked him whether the films they were showing in the kinetoscopes could be projected onto a screen. The answer was yes.

The Lathams set about devising a projection machine as

well as a motion-picture camera. Because their projector—for which, incidentally, they received suggestions from William Kennedy Dickson—only copied the principle of the kinetoscope, it was of less significance than their camera. In the kinetograph, the film was wound and unwound directly from one reel to another. Since the resulting strain of more than forty or fifty feet of film would break the film, the kinetograph could not take a continuous picture of more than about fifteen seconds in length. Enoch Rector devised a sprocket which slackened off enough film in a loop to prevent the stop-and-go motion from tugging at the unwinding reel. Allowing the camera to take as long a film as a reel would hold, this little device—called the Latham Loop—was an important contribution to the motion pictures.

At the time Edison applied for a United States patent on the the kinetoscope, he was asked whether he wished to take out foreign patents on it as well. When told that foreign patents would cost $150 more, Edison is said to have replied, "It isn't worth it." Thus when Robert W. Paul, a London manufacturer of scientific instruments, was asked, in 1894, to duplicate the kinetoscope, he not only did so but—finding to his amazement that it was not patented in England—manufactured and sold, within the next two years, about sixty of the machines. Then, to supply his customers with films, he built a camera which not only incorporated a stop-motion device similar to that originated by Edison and Dickson but was portable. He also built a projector—the bioscope—which took into account the all-important principle of persistence of vision and thus effected the necessary intermittent motion. As the film passed through the projector, it was made to pause longer at each frame than between frames and thereby allowed the eye time to "take in" each picture. He demonstrated this machine, for the first time, at Finsbury Technical College, in February of 1896.

Meanwhile, in Germany, Max Skladanowski had built and patented a motion-picture machine which he modeled, like Paul's, after the kinetoscope and which he also called the bioscope. In November of 1895, Skladanowski demonstrated it as the concluding number on a variety bill at the Wintergarten in

Berlin. The showing consisted of two films of about forty-eight frames each.

In France, the Lumière brothers—Auguste and Louis—manufacturers of photographic equipment, had also been experimenting with motion pictures. Beginning, as Paul did, with the kinetoscope, which was shown in France for the first time in 1894—only a few months after it had been introduced in the United States—they found out that the continuous motion in the kinetoscope would not do for a projection machine. Accordingly, they built a stop-motion device. They also built a camera, which differed from Edison's kinetograph in the speed at which the film was fed through it, that is, in the number of pictures, or frames, it recorded each second. Whereas the kinetograph took forty-eight frames per second, the Lumières decided on sixteen as the proper rate.[1] By early 1895, they had completed both projector and camera and had taken some pictures, and on March 22, at their factory in Lyons, they demonstrated their accomplishment. They called their projector the *Cinématographe*, a name reminiscent of Sellers' paddle-wheel machine and anticipating the universal word for the motion pictures—*cinema* (Gr. *kinema, kinematos,* motion).

Although the Lumières, like Edison, had little faith in the commercial future of the motion pictures, they decided to open an establishment in Paris for showing films. The enterprise was under the direction of their father, Antoine Lumière, who had given up the management of the Lyons factory. A basement room in the Grand Café on the Boulevard des Capucines was rented for the occasion, and here, on December 28, 1895, the showing took place. Each film, like Edison's, was fifty feet long, and there were about ten films. Included were *Lunch Hour at the Lumière Factory*, which shows workers leaving the plant at Lyons, *Arrival of a Train at a Station,* in which the oncoming locomotive is said to have terrified the spectators, *A Game of Cards,* in which the players are Antoine Lumière, the conjurer Trewey, who sits opposite him and is the dealer, and Louis Lumière's father-in-law, Winckler, the Lyons brewer, who pours out some beer,

[1] The standard rate has since been established as twenty-four.

Baby's Lunch, a picture which Louis Lumière had taken of Auguste and Mme Lumière with their infant daughter on the walk beside the Lumière house, *Blacksmiths, The Rue de la République,* a Lyons traffic scene, and *Bathing Beach,* in which the waves break on the shore. Admission was one franc, and the receipts on that opening day were thirty-five francs. The essential principles of motion-picture photography and projection having at last been applied in a commercial enterprise, the motion pictures were born.

The idea that Edison had begun investigating eight years before had thus become a reality. Edison originated the idea, which, with the ingenious help of Dickson, took the form of the kinetoscope; but the kinetoscope became the motion pictures independently of Edison, in a way that he had not originally intended and over a course that he could not have foreseen. The extent to which even the kinetoscope is solely Edison's invention is uncertain. First, there was Dickson; and besides Dickson, other inventors contributed to the progress which led deviously from the laboratory in West Orange, New Jersey, to the Grand Café in Paris, from the peep-show box to the motion pictures.

Then there were those who, although they were off the path of this progress, were experimenting with motion pictures at the time. There was, for example, William Friese-Greene, a photographer of Bath, England. Friese-Greene's epitaph describes him as "The Inventor of Cinematography," and attempts have been made to support this claim. Together with John Rudge, an optician, and Mortimer Evans, a civil engineer, Friese-Greene built a motion-picture camera and applied for a patent on it in 1889; but it has not been established that he effected the successful projection of motion pictures onto a screen. Although Friese-Greene apparently wrote to Edison suggesting that the motion pictures might be made a part of the phonograph—after Edison already had this idea—he neither completed a machine for this purpose nor directly contributed to the course leading from the kinetoscope to the motion pictures as perfected by the Lumières.

The tendency to simplify has given Edison credit as the inventor of the motion pictures. To point out that he was not, that in fact no one individual may be said to have been the sole inventor, is not to minimize the importance of his idea or even of the kinetoscope. That it was the Lumières who first built a machine incorporating the progress made by other inventors, who improved the rate of speed at which a film should pass through a camera, and who first demonstrated the completed machine as a commercial reality is a fact that those who would simplify cannot disregard. Ironically, however, if the *première* at the Grand Café late in 1895 had been delayed only four months, Edison would have had the distinction not only of originating the idea that led to the motion pictures but also of introducing the motion-picture machine to the world. As it was, on April 23, 1896, he introduced the device to the United States.

Even though, at the time he was working on the kinetoscope, Dickson had effected the projection of a motion picture onto a screen, Edison had refused to put projection machines on the market. When Norman Raff proposed that they do so, Edison is reported to have replied that the company was selling kinetoscopes for $300 to $350 apiece and making money and that if they sold machines which would enable a large group of people to see the films simultaneously, there would be use for only about ten of them in all the United States. But now the Lathams had a projector, which, as the pantopticon, they demonstrated publicly on May 20, 1895, in New York City. The pantopticon operated on the principle of the kinetoscope—that is, in its continuous motion—but it projected a four-minute film of a boxing match which Otway Latham had directed on the roof of Madison Square Garden. Here was competition. Edison assigned one of his assistants, Charles H. Kayser, to the project of building a machine that would be better than the Lathams'. Meanwhile, however, Thomas Armat, of Washington, one of those inventors who were also experimenting with the motion pictures, had constructed a stop-motion mechanism for a projector, which he demonstrated at the Cotton States Exposition in Atlanta, Georgia, in September of 1895. Edison was informed of Armat's invention, and, early in 1896, an agreement was reached whereby Edison would manufacture a projection machine incorporating Armat's device. The machine would be marketed under the Edison name but would be labeled "Armat designed." The name chosen for the new machine was vitascope.

On April 14, 1896, under the ambiguous headline "Edison's Latest Triumph," the *New York Times* reported:

> Thomas A. Edison and Albert Bial have perfected arrangements by which Edison's latest invention, the vitascope, will be exhibited for the first time anywhere at Koster & Bial's Music Hall. Edison has been at work on the vitascope for several years.
>
> The vitascope projects upon a large area of canvas groups that appear to stand forth from the canvas, and move with great facility and agility, as though actuated by separate impulses. In this way the bare canvas before the audience becomes instantly a stage upon which living beings move about.
>
> Mr. Bial said yesterday: "I propose to reproduce in this way at Koster & Bial's scenes from various successful plays and operas of the season, and well-known statesmen and celebrities will be represented as, for instance, making a speech or performing some important act or series of acts with which their names are identified. No other manager in this city will have the right to exhibit the vitascope."

Five days later, the first newspaper advertisement of a moving picture appeared in the *Times*. At the foot of Koster & Bial's theatre announcement of their current attraction—the monologuist Albert Chevalier "together with all the other Great Foreign Stars"—could be read: "Extra—Due notice will be given of the first public exhibition of Edison's latest marvel, THE VITASCOPE." The "due notice," appearing two days later, gave the date of the *première*—April 23—and on that morning the Koster & Bial advertisement gave the vitascope top billing, Chevalier and the "Great Foreign Stars" being summarily relegated to second place.

The *première* of the vitascope was more auspicious than that of the *Cinématographe* on that winter evening four months before in the basement room on the Boulevard des Capucines. Koster & Bial's, in Herald Square, was one of New York City's popular music halls. Edison himself came over from New Jersey for the occasion and occupied a box seat. Armat was there, too, taking charge in the projection booth, set up in the second balcony.

The next morning, the *Times* reported as follows:

The new thing at Koster & Bial's last night was Edison's vitascope, exhibited for the first time. The ingenious inventor's latest toy is a projection of his kinetoscope figures in stereopticon fashion, upon a white screen in a darkened hall. In the center of the balcony of the big music hall is a curious object, which looks from below like the double turret of a big monitor. In the front of each half of it are two oblong holes. The turret is neatly covered with the blue velvet brocade which is the favorite decorative material in this house. The white screen used on the stage is framed like a picture. The moving figures are about half life size.

When the hall was darkened last night a buzzing and roaring were heard in the turret, and an unusually bright light fell upon the screen. Then came into view two precious blonde young persons of the variety stage, in pink and blue dresses, doing the umbrella dance with commendable celerity. Their motions were all clearly defined. When they vanished, a view of an angry surf breaking on a sandy beach near a stone pier amazed the spectators. The waves tumbled in furiously and the foam of the breakers flew high in the air. A burlesque boxing match between a tall, thin comedian and a short, fat one, a comic allegory called "The Monroe Doctrine", an instant of motion in Hoyt's farce, "A Milk White Flag," repeated over and over again, and a skirt dance by a tall blonde completed the views, which were all wonderfully real and singularly exhilarating. For the spectator's imagination filled the atmosphere with electricity, as sparks crackled around the moving lifelike figures.

So enthusiastic was the appreciation of the crowd long before the extraordinary exhibition was finished that vociferous cheering was heard. There were loud calls for Mr. Edison, but he made no response.

Of the films included in that first showing of the vitascope, it was, the *Times* reported in its Sunday edition two days later, the waves tumbling in on a beach and about a stone pier that caused the spectators to cheer and marvel most of all. Big rollers broke on the beach, foam flew high, and weakened waters poured far up on the beach. Then great combers arose and pushed each other shoreward, one mounting above the other, and they seemed to fall with mighty force and all together on the shifty sand, whose yellow receding motion could be plainly seen.

Edison apparently realized, however, that the use of motion pictures to provide entertainment by the sheer novelty of the device itself could not be exploited for long. The *Times* announced:

> Mr. Edison is working hard for the absolute perfection of his machine, and at the same time is arranging for the securing of pictures the like of which, in other than inertness, the public has never seen.
>
> He has bought, for about $5000, two ancient, but still serviceable locomotives and several dozen flat cars. He has built about a quarter of a mile of railroad track in a secluded spot, not far from his laboratory. In a few weeks he will start a train from each end of the track, and will run them to a crash. The engines and cars will be manned, just as trains are in active service, and all the incidents of a train wreck will be caught by machines stationed at short intervals near the track.
>
> Machines have been sent to Rome, and in a short while the entire stage at Koster & Bial's will be occupied by a realistic representation of Pope Leo XIII, saying mass in the Sistine Chapel.

This kind of use of the motion pictures had, in fact, been predicted a year before. After the Lathams had publicly projected their boxing-match picture, Howard B. Hackett wrote in the *New York World:*

> You will sit comfortably and see fighters hammering each other, circuses, suicides, hangings, electrocutions, shipwrecks, scenes on the exchanges, street scenes, horse races, football games —almost anything in fact in which there is action, as if you were on the spot during the actual event.

Hackett's prediction was coming true. In 1896, when the motion pictures had become a practical reality, when they had evolved into the device essentially as it was to remain—the device for recording and projecting a film of sufficient magnitude to constitute art—their future lay, it seemed, in providing entertainment by presenting scenes of actuality.

On the other hand, Charles Frohman, the theatrical producer, saw how this use might be extended to the theatre. After attending that first showing of the vitascope, he declared:

> That settles scenery. Painted trees that do not move, waves that get up a few feet and stay there, everything in scenery we simulate on our stages will have to go. When art can make us believe that we see actual living nature, the dead things of the stage must go.
>
> And think what can be done with this invention! For instance, Chevalier comes on the screen. The audience would get all the pantomime of his coster songs. The singing, words fitted to gestures and movements, could be done from the wings or behind the curtain. And so we could have on the stage at any time any artist, dead or alive, who ever faced Mr. Edison's invention.

Whether the invention may be called "Mr. Edison's" is—as the records show—open to question. But there is no question about the motion pictures' having originated, not as an art, but as a machine. The ingenuity and effort, not of artists, but of inventors, mechanics, photographers, engineers, and manufacturers, made the machine possible. The purpose of these men— from Muybridge with his pictures of Leland Stanford's horses to Edison with his vitascope—was not artistic, but utilitarian—to perfect a machine that would have a use. The machine is still being perfected, but in Edison's vitascope, or in the Lumières' *Cinématographe,* the invention culminated. The machine was invented before the motion pictures started to become an art, and it is significant that the first motion-picture show at Koster & Bial's was advertised as a machine—"Edison's latest marvel, THE VITASCOPE." The machine made possible the development of motion pictures as an art.

2. "Arranged Scenes"

Among those persons who attended the first public showing of the Lumière films was the proprietor and director of the Théâtre Robert-Houdin, on the Boulevard des Italiens in Paris. He was Georges Méliès, and his theatre specialized in shows of magic and transformations. His introduction to the *Cinématographe* was to result in a transformation far greater than any he had ever effected on the stage.

Méliès was a man of amazing versatility. He was not only proprietor and director of the Robert-Houdin but also its stage manager, scene designer, and principal actor. He understood machinery, was himself a mechanic, and constructed machines for his trick effects. He was a cartoonist and satirist. Somehow his background, inclination, and experience had prepared him better than anyone else—including the Lumières—to appropriate the motion-picture machine and start the motion pictures on their way to becoming art.

Méliès was born in Paris on December 8, 1861, the son of a well-to-do shoe manufacturer. Early in his school life he became possessed, as he said, by the demon of drawing. He drew portraits and caricatures of his teachers and his fellow students and sketches of landscapes that had the appearance of theatre-like decor. By the time he was ten years old, he was constructing puppet shows and theatre scenery of cardboard. After a year of military service, he returned to Paris, intending to enter the École des Beaux-Arts and become a painter. But his father wanted him to become an industrialist. How could anyone, he asked his son, enter such a profession as painting and keep from starving? So Méliès entered his father's factory. Here he occupied himself with machinery and thus acquired a dexterity in mechanics. A year in London, where he went to learn English, also contributed to the preparation for the time when the motion-picture machine would be ready for him. Not understanding the language well enough to appreciate plays in the London theatres, he used to go to Egyptian Hall, where the famous conjurer Maskelyne presented scenic illusions and other shows of magic. After returning to Paris, he was a frequent spectator at the "theatre of illusions," the Robert-Houdin, presided over by the magician Houdin himself. Merely by watching Houdin's automatons from a seat in the audience, Méliès reconstructed them and actually made them work. Soon he was giving performances of magic himself, at first in *salons* and then in public theatres. His sense of humor gave his performances a comic slant that was later to be evidenced in his films. He became an illustrator for the satirical journal *La Griffe,* in which his caricatures of General Boulanger were said to have contributed largely to the failure of the General's attempt to overthow the Republic and establish a dictatorship. In 1888, having come into considerable means, Méliès bought the Théâtre Robert-Houdin. Now he was in his element. He renovated the establishment and began there a proprietorship that was to last for thirty-six consecutive years.

A man of the theatre, and of his kind of theatre in particular, Méliès was fascinated on that December afternoon in 1895 as he watched the Lumière films projected onto the screen in the basement room of the Grand Café. He realized at once that here was a way of extending the unsophisticated entertainment he was providing at the Robert-Houdin. He had, in fact, already introduced there a sort of screen entertainment by concluding each performance with the projection of a series of pictures on colored glass in a machine similar to the magic lantern—travel scenes, hand-painted cartoons, snowfalls, day-and-night effects, lightning, and decorated rosettes which revolved. By a special lighting device, scenes were made to dissolve one into another. Méliès saw in the motion-picture machine an apparatus even more magical than the magic lantern. He offered at once to buy or rent the *Cinématographe.* He said, years later, that Antoine

Lumière, who refused not only Méliès' offer of 10,000 francs but also 50,000 francs offered by the director of the Folies-Bergère, gave as the reason for his refusal his wish to exploit the machine himself. Louis Lumière, on the other hand, is reported to have said that his father refused because he thought it dishonest to sell an invention which in his opinion had no commercial future whatsoever.

Méliès decided to build a motion-picture machine himself. He learned, however, that Robert Paul had come to the continent from London to sell his bioscope, which would project Edison kinetoscope films. Méliès bought one of Paul's machines, procured some Edison films, and, early in 1896, opened at the Robert-Houdin the first cinema theatre in the world. He even improved on the bioscope by designing a loop device, similar to the Lathams', to prevent the film's breaking.

Now came the great step. Dissatisfied with the films he could buy, Méliès decided to make motion pictures himself. He was aware that the *Cinématographe* was reversible, and, understanding the mechanism, he made a camera out of the bioscope. Then he was faced with another obstacle: no film stock was available to him in France.

Méliès has been called a film pioneer. He had the temperament of the pioneer in being undaunted by obstacles and ingenious in surmounting them. The difficulty about film stock was minor compared to obstacles that Méliès was to face throughout his career. Having heard that Paul had some film in London, Méliès went there, but Paul would sell him no less than a case of Eastman film, and a case cost 45,000 francs. Not knowing whether he could ever recoup 45,000 francs invested in blank film but having faith that he could, Méliès bought a case. The case being hermetically sealed, he did not discover until he got back to Paris that the film was not perforated. However, he had an instrument for perforating film made, and although the instrument was crude, Méliès patiently perforated some film with it and set out to take his first pictures. Then he encountered still another obstacle: equipment he had used for developing film, as an amateur photographer, could not be employed for films as long as Eastman's. At first he tried cutting the films into strips short enough to develop in his photographic trays, fusing them after they were dry. Then he devised a developing machine consisting of a drum around which he wound the film and which, operated by a crank, revolved in a semicircular tub of developing solution.

The first motion pictures which Méliès made were like others of the time—brief depictions of the passing scene. His very first film, which he called *A Game of Cards* and which he made in the spring of 1896 on the grounds of his house at Montreuil sous Bois, a Paris suburb, is similar to the Lumière film of the same subject. With his portable camera, he was not restricted to Montreuil and was soon photographing uncomplicated incidents in and about Paris—street scenes, a train arriving at a station, boats on the Seine, etc. He went to Le Havre and took pictures of the seashore. Inasmuch as the film could not be removed from the camera in daylight and the camera held only sixty-five feet of film, Méliès had to make many tiring trips between the shore and a Le Havre photographer's. One of Méliès early films is a primitive newsreel: the Czar of Russia and his cortege going to Versailles.

Méliès' career was inevitably leading him to an attempt to bring the stage and the motion pictures together. Even in 1896, he made some films more suggestive of the kind of entertainment he was providing at the Théâtre Robert-Houdin than of actuality; *Conjuring, Conjurer Making Ten Hats in Sixty Seconds, The Vanishing Lady,* and *The Haunted Castle.* These were, essentially, pictures Méliès made of acts on the bills at the Robert-Houdin, except that he had not photographed them in the theatre but outdoors. They represented the first steps away from films of actuality toward scenes arranged especially for the camera. In *The Haunted Castle,* even the scenery was arranged, the background representing the first *mise en scène* Méliès ever filmed, if not the first in the history of the motion pictures.

Of the films Méliès made that first year, the most interesting cinematically is *The Vanishing Lady.* Although it is ostensibly a motion picture of a magician's trick, Méliès made the lady vanish, not by a stage device, but by manipulation of the camera. He had discovered this kind of manipulation by accident. One day in the fall of 1896, as he was prosaically photographing traffic in la Place de l'Opéra, the mechanism in his camera jammed. In the minute that it took him to re-engage the film, the scene changed, and when he projected the resulting picture, he was startled to notice that an omnibus suddenly changed into a hearse, and men into women. Méliès the magician realized that he had inadvertently performed with his camera a trick as amazing as any he had ever performed in the theatre. As a result, in *The Vanishing Lady* the lady vanishes, not through a trap door, but by a stopping of the camera. Méliès had discovered that the arrangement which characterizes the motion pictures is more than the arrangement of the objects photographed. He had discovered that he could not only photograph the magic he made on his stage but also make magic with the motion-picture machine itself. That he exploited this possibility only slightly is due to his being a man of the theatre. That he incorporated the trick in his films at all is due to his being a magician.

He made *The Vanishing Lady* and other films for exhibition at his theatre, but he was soon selling films to other exhibitors, too. He associated himself with a man named Reulos, and in October of 1896, their advertisements appeared in the newspapers: "Animated photographs for sale every day at the Théâtre Robert-Houdin." They called their organization Star Film. Its trade-mark, a star, which appeared on all its film titles, was the precursor of the Pathé rooster, the Metro-Goldwyn-Mayer lion, etc. With Reulos and Korsten, a mechanic at the Robert-Houdin, Méliès built a projector, patented it as the *Kinetographe,* and put it on the market. He opened a sales shop in the autumn of 1896 at 14, Passage de l'Opéra. The venture with the *Kinetographe,* however, did not last a year. Méliès even gave up using the *Kinetographe,* which could be converted into a camera, in making his own pictures, in favor of a Demeny-Gaumont machine and, later, of a Lumière *Cinématographe.*

One day early in 1897, the singer Paulus came to Méliès with an interesting request. It will be remembered that Charles

23

Frohman, after seeing Edison's vitascope, had suggested that Chevalier be photographed singing and that the film be projected while Chevalier sang from the wings. Whether Paulus had gotten the idea from Frohman or thought of it himself, he presumably asked Méliès to make motion pictures of him singing some of the songs that had made him famous so that the pictures might be shown to the accompaniment of his off-stage singing. The plan was for Paulus to appear before the camera as he sang in the music halls, that is, in costume and make-up, and in front of scenery appropriate to the songs. Realizing that taking the pictures outdoors at Montreuil would be unsatisfactory, not only because the scenery would be crude, but also because the limited time during which the sun's rays would be favorable might oblige Paulus to make several trips from Paris before the project could be completed, Méliès decided to take the pictures at the Théâtre Robert-Houdin. He arranged on the stage there the appropriate scenery and rigged up electric arc lights, which he had used for trick effects. The arc light was not yet perfected, but by careful attention to the mechanism which brought the carbon to combustion, Méliès maintained a light constant enough to take a picture of about one minute's duration. Thus he filmed Paulus singing five of his songs. These were the first films made under electric light.

Those five little films represent Méliès last groping step toward bringing the camera into the theatre. Now he was to proceed directly. Making the films of Paulus had demonstrated that what was needed was an arrangement whereby stage equipment could be utilized without dependence on the impractical arc lights—in other words, the need for a theatre illuminated by sunlight. It would be a photographer's studio equipped with stage properties and stage scenery.

That spring, Méliès built such a studio on the grounds of his house at Montreuil. It was a rectangular structure (about 56 feet by 18 feet) with glass sides and a gable roof. The camera was set up at one end and scenery at the other.

Transformation had been in Méliès' repertoire at the Robert-Houdin. Having effected a transformation by accident when he projected his film of the traffice scene, he subsequently made the trick film *The Vanishing Lady* by photographing the subject outdoors. Now, having a studio for theatre-like staging, he effected transformations even more theatrical and more astonishing. He expanded on the trick of transformation in a variety of ways. In the sixty-five-foot film *The Magical Box,* Méliès used this trick at least five times. First, a magician makes a box suddenly appear on a table. A boy jumps out of the box and is cut in half at a touch of the magician's wand. The two halves are transformed into two boys, who begin wrestling. At another touch of the wand, one of the boys disappears; the other, whom the magician picks up, is transformed into two flags. In his film *The Adventures of William Tell* (1898), a suit of armor comes to life, and *The Devil in a Convent* (1899) involves transformations of scenery as well as of actors. It is no wonder that Walt Disney has been called Méliès' heir.

Also by accident, Méliès discovered the fade, the device by which a scene is gradually disclosed on the screen as the intensity of light increases—a fade-in—or is made to disappear gradually as the intensity of light decreases—a fade-out. It had been Méliès' practice to decrease the aperture of the lens toward the end of each scene to prevent the film's being fogged. When the film was edited, this part was discarded. But one day, by mistake, an uncut film was projected. Méliès noticed that the fading of the scene made a more effective transition—like the slow closing of a theatre curtain at the end of a scene—than an abrupt cut. It was a fade-out, which gave him the idea of introducing the scene with a fade-in.

Méliès knowledge of still photography and his experience with the motion-picture camera led him to the discovery of other ways in which the camera could effect tricks. One of these ways was the dissolve. By applying the principle of double exposure to the motion pictures, Méliès discovered the dissolve, a linking device whereby as one scene fades out, another fades in—in other words, a simultaneous fade-out and fade-in. He also adapted to the motion pictures the photographic techniques of the vignette and photography upon a black ground. These techniques illustrated what Méliès meant when he declared that in motion pictures it is possible to do the impossible.

He reconstructed and filmed in his studio actual events such as *The Dreyfus Affair* (1899) and *The Coronation of Edward VII* (1902).

The reconstruction of actuality led Méliès to employ two other devices: the small model and the taking of pictures through an aquarium. The first of these was not Méliès' invention. The second was an adaptation of a theatre trick. To effect the trick for the motion pictures, Méliès merely placed a large aquarium, containing seaweed and fish, in front of the subject of the camera.

The film that Méliès was making in his studio at that time continued to represent a transference to the screen of the tricks he had performed on the stage at the Robert-Houdin. Most of them were short films, like *Conjuring*, in which Méliès acted the magician. A few comprised two or more 65-foot films in one —such as *The Laboratory of Mephistopheles* (1897) and *The Devil in a Convent*, each a 195-foot film.

It occurred to Méliès that the motion pictures would permit the joining of strips of film to make up not only the same scene but also a number of scenes relating to one subject. Accordingly, *The Dreyfus Affair* comprises twelve scenes, each representing an episode in the case of the falsely accused officer. Méliès had already made some short films of reconstructed actuality—such as *Sea Fighting in Greece* and *The Blowing up of the Maine in Havana Harbor* (1898), each 130 feet in length—but *The Dreyfus Affair*, composed of thirteen sixty-five-foot films, took fifteen minutes to screen.

Cinderella (1899) produced just after *The Dreyfus Affair,* was the kind of film with which Méliès was most successful. It was one of those films of "artificially arranged scenes" which represent his attempt to produce and film in his studio the kind of entertainment he staged at his theatre. Méliès was unequaled in reproducing the magic effected by combining theatrical tricks with cinematic ones. No print of *Cinderella* has been preserved, but from the Star Film catalogue one learns that it was "a production in grand spectacle illustrating each of the scenes of the fairy tale" and that it was "augmented by marvelous tricks, scenic effects, dissolving views, ballets, marches, etc., in which more than thirty-five persons participate." The titles of the 20 scenes, totaling 410 feet of film, are also suggestive of what the film was like, including trick devices that Méliès had incorporated in earlier films:

1. Cinderella in Her Kitchen.
2. The Fairy, Mice, and Lackeys.
3. The Transformation of the Rat.
4. The Pumpkin Change to a Carriage.
5. The Ball at the King's Palace.
6. The Hour of Midnight.
7. The Bedroom of Cinderella.
8. The Dance of the Clocks.
9. The Prince and the Slipper.
10. The Godmother of Cinderella.
11. The Prince and Cinderella.
12. Arrival at the Church.
13. The Wedding.
14. Cinderella's Sisters.
15. The King, Queen, and Lords.
16. The Nuptial Cortege.
17. The Bride's Ballet.
18. The Celestial Spheres.
19. The Transformation.
20. The Triumph of Cinderella.

Cinderella was something new in the motion pictures. In *The Dreyfus Affair,* the camera had not exactly recorded actuality, but it had recorded reconstructed actuality. In *Cinderella,* the motion pictures created.

Some of Méliès' other films of arranged scenes are based on literary sources, fairy tales, or folklore, as, for example, *Little Red Riding Hood* (1901), *Robinson Crusoe* (1902), *The Damnation of Faust* (1903), *Faust and Marguerite* (1904), *The Palace of the Arabian Nights* (1905), and *Rip's Dream* (1905).

Méliès found his studio too small and decided to enlarge it. Over the playing space he built a stage house high enough to accommodate a grid, on which stage hands could manipulate

27

scenery and special effects. He flanked the playing space with wings, each extending about ten feet, thereby widening this part of the studio to about forty-eight feet. Behind the wings and the playing space, the addition provided for scene docks and dressing rooms. A pit, ten feet deep, under the playing space, allowed for the use of trap doors. To soften the hard shadows cast by the iron framework as the sun beat through the glass, Méliès arranged cloth shades. A shedlike wing at the opposite end of the studio from the playing space housed the camera. It is not known whether or not Méliès ever moved the camera during the filming of a scene. In *The Man with the Rubber Head*, a trick involves the apparent inflation of a man's head until it bursts, and it has been suggested that the trick was effected by the camera's being moved toward the head. But among Méliès' drawings, a plan for this particular trick indicates a man seated on a dolly and concealed except for his head, and the dolly is on an inclined plane leading up to the camera.

Adjoining the studio, Méliès built a replica of the main wing, except that it had a concrete floor and, instead of roof and sides, a framework over which awnings were stretched for protection against rain. Here the scenery was built and sometimes filming done.

All of the scenery, properties, set pieces, and trick machinery that Méliès had employed at the Théâtre Robert-Houdin he reconstructed in his studio. He designed the models of the scenery, which was then built and painted by his decorator and assistants. Méliès found that for motion-picture scenery he had to modify the use of paint. Whereas in the theatre he obtained innumerable color effects, his camera recorded only various shades of gray, from black to white. Blue, he discovered, would become white in the film, and red, green, and yellow, black. His films were colored by hand, on the prints themselves, but all of the photographed objects—scenery, furniture, properties, and even carpets—were painted in grisaille. Ready for filming, they looked, Méliès said, like funeral decorations.

Mme Thuillier supervised all of the coloring of Méliès' films from 1897 to 1912. Each of her twenty assistants was a specialist in one color. A change from one frame to the next was another means of effecting a trick. An actor would thus in a flash be made to change costumes. Color for films was not, however, an invention of Méliès', since it had been used in still photography and in 1894 by Edison in the film *The Dance of Annabelle*.

Costumes had to be of a particular fabric, not only to photograph well, but to take the proper colors. The studio contained an enormous store of costumes of all kinds, of various periods and countries, together with accessories such as hats, wigs, armor, and ornaments.

The complex establishment at Montreuil epitomized what motion-picture studios were to become: the main studio, with its elaborately equipped playing space; the costume room, with its many workers, presided over by Mme Méliès; the studio for building of scenery, machinery, and properties; a printing laboratory in Paris and, later, another one on the grounds at Montreuil; an auxiliary laboratory where films were colored; and Méliès' offices in le Passage de l'Opéra.

The success of *The Dreyfus Affair* and *Cinderella* encouraged Méliès to make other long films. In 1900, he produced *Joan of Arc* (813 feet) and *A Christmas Dream* (520 feet) and, the next year, *Little Red Riding Hood* (520 feet) and *Bluebeard* (690 feet). During this time, however, he continued to make short films.

To Méliès, the motion pictures were a means of presenting on a screen the kind of entertainment he presented on the stage of the Robert-Houdin. In the films in which he plays the magician, he makes an entrance and bows as to the audience and bows again before making an exit. In the long films, the scenes are presented in sequence, as in a theatre. The dissolves which link them are a trick device used in place of scene shifting. The position of the camera never changes. One sees all the scenes as from a centrally located theatre seat.

Because Méliès thought of the motion pictures in terms of the stage, he brought to them the organization of the theatre and consequently the conception of the director as the unifying artist. But as he worked with this new medium, he discovered

29

that there are differences as well as likenesses between the method of the stage and that of the motion pictures. The *mise en scène* for a film, he said, is quite like that for the stage, except that the artist ought to know how to combine everything on paper and consequently to be author, stage manager, designer, and, often, actor. Differentiating between acting for the stage and acting for the screen, he observed that a good cinema actor is one who knows how to be understood without speaking and whose gestures, although necessarily exaggerated, must be precise. Although Méliès thought of the camera primarily as a machine to record his arrangements on the stage, he realized that what the spectator sees in the theatre and what the camera records are significantly different. He cautioned that, since figures in photographs hide one another, the greatest care must be taken to show off the principal characters in front and moderate the activity of secondary characters, always guarding against gesticulating at the wrong time, that otherwise the picture will give the impression of a jumble of people who keep moving, and that the audience, not knowing which to watch, will not understand the action. Only the camera is the spectator, he said, and nothing is worse than the actor's looking into it and being concerned with it while he plays, as invariably happens to actors used to the stage and not to the screen.

At first, Méliès had difficulty in obtaining actors for films because the actors felt that motion pictures were beneath their dignity. In his early films, he employed workers at the Robert-Houdin, his neighbors, members of his family, and even his domestic servants. But the poorly paid dancers at the Châtelet accepted Méliès' offer to appear in films. Then opera dancers followed suit, and finally actors of the Comédie Française. Méliès built up a classification of performers according to their capacities. But in the trick scenes, he played the principal roles himself because, with the exception of an acrobat named André Deed, he could never make his comedians understand the one thousand and one fine points that meant the good execution of a complicated trick.

Méliès worked meticulously. Although D. W. Griffith was

later to be credited with being the first motion-picture director to rehearse scenes—the "once-again method," it came to be called —it was not unusual for Méliès to spend eight or nine hours on a tableau which would last only two minutes in screening.

Not only was Méliès author, stage manager, designer, and actor—as he said the motion-picture artist should be—but he was also choreographer, creator of special effects, costumer, and property man. He was, in addition, producer and distributor. No worker in the motion pictures ever encompassed more.

After he built his studio, Méliès decided to make a cinema theatre of the Robert-Houdin. His advertisements in September of 1897 read:

> Henceforth the shows of prestidigitation will not take place except at matinees, on Sundays and holidays, at half past two. Evenings will be reserved for cinematography. The single price of admission in the evening is fixed at 0 fr., 50.

However, before the end of the year, he resumed his stage performances. For a while in 1898, he devoted Sunday evenings to cinema at the Robert-Houdin, but after that, he presented films only as part of his shows of magic.

In 1900, Méliès founded the Trade Committee of Motion Picture Producers, the headquarters of which were the foyer of the Robert-Houdin. Elected president, he served in that capacity until 1912.

In 1908 and 1909, he presided at the first two International Congresses of the Cinema. At the first of these, he proved—against the resistance of other producers—the necessity of establishing an international standard of perforation of film. It was also at this Congress that Méliès balked an attempt to impose a single price for the sale of films, contending that a uniform price would result in mediocre motion pictures. To the charge of a representative of one of the large companies that, being only an artist, Méliès did not understand that to build up a business one must have the largest possible market, he replied, as he says in his memoirs:

> I am only an artist, so be it. That is something. But it is for

31

just that reason that I cannot agree with you. I say the cinema is an art, for it is the product of all the arts. Now either the cinema will progress and perfect itself to become more and more an art, or if it remains stationary and without possible progress, if the price of sale is fixed, it will go down in ruin at short notice. That is what concerns me. Do not think that I consider myself lowered in being scornfully called an artist. For if you, a businessman, do not have artists to make films for you, I ask, what can you sell?

After the extensive counterfeiting of his film *A Trip to the Moon* in the United States, Méliès opened a branch office in New York under the direction of his brother Gaston. On taking charge, Gaston Méliès published as a preface to the Star Film catalogue a warning to infringers. The preface constitutes a succinct appraisal of Méliès' importance in the history of the motion pictures:

> Georges Méliès, proprietor and director of the Théâtre Robert-Houdin in Paris, is the originator of this genre of films composed of artificially arranged scenes. The creation of this kind of film has given a new life to commercial films at a time when they were dying out. He conceived the idea of representing comic, magic, and mystery views, and his creations have since often been imitated without success.
>
> A great number of American, French, and English film manufacturers, looking for novelty but lacking the necessary talent to create it, have deemed it easier and more economical to counterfeit the Star films and to advertise their shameless counterfeits. That explains the simultaneous appearance in a well-known New York newspaper of advertisements of four or five different firms for the celebrated *Trip to the Moon*. Each of these firms pretended to be the real creator. All of these pretensions were uniformly false.
>
> *Gulliver's Travels, The Dream of an Astronomer, Cinderella, Little Red Riding Hood, Bluebeard, A Christmas Dream* are some of the personal creations of M. Georges Méliès, who himself originated the ideas, painted the scenery, conceived the accessories, and played the scenes.
>
> In opening a branch in New York we are ready and ener-

The Interior of Georges Méliès' Studio at Montreuil, France

"All of the scenery, properties, set pieces, and trick machinery that Méliès had employed at the Théâtre Robert-Houdin he reconstructed in his studio at Montreuil."

One of Méliès' Drawings for *A Trip to the Moon,* 1902

"A Trip to the Moon tells, in thirty scenes, the story of a journey taken to the moon and back by members of the Scientific Congress."

getically resolved to engage suits against all infringers and other pirates. We will not repeat it; we will act.

After founding the New York branch, Méliès built a printing laboratory on his property at Montreuil so that a film could be processed immediately after the photographing of a scene. Previously, films had to be taken into Paris for development, with the result that when a film turned out to be unsatisfactory, Méliès was put to the additional expense of calling the cast together again for a retake.

Méliès had taken his first pictures himself. Then he trained a professional operator. Méliès made his negatives in duplicate so that one of them could be shipped to New York, where positive prints were made for distribution in the United States. He obtained two negatives by having two cameras functioning side by side simultaneously. His daughter Georgette became the operator of the second camera.

Méliès continued to make films until 1914. Then disaster struck him. That was the year the war began, and its immediate and first effect on Méliès was the closing of the Théâtre Robert-Houdin. Méliès established a theatre of "Artistic Varieties" at Montreuil, and with his son, his daughter, and a troupe of Parisian performers played there, until 1923, as he says in his memoirs, "all the chief masterpieces in the repertory of opera, comic opera, and operetta, and a number of dramas, vaudeville acts, and comedies." Méliès himself played more than ninety-eight of the most varied roles.

Meantime, all was not going well with the merchandising of his films. Other producers were now renting, instead of selling, films. But Méliès, who had put his profits into buildings and equipment and who had no business partners, was not able to finance a rental plan. Furthermore, Gaston Méliès had decided, without consulting his brother, to make motion pictures himself and inaugurated his plan by going west with a large troupe of cowboys and Indians. In a year, he lost so much of his brother's money that the New York branch had to close.

By 1923, Méliès was bankrupt. The receipts from the The-

33

atre of Varieties had not even met his general expenses, and all of his property had to be sold. His poignant account in his memoirs documents a part of motion-picture history:

> One can imagine his chagrin when he had to quit his family property, where he had lived for sixty-one years and in which he had passed his prime with all the members of his family. What heartbreak when he was forced to abandon the cinematography which he loved, and what pain when for more than a month he saw carried away by the secondhand dealers, dealers in old furniture and scrap, all the valuable material which had cost him twenty years of hard labor and which, naturally, was bought for nothing. It was the same with the laboratories, the shops, and installations at the Passage de l'Opéra and with those at Montreuil. These last included a number of buildings, stores of costumes, and sheds where the most cumbersome and baroque objects, of which only the stores of the Châtelet could give an idea, were accumulated: aeroplanes, balloons, dirigibles, helicopters, tramways, automobiles, railroads, locomotives, staircases, and practicable props, carpentry work of all kinds, weapons, accessories of all sorts, in brief, more than one can imagine. The pity was that his lyric theatre, his last means of sustenance, situated on the grounds of his property, was razed as a result of the conveyance of the land, thus taking away his last resources. This voluminous mass of material proved above all the fact that Méliès was the first to institute, in his films, gigantic constructions, elegantly built in flats and in staff and decorated to represent rocks, glaciers, grottoes, infernal and celestial regions, in which locomotives, automobiles, or other vehicles were in his films, victims of the most burlesque and fantastic accidents.
>
> In 1923 Méliès, his daughter, his son, his son-in-law, and their two little girls, the last hardly four months old, finally quitted the family home, without hope of ever seeing it again. For this vast property, containing a magnificent park, was broken up into parts and sold by lots. At the same time, his theatre in Paris, the Théâtre Robert-Houdin, was being demolished for the building of the Boulevard Haussmann, and Méliès was suddenly obliged to remove the furnishings of that theatre as well as all the equipment at the Passage de l'Opéra, also included

in the demolitions. The misfortune overwhelmed him. What to do with all the cases containing the hundreds of negatives on which he had so painstakingly worked, inasmuch as he had not the least place in which to put them, and because for lack of funds he could not longer continue his profession of the cinema? In a moment of anger and exasperation he ordered the destruction of all of that precious material.

Although destitute, Méliès did not give up. He organized concerts at the seaside resorts, sometimes playing in light opera, sometimes giving interludes of magic. Then, when the season was over, he toured the provinces. In 1924, he was employed for five months re-equipping the stage of a Sarrebruck Theatre, which was being restored after its destruction during the war. The next year he returned to Paris and obtained a little stand for the sale of candy and toys in the Gare Montparnasse. It was here, in 1929, that he was discovered, long after those who had known him in his motion-picture days had supposed him dead. Léon Druhot, the editor of the *Ciné Journal,* was passing through the station one day and heard Méliès called by name. He walked over to the man spoken to and said, "Pardon, Monsieur, I just heard your name. Could you by chance be a relative of Georges Méliès', who worked in the motion pictures before the war?"

"Why certainly, Monsieur," Méliès replied. "I am even his nearest relative, for I am Georges Méliès!"

After questions and explanations, Druhot said, "But you cannot stay here at your age. You are an illustrious Frenchman and world renowned in the motion pictures. Listen. I am going to undertake at once a campaign that I hope will have results."

In his paper the next day, Druhot announced his discovery. Reporters and photographers descended upon the stand in the railway station, and Méliès was famous again. Some of his films were found and shown at a series of gala soirees. Méliès was made a Chevalier of the Legion of Honor, having chosen Louis Lumière as his sponsor. At the annual banquet of the French Motion-Picture Syndicate, the president declared that the motion-picture industry owed Méliès a place. This, incidentally, he never received. In fact, it was two years before a pension was

35

obtained for him, whereby he could quit the stand and, with his wife and his granddaughter, take up residence in a château maintained by the Mutual Organization of the Cinema at Orly, near Paris. Here Méliès spent his last years classifying cinematic documents and writing his memoirs. He died on January 21, 1938.

During his career in the moving pictures, Méliès made about five hundred films, and of the barely fifty which have been preserved, the best is *A Trip to the Moon*.

The title is literal. *A Trip to the Moon* tells, in thirty scenes, the story of a trip the members of the Scientific Congress take to the moon and back. The film opens with the astronomers' meeting at which the trip is planned, then shows the building of the shell in which the astronomers are to travel and of the monster gun that is to project the shell, the take-off from the earth, the arrival on the moon, the adventures with the hostile lunar inhabitants, the escape to the shell and return to earth, and concludes with a reception in the astronomers' honor.

The scenes are said to be based on Jules Verne's *From the Earth to the Moon* and H. G. Wells's *The First Men in the Moon*, but Méliès' treatment is so original that any connection is superficial. The plot is similar to that on which Méliès based at least two other films—*The Impossible Voyage* (1904) and *The Conquest of the Pole* (1912), each presenting a professional group planning a fantastic trip, the construction of the means of travel, the departure, the arrival, bizarre adventures, the return, and the reception.

The scenes of *A Trip to the Moon* are described in the Star Film catalogue as follows:

1. The Scientific Congress at the Astronomic Club.
2. Planning the Trip. Appointing the Explorers and Servants. Farewell.
3. The Workshops; Constructing the Projectile.
4. The Foundries. The Chimney-stack. The Casting of the Monster Gun.
5. The Astronomers Enter the Shell.
6. Loading the Gun.

7. The Monster Gun. March Past the Gunners. Fire!!! Saluting the Flag.
8. The Flight Through Space. Approaching the Moon.
9. Landed Right in the Eye!!!
10. Flight of the Shell into the Moon. Appearance of the Earth from the Moon.
11. The Plain of Craters. Volcanic Eruption.
12. The Dream (the Bolies, the Great Bear, Phoebus, the Twin Stars, Saturn).
13. The Snowstorm.
14. 40 Degrees below Zero. Descending a Lunar Crater.
15. In the Interior of the Moon. The Giant Mushroom Grotto.
16. Encounter with the Sélénites. Homeric Flight.
17. Prisoners!!
18. The Kingdom of the Moon. The Sélénite Army.
19. The Flight.
20. Wild Pursuit.
21. The Astronomers find the Shell again. Departure from the Moon.
22. Vertical Drop into Space.
23. Splashing into the Open Sea.
24. At the Bottom of the Ocean.
25. The Rescue. Return to Port.
26. Great Fete. Triumphal March Past.
27. Crowning and Decorating the Heroes of the Trip.
28. Procession of Marines and Fire Brigade.
29. Inauguration of the Commemorative Statue by the Mayor and Council.
30. Public Rejoicings.

The style of *A Trip to the Moon* is typical of Méliès. Its phantasmagoria represents his particular blend of theatre and cinema, and its satire of the scientists and their ideas of the universe manifests his humor. The first film about interplanetary travel, it has a freshness and wit lacking in its current solemn counterparts about rockets and space ships. The meeting of the bearded astronomers, got up in medieval robes and tall pointed caps, turns into a lively squabble. As the voyagers go aboard the shell, it is pushed into the gun by a line of buxom chorus girls,

37

who take off their hats and wave them as though at the audience. The astronomers' dream could have been dreamed only by Méliès, and only he could have staged it for the camera. The film contains no subtitles—and needs none. In its dependence only on pictures to tell the story, *A Trip to the Moon* is cinematic.

The film is characteristic of the way Méliès' experiments seemed inevitably to lead. It is a series of arranged scenes incorporating elaborate theatre decor and trick devices. In the Museum of Modern Art print of the film, the last five "views" are missing. The other twenty involve fifteen different sets, most of them elaborately represented on back cloths and cutouts. The astronomers meet in a castle-like hall with fluted columns and leaded windows. The factory scene has a glass-windowed background somewhat like the roof and sides of the Montreuil studio. The scene for the foundries is represented as being viewed from roof tops, which form the lower part of the set. In the following scene, the shell is resting on roof tops too, but not on the same roof tops. There is even a different set for the scene in which the gun is fired, the backing for this scene being a perspective of rough terrain and sky. For the scenes on the moon, the sets are particularly original in their representation of giant mushrooms and other strange fauna, bizarre peaks, and lunar craters.

The sets represented something new in the motion pictures, and Méliès' magic touch made them original and startling. Smoke pours from the chimneys of the gun factories. When the shell strikes the moon in the eye, the moon winces and drops tears. The scenery on the moon's horizon descends like a Henri Rousseau forest scene in sudden animation, and beyond it the earth rises. In the astronomers' dream a comet crosses the sky, faces appear in the stars of the Great Bear, a figure leans out the window of a planet, and snow falls. An umbrella that has been turned into a mushroom grows tall in a few seconds. And when the shell falls into the ocean, there is an underwater scene which adapts Méliès' trick of photographing through an aquarium.

Although the acting in *A Trip to the Moon* seems, by modern standards, crude, it must be remembered that the film was made not only a quarter of a century before motion pictures talked but also at a time when, except for Méliès, motion-picture directors were little concerned with a distinction between acting for the screen and for the stage. But even *A Trip to the Moon,* which Méliès made early in his career, evidences the hand of the director who formulated rules for motion-picture acting.

Since *A Trip to the Moon,* like all of Méliès' films, was printed without credit titles, actors were not identified with particular roles. Méliès, however, is recognizable as the leader of the expedition. Years later, Méliès recalled, in a letter to Jean LeRoy, that the woman on the crescent was played by Bluette Bernon, a music-hall singer; the Sélénites were acrobats from the Folies-Bergère; the stars, ballet girls of the Théâtre du Châtelet; and the principal men, Victor André of the Cluny Theatre and Delpierre and Farjaux-Kelm-Brunnet, music-hall singers. Méliès designed the costumes as well as the sets. Particularly original are costumes for the Sélénites—part bird, part man, and part lobster.

All of the shots in *A Trip to the Moon* are, of course, long. The scenes represent, as nearly as Méliès could contrive them, what they would have looked like on a stage, observed from a center seat in the orchestra. Even the scene in which the shell approaches the moon, in the manner of a zoom shot, was effected more likely by a plaster-of-Paris moon's having been moved up to the camera—as in Méliès' plan for *The Man with the Rubber Head*—than by the camera's having been moved. The limited playing space in the Montreuil studio and the unvarying distance of the camera from this area tended to keep the acting in profile —particularly noticeable in entrances and exits and in groupings of crowd scenes.

Although *A Trip to the Moon* is primarily a series of arranged scenes photographed by the motion-picture camera, it incorporates cinematic elements. Méliès makes the Sélénites vanish suddenly, changes an umbrella into a mushroom, and links the scenes by dissolves. But cinematic though these devices may be, Méliès regarded them only as part of the abracadabra of his show. To him, they were one with the smoke-belching chimneys, the descending horizon, and the moving planets. He had happened on stop-motion photography and the dissolve, and he used these techniques in *A Trip to the Moon* because they were effective tricks.

A Trip to the Moon was one of the first films, if not the first, for which a musical score was especially composed. The music, written for it by the orchestra leader of the Olympia Theatre, is said to have pleased the public so much that the style became *à la lune*.

When the film was completed, Méliès invited exhibitors to a special screening. Here he met with another obstacle. Shortly before his death, he recorded what happened, and his account not only explains how he got his film before the public but is a commentary on the little world of the Paris boulevards at the turn of the century, and particularly on the perseverance and ingenuity of a remarkable entrepreneur:

> A score of spectators were present (those who at the time were established in the suburbs or in Paris itself). I sat down at the piano and improvised an accompaniment, and the film was projected. I expected an immediate success, for seeing it that morning myself, I had found it amusing.
>
> To my great surprise the screening terminated in a glacial silence. Needless to say, I was distressed at the result after the long, difficult, and expensive work. I said to myself, there's no doubt about it, it's a beautiful failure. One of them finally made up his mind and shot at me, "How much do you sell that for?"
>
> I replied, "Why at the same price as other films, 1 franc, 50 centimes per metre in black, 3 francs in color. There are 280 metres. That makes 420 francs in black and 840 francs colored."
>
> I can say that never in my life have I had such exclamations of reprobation concerning a screening. Consider, films up to that time had been between 20 and 60 metres at the most, and I had made a film 280 metres long, the first of that consequence.[1]
>
> I must certainly have given my spectators the impression that I was a candidate for an insane asylum. Exclamations rained

[1] As Georges Sadoul points out, there are errors of fact in Méliès' account. *A Trip to the Moon* was not the longest film up to that time, Pathé having already made longer ones and Méliès himself having produced a film of the Paris Exposition, totaling 1105 feet, in 1900. The catalogue of the Star Film indicates that *A Trip to the Moon* was apparently nearer 260 than 280 metres long.

from everywhere: "It's ridiculous, a film at that price!" "It's never happened before!" "You won't sell a single one!" "Anybody would be ruined with pictures at that price!" etc.

And the procession toward the exit commenced and grew. I detained one of them by the arm and said to him, "Listen, will you make a deal?" He was nonplussed, and I asked, "Where are you located now?"

"At the Foire du Trône," he replied.

"Good. Now I am hastily going to make you a large sign, painted in distemper like the scenery, with an enormous moon receiving the shell in the eye, accompanied by the title of the film and the inscription *Unpublished and sensational.* I will bring it to you at six o'clock. You will post it. I will let you have the film for the evening. You will project it at each show. I will not ask a cent of you, but I wish to see the effect on the public. At midnight, if it is a failure I will take the film back and that is that. If the film pleases, I will sell it to you, if you wish it of course. I will take it back if you do not want it. There. Does that suit you?"

"Well, all right."

That was his reply, curt and poetic.

That evening all was ready. The crowd started to arrive, the promenading got under way, the public congregated in front of the large moon, but the sign, which made them all laugh, was received by the most jesting remarks: "It's a joke." "It's a hoax." "Do they take us for fools in this establishment?" "Do you think anybody could go to the moon to take photographs?"

(The public at that time, not yet initiated into the faking of the cinema, imagined that only real things could be photographed.)

The result was that, in spite of the depreciatory remarks of the critical, there were at the first screening about fifteen slightly sympathetic spectators ready to see the presentation, as if something had mystified them.

After a series of films of twenty or thirty metres in length, the famous *Trip,* announced outside, finally came on.

During the first scene the audience kept silent. During the second they began to be interested. At the third, there were some laughs; at the fourth, the fifth, and the sixth they became louder and louder, not stopping until the end. At the last scenes

41

it was frantic. No one had ever seen a film like it, for it was the first of its kind, which explains the effect produced.

On going out, the spectators made an enthusiastic verbal advertisement for the newcomers who, at the sound of the applause, had gathered outside the little establishment. From that moment there was an incredible stampede of crowded houses until midnight. They even had to curtail the series of little films to increase the number of showings. In short, the receipts were more impressive than any of my exhibitors had ever received.

* * * *

I have never learned how, in the world of exhibitors, the news spread with such incredible rapidity. It is certain that the next day all the exhibitors in France were informed of the triumphant success of *A Trip to the Moon,* and orders flowed in from all sides.

No film had ever been so successful. It was soon being shown throughout Europe and the United States. In 1902, when Thomas L. Tally opened his Electric Theatre in Los Angeles, California, his program included *A Trip to the Moon.* Tally's print, incidentally, had not been licensed by Méliès' office. Three prints of the film had been bought from Méliès and sent to the United States, where unauthorized copies were made and exploited by the hundreds, film copyrights not yet having been established. As a result, Méliès' own sale of the film stopped before he had recouped its cost of about 10,000 francs. But, as he good-naturedly observed later, thanks to infringers like Thomas Edison, the name of Méliès became known throughout the world, even though the publicity was a little costly.

A Trip to the Moon and other films which Méliès made in the same manner demonstrated that the scope of the motion pictures was not limited to actuality. These films implied more than a camera recording the passing scene. Arranged scenes implied an arranger, a director—the artist. Working in the medium of the theatre, the artist was confined only by his imagination and capacity to create. Méliès created theatre-like subjects and recorded them by the device of the motion pictures. In this way he brought to the screen the organization of the theatre, the involved organization that united the arts and crafts of many work-ers—the author, the director, the stage manager, the scene de-signer, the actor, and the producer. Being all of these specialists himself, Méliès anticipated not only the complexity of the mo-tion-picture industry but also its specialization. That is enough to justify his epithet: "motion-picture pioneer." In addition, Méliès the magician discovered that tricks can be performed with the camera, that the artist can manipulate not only the scene but also the medium of the motion pictures. He discovered that the motion pictures are more than a device. Of Méliès, D. W. Griffith said, "I owe him everything."

3. Arranged Shots

U p to the time that Méliès produced *A Trip to the Moon,* no comparable films had been made. In the United States, the motion pictures had been exploited primarily as a novelty. To maintain the novelty, the Edison Company and rival producers varied the subjects of their cameras, but the variety of the subjects was limited for the most part to the passing scene. The camera was only a device.

There was, however, variety in the way the device was exploited. After the introduction of the vitascope, Raff & Gammon took pictures on the roof of their office building on Twenty-eighth Street so that their actors would not have to make the trip over to the Black Maria in West Orange. On this roof-top studio, which was just a platform set up in front of the camera, they filmed an incident from the current stage hit *The Widow Jones.* A fifty-foot film, it was a close-up of the two principal players, May Irwin and John C. Rice, and its title, *The Kiss,* is completely descriptive. It was the motion-picture sensation of 1896. In March of 1897, Enoch Rector exposed 11,000 feet of film in recording the Corbett-Fitzsimmons prize fight at Carson City, Nevada—the longest film that had ever been made of a single event. A play produced in New York that summer—*The Good Mr. Best,* by John M. McNally—included motion-picture scenes to show what was taking place in various rooms of a house. This film had been made by J. Stuart Blackton, a newspaper reporter and illustrator, and Albert E. Smith, an entertainer, who had bought a projecting kinetoscope from Edison—calling it the "American vitagraph"—and gone into the motion-picture business together. In the fall, Blackton and Smith produced, on the roof of the Morse Building on Nassau Street in New York, a forty-five-foot film, *The Burglar on the Roof*, with Blackton in the title role. The following winter, in competition with a motion picture of the Passion Play enacted in Horitz, Bohemia, and exhibited in Philadelphia, Pennsylvania, a Passion Play was filmed on the roof of the Grand Central Palace. The American version, 2100 feet long, was exhibited in January of 1898 at the Eden Musée to the accompaniment of a "lecturer" who recited the text. The following April, war with Spain having been declared, Blackton and Smith made a motion picture which they called *Tearing Down the Spanish Flag*. This little film, in which two eighteen-inch flags were interchanged on a pole, represented a groping toward the creative use of the motion pictures: although the film was purported to be a presentation of reality, the subject was expressly composed for the camera. A year later, Blackton and Smith filmed the Windsor Hotel fire in New York and thereby produced a newsreel. In 1902, Thomas L. Tally opened his Electric Theatre in Los Angeles, presenting an hour's program of films for ten cents—"up to date high class moving picture entertainment, especially for ladies and children." This was the first theatre in the United States devoted exclusively to motion pictures. At the St. Louis Exposition in 1903, George C. Hale, a former chief of the Kansas City Fire Department, presented a novel exhibit of travel films which had been photographed from moving trains—novel because to obtain the illusion of travel Hale screened his *Tours and Scenes of the World* in a theatre built to resemble a railway coach, seating arrangement and all. The ticket taker was costumed as a conductor. After the patrons had gone aboard, a locomotive bell rang, a whistle blew, the car rocked, and the pictures appeared on a screen at the end of the car. When the Exposition closed, Hale took his *Tours and Scenes of the World* about the country for two years, to his immense profit.

Such is the extent to which the production of motion pictures in the United States had progressed almost a decade after the appearance of the kinetoscope. In the fall of 1903, Edwin S. Porter produced *The Great Train Robbery*—the first really cinematic film.

45

There is nothing in Porter's background and early life to distinguish him from other motion-picture pioneers, who—with the exception of Méliès—were not artists, but mechanics, manufacturers, inventors, and entrepreneurs. Porter was born in Connellsville, Pennsylvania, on April 21, 1870, the son of a merchant. He had a public-school education, but by the time he was eighteen he had been a plumber, an exhibition skater, a sign painter, a custom tailor, and a telegrapher. In the spring of 1898, after three years in the Navy, where he is said to have impressed his superiors by inventing electrical devices for the improvement of communications, he came to New York and began his career in the motion pictures. In the spring of 1896, the motion pictures, in the form of the vitascope, were beginning too. Porter obtained a job operating the vitascope for Raff & Gammon. But before the year was out, having his doubts that the vitascope would succeed as a monopoly, Porter was persuaded by Harry Daniels to form a partnership for the exhibition of motion pictures in the British West Indies and Central America with a rival machine, Kuhn and Webster's projectorscope. The following spring, however, Porter was again in New York showing Kuhn and Webster films on a projectorscope in Herald Square to advertise, among other commodities, Scotch whiskey.[1] This was the first use of the motion pictures in advertising. After another tour with the projectorscope, this time to Canada, Porter became the operator of the projector at the Eden Musée. Then he returned to the Edison Company. As Edison's cameraman, Porter photographed the yacht races for the Americas Cup and obtained some startlingly effective back-lighted pictures because he had been jockeyed into a position on the referee's boat from which he had had to photograph against the sun.

Porter made pictures typical of those of the time—vaudeville turns, uncomplicated incidents contrived for approximately fifty feet of film, travel scenes, and newsreel-like films such as those of yacht races and prize fights. Méliès' films were, of course, being shown in the United States, were, in fact, being duplicated

[1] Operating the projector from behind a screen overlooking Broadway, Porter was arrested for blocking traffic.

46

by the Edison Company and sold at considerable profit. Impressed with the series of scenes in Méliès' film—arranged to tell a story—Porter decided to make a narrative film by joining together motion pictures already made. Many of the films in the Edison Company's collection were of fire-department activities; he began with these and, in 1902, produced *The Life of an American Fireman.*

A description of this film appeared in the Edison Catalogue of 1903. A short scenario, it indicates—as Méliès' descriptions of films do not indicate—details of action:

SCENE 1: The Fireman's Vision of an Imperiled Woman and Child
The fire chief is seated at his office desk. He has just finished reading his evening paper and has fallen asleep. The rays of an incandescent light rest upon his features with a subdued light, yet leaving his figure strongly silhouetted against the walls of his office. The fire chief is dreaming, and the vision of his dream appears in a circular portrait on the wall. It is a mother putting her baby to bed, and the impression is that he dreams of his own wife and child. He suddenly awakens and paces the floor in a nervous state of mind, doubtless thinking of the various people who may be in danger from fire at the moment.
Here we dissolve to a picture of the second scene.

SCENE 2: Close View of a New York Fire-Alarm Box
Shows lettering and every detail in the door and apparatus for turning in an alarm. A figure then steps in front of the box, hastily opens the door, and pulls the hook, thus sending the electric current which alarms hundreds of firemen and brings to the scene of the fire the wonderful apparatus of a great city's Fire Department.
Again dissolving the picture, we show the third scene.

SCENE 3: Sleeping Quarters
A row of beds, each containing a fireman peacefully sleeping, is shown. Instantly upon the ringing of the alarm the firemen leap from their beds and, putting on their clothes in the record time of five seconds, a grand rush is made for a large circular opening in the floor through the center of which runs a brass pole. The first fireman to reach the pole seizes it and, like a flash,

47

disappears through the opening. He is instantly followed by the remainder of the force. This in itself makes a most stirring scene.

We again dissolve the scene to the interior of the apparatus house.

SCENE 4: Interior of Engine House

Shows horses dashing from their stalls and being hitched to the apparatus. This is perhaps the most thrilling and in all the most wonderful of the seven scenes of the series, it being absolutely the first moving picture ever made of a genuine interior hitch. As the men come down the pole and land upon the floor in lightning-like rapidity, six doors in the rear of the engine house, each heading a horse-stall, burst open simultaneously, and a huge fire horse, with head erect and eager for the dash to the scene of the conflagration, rushes from each opening. Going immediately to their respective harness, they are hitched in the almost unbelievable time of five seconds and are ready for their dash to the fire. The men hastily scamper upon the trucks and hose carts, and one by one the fire machines leave the house, drawn by eager, prancing horses.

Here we again dissolve to the fifth scene.

SCENE 5: Apparatus Leaving Engine House

We show a fine exterior view of the engine house, the great door swinging open and the apparatus coming out. This is the most imposing scene. The great horses leap to their work, the men adjust their fire hats and coats, and smoke begins pouring from the engines as they pass our camera.

Here we dissolve and show the sixth scene.

SCENE 6: Off to the Fire

In this scene we present the best fire run ever shown. Almost the entire fire department of the large city of Newark, New Jersey, was placed at our disposal, and we show countless pieces of apparatus, engines, hook-and-ladders, hose towers, hose carriages, etc., rushing down a broad street at top speed, the horses straining every nerve and evidently eager to make a record run. Great clouds of smoke pour from the stacks of the engines, thus giving an impression of genuineness to the entire series.

Dissolving again, we show the seventh scene.

George Barnes in *The Great Train Robbery*
Directed by Edwin S. Porter for the Edison Co. in 1903.

"Scene 14: A life-size picture of Barnes, leader of the outlaw band, taking aim and firing point-blank at the audience. The resulting excitement is great. This scene can be used to begin or end the picture."—*Edison Catalogue,* 1904.

Lou Tellegen as Essex in *Queen Elizabeth*
Directed by Louis Mercanton for Histrionic Film Co. in 1912.

"Even the outdoor scenes are more suggestive of the theatre than of reality."

SCENE 7: Arrival at the Fire

In this wonderful scene we show the entire fire department as described above, arriving at the scene of action. An actual burning building is in the center foreground. On the right background the fire department is seen coming at great speed. Upon the arrival of the different apparatus, the engines are ordered to their places, hose is quickly run out from the carriages, ladders are adjusted to the windows, and streams of water are poured into the burning structure. At this crucial moment comes the great climax of the series. We dissolve to the interior of the building and show a bed chamber with a woman and child enveloped in flame and suffocating smoke. The woman rushes back and forth in the room, endeavoring to escape, and in her desperation throws open the window and appeals to the crowd below. She is finally overcome by the smoke and falls upon the bed. At this moment the door is smashed in by an ax in the hands of a powerful fire hero. Rushing into the room, he tears the burning draperies from the window and smashes out the entire window frame, ordering his comrades to run up a ladder. Immediately the ladder appears, he seizes the prostrate form of the woman and throws it over his shoulder as if it were an infant and quickly descends to the ground. We now dissolve to the exterior of the burning building. The frantic mother having returned to consciousness, and clad only in her night clothes, is kneeling on the ground imploring the firemen to return for her child. Volunteers are called for, and the same fireman who rescued the mother quickly steps out and offers to return for the babe. He is given permission at once to once more enter the doomed building and without hesitation rushes up the ladder, enters the window, and after a breathless wait, in which it appears he must have been overcome by smoke, he appears with the child in his arms and returns safely to the ground. The child, being released and upon seeing its mother, rushes to her and is clasped in her arms, thus making a most realistic and touching ending of the series.

As the scenario implies, the film turned out to be not so much a joining together of motion pictures that Porter had found in the Edison collection but scenes filmed expressly to tell the story and then joined together somewhat in the manner of

49

A Trip to the Moon and similar films by Méliès. There is, however, in Porter's film, a difference in the joining. Whereas Méliès' films of arranged scenes are narrative in the way that Hogarth's paintings *Marriage à la Mode* and *The Rake's Progress* are narrative, *The Life of an American Fireman* implies—particularly in the last scene—a different kind of narration. The scene is not presented in a single shot but is broken down into three shots. *The Life of an American Fireman* represents a step toward the principle of editing, which is the basis of motion-picture art.

The uncomplicated story that the film tells is germane to the medium. Rescue from peril has become the stock in trade of the motion pictures, and the technique by which excitement and suspense are increased in the presentation of such situations is familiar. It is easy to imagine how the incident which comprises *The Life of an American Fireman* would be presented in a motion picture today. The film would crosscut between the people in the burning house to the firemen coming to the rescue. Each shot of the interior of the house would present the danger as being increasingly intense, and each shot of the firemen would bring them nearer. The shots would vary in other ways, too. There would be close-ups of the principal characters and close shots of sections of the speeding fire engine. Porter's film does, in part, anticipate this type of treatment. There is even a close shot—of a fire-alarm box as a hand reaches up to turn in the alarm. The vision of the fire chief's dream "appears in a circular portrait on the wall." This is the device of the dream balloon, a device borrowed from the cartoonist, who represents a character's thoughts by picturing them in a circle above the character's head. It is a rudimentary form of crosscutting, but in depicting the scene of the rescue itself, it did not occur to Porter to show simultaneous action by crosscutting between the interior and the exterior of the building, between the woman and the child about to be rescued and the fireman about to rescue them. Even after the fireman had carried the woman out the window, the camera remains on the interior scene until he reappears and rescues the child. The treatment of the last shot is similar. The fireman enters the building, and the camera remains on the exterior scene during "a breathless wait." The situation presented in these last three shots is, of course, the very material for motion-picture editing—a discovery, however, which would have to wait until Porter made *The Great Train Robbery*.

Meanwhile, however, Porter was occupied in turning out other films for the Edison Company, including *Uncle Tom's Cabin* and *The Road of Anthracite*. The advertisement for *Uncle Tom's Cabin* announced that "every scene has been posed in accordance with the famous author's version." The film was 1100 feet long, longer than any other that had been made previously in the United States. Influenced by the method of the play *Uncle Tom's Cabin,* rather than by that of Harriet Beecher Stowe's novel, from which the play had been adapted, Porter built up the film to a series of fourteen scenes, together with a prologue. This film was accordingly no more cinematic than Méliès' arranged scenes. *The Road of Anthracite,* made to advertise the cinder-free travel on the Delaware, Lackawanna & Western Railroad, is composed of three shots of the mythical Phoebe Snow, "all in white who rode on the road of anthracite": Phoebe Snow getting onto the train, Phoebe—in a medium-close shot—seated in what appears to be the interior of a Pullman, and Phoebe—still immaculately white—getting off the train. Marie Murray, a photographer's model, played Phoebe Snow, and Porter made the film on the Lackawanna Railroad.

Then, in the fall of 1903, Porter made *The Great Train Robbery*. It has been contended that Porter's inspiration for *The Great Train Robbery* was not the films of Méliès but certain British films—in particular, *Attack on a China Mission*— and that several episodes in *The Great Train Robbery* plagiarize another British film, *Robbery of the Mail Coach*—said to have been produced by the Sheffield Company earlier in 1903 than the Porter film. This assertion of Porter's indebtedness is based, however, only on catalogue descriptions of these films, which have been lost. But catalogue descriptions, which tend to represent films as being more exciting and complicated than they are, may imply editing that is not in them. Whether or not Porter ever saw *Attack on a China Mission* and *Robbery of the Mail Coach* and whether or not these films were actually as the catalogue represents them have not been established. But of films still in existence, *The Great Train Robbery* is the first that is essentially cinematic.

Train robberies were familiar occurrences in the West in the early 1900's and were prominently written up in newspapers and magazines. There had even been a play called *The Great Train Robbery,* from which Porter borrowed the title for his film, but not the plot. Porter's plot, according to the 1904 Edison Catalogue, is as follows:

SCENE 1: Interior of a Railroad Telegraph Office
Two masked robbers enter and compel the operator to get the "signal block" to stop the approaching train, and make him write a fictitious order to the engineer to take water at this station, instead of "Red Lodge," the regular watering stop. The train comes to a standstill (seen through window of office), the conductor comes to the window, and the frightened operator delivers the order while the bandits crouch out of sight, at the same time keeping him covered with their revolvers. As soon as the conductor leaves, they fall upon the operator, bind and gag him, and hastily depart to catch the moving train.

SCENE 2: Railroad Water Tower
The bandits are hiding behind the tank as the train, under the false order, stops to take water. Just before she pulls out they stealthily board the train between the express car and the tender.

SCENE 3: Interior of Express Car
Messenger is busily engaged. An unusual sound alarms him. He goes to the door, peeps through the keyhole, and discovers two men trying to break in. He starts back bewildered, but, quickly recovering, he hastily locks the strong box containing the valuables and throws the key through the open side door. Drawing his revolver, he crouches behind a desk. In the meantime the two robbers have succeeded in breaking in the door and enter cautiously. The messenger opens fire, and a desperate pistol duel takes place in which the messenger is killed. One of the robbers stands watch while the other tries to open the treasure

52

box. Finding it locked, he vainly searches the messenger for the key and blows the safe open with dynamite. Securing the valuables and mail bags they leave the car.

SCENE 4: This Thrilling Scene Shows the Tender and Interior of the Locomotive Cab, While the Train is Running Forty miles an Hour

While two of the bandits have been robbing the mail car, two others climb over the tender. One of them holds up the engineer while the other covers the fireman, who seizes a coal shovel and climbs up on the tender, where a desperate fight takes place. They struggle fiercely all over the tank and narrowly escape being hurled over the side of the tender. Finally they fall, with the robber on top. He seizes a lump of coal and strikes the fireman on the head until he becomes senseless. He then hurls the body from the swiftly moving train. The bandits then compel the engineer to bring the train to a stop.

SCENE 5: Shows the Train Coming to a Stop

The engineer leaves the locomotive, uncouples it from the train, and pulls ahead about 100 feet while the robbers hold their pistols to his face.

SCENE 6: Exterior Scene Showing Train

The bandits compel the passengers to leave the coaches, "hands up," and line up along the tracks. One of the robbers covers them with a revolver in each hand, while the others relieve the passengers of their valuables. A passenger attempts to escape and is instantly shot down. Securing everything of value, the band terrorize the passengers by firing their revolvers in the air, while they make their escape to the locomotive.

SCENE 7

The desperadoes board the locomotive with this booty, compel the engineer to start, and disappear in the distance.

SCENE 8

The robbers bring the engine to a stop several miles from the scene of the "hold up" and take to the mountains.

SCENE 9: A Beautiful Scene in a Valley

The bandits come down the side of a hill, across a narrow stream, mounting their horses, and make for the wilderness.

53

SCENE 10: Interior of Telegraph Office
The operator lies bound and gagged on the floor. After struggling to his feet, he leans on the table and telegraphs for assistance by manipulating the key with his chin and then faints from exhaustion. His little daughter enters with his dinner pail. She cuts the rope, throws a glass of water in his face, and restores him to consciousness, and, recalling his thrilling experience, he rushes out to give the alarm.

SCENE 11: Interior of a Typical Western Dance Hall
Shows a number of men and women in a lively quadrille. A "tenderfoot" is quickly spotted and pushed to the center of the hall and compelled to do a jig, while bystanders amuse themselves by shooting dangerously close to his feet. Suddenly the door opens, and the half-dead telegraph operator staggers in. The dance breaks up in confusion. The men secure their rifles and hastily leave the room.

SCENE 12: Shows the Mounted Robbers Dashing Down a Rugged Hill
at a terrific pace, followed closely by a large posse, both parties firing as they ride. One of the desperadoes is shot and plunges headlong from his horse. Staggering to his feet, he fires at the nearest pursuer, only to be shot dead a moment later.

SCENE 13
The three remaining bandits, thinking they have eluded the pursuers, have dismounted from their horses, and after carefully surveying their surroundings, they start to examine the contents of the mail pouches. They are so grossly engaged in their work that they do not realize the approaching danger until too late. The pursuers, having left their horses, steal noiselessly down upon them until they are completely surrounded. A desperate battle then takes place, and after a brave stand all the robbers and some of the posse bite the dust.

SCENE 14: A Life-Size Picture of Barnes,
leader of the outlaw band, taking aim and firing point-blank at the audience. The resulting excitement is great. This scene can be used to begin or end the picture.

In making *The Great Train Robbery*, Porter hit on elements which directors who came after him were to refine and elaborate as peculiar to the art of the motion pictures. There is, for example, the story itself. Being 800 feet long and taking almost twelve minutes to screen, *The Great Train Robbery* tells a story that was—and still is—a popular one, of a conflict between law and order, in particular, a conflict presented in a vigorous physical action—holdups at gun point, the frenzied alarm, flight and pursuit on horseback, and a gun battle in which "after a brave stand all the robbers and some of the posse bite the dust." The Edison Catalogue states that the life-size picture of the outlaw leader taking aim and firing point-blank at the audience may be used to begin or end the picture, that "the resulting excitement is great." But the significance of this close-up of the outlaw is more than that of excitement. As John Howard Lawson points out, it forces the spectator to identify himself more closely with what has taken place. Later, when the camera was to become more flexible, tilting and panning were to give meaning to scenes in a way that the stage could not. In the scene in which the robbers climb down from the locomotive and take to the mountains, the camera pans with them as they cross the roadbed and then tilts to follow them down the embankment. The next scene opens as they come running through the woods from the background toward the camera. Then, as they turn left, the camera pans with them again, this time to reveal what they are running toward—their horses. In the mail-car scene, back projection gives the illusion of scenery flashing past the open door. On the other hand, in filming "the tender and interior of the locomotive cab, while the train is running forty miles an hour," Porter shot the scene on the train itself. This shot represents an early but effective use of the cinematic device of the moving camera.

But what gives *The Great Train Robbery* the distinction of being the first really cinematic film is the way in which the shots are arranged. Each of the fourteen scenes is not played out to the end as in a Méliès film, for Porter discovered that the motion pictures permit—with a flexibility that a play does not— the cutting of a scene before it is completed and sudden transference to another one. With the exception of the dream balloon, *The Life of an American Fireman* tells its story in the manner of *A Trip to the Moon*. In *The Great Train Robbery,* however, there is a tendency toward what has come to be understood in motion-picture making as editing. At the end of Scene 9, the bandits "make for the wilderness"; Scene 10 shows what is happening meanwhile in the telegraph office; and Scene 11 implies simultaneous action in still a third place—the dance hall. Furthermore, these three successively presented scenes unite the three main lines of action.

The Great Train Robbery, which Porter not only wrote but also directed, photographed, and edited, is called the first western. None of the scenes, however, were shot farther west than New Jersey. His association with the officials of the Lackawanna Railroad when he was making *The Road of Anthracite* stood Porter in good stead. When he began work on *The Great Train Robbery,* the Lackawanna lent him a train. He shot the train scenes on the Lackawanna track in the vicinity of Patterson, New Jersey, and the scenes of the chase and pursuit on horseback in Essex County Park, near West Orange.

Porter's actors included Frank Hunaway, a former United States cavalryman; Max Aronson, who had already appeared in Edison films; and George Barnes, a performer at Huber's Museum, a New York variety house. Barnes is the robber who fires point-blank at the audience; Aronson played several parts, including a bandit, a passenger on the train, and the fireman. Aronson, who later became famous as the screen cowboy Bronco Billy Anderson, is said to have missed the first day of shooting of *The Great Train Robbery* because, riding out to location from a West Orange livery stable, he was thrown from his horse. Employees of the Edison plant at West Orange were supers in the scene in which the passengers are held up. Marie Murray, the Phoebe Snow of *The Road of Anthracite,* appears in the dance-hall scene.

Evaluated by modern standards of motion-picture production, *The Great Train Robbery* is obviously crude. With the exception of the close-up of Barnes, all of the shots are long. The interior scenes are theatre-like because of the unvarying angle of the camera. The realism of the outdoor scenes contrasts strangely with the staginess of the interior ones—the unconvincing backgrounds for the telegrapher's office and the mail car and the lamp and stove painted on the set for the dance-hall scene. In the interior scenes, the actors play in profile, and some of their gestures are so broad that they are ludicrous. In the acting, there is a general lack of what is called the illusion of the first time. The dance-hall scene, in which the telegrapher's entrance is lost in the confusion of the crowd, violates Méliès' admonition that "the greatest care must be taken to show off the principal characters in front and moderate the ardor of secondary characters, always guarding against gesticulating at the wrong time, which in photographing gives the effect of a jumble of people who keep moving." Finally the substitution of a dummy to represent the fireman thrown off the speeding train is hardly deceptive.

The arranged scenes of *A Trip to the Moon* are more artistic than the staging in *The Great Train Robbery*. But the importance of *The Great Train Robbery* to the history of the motion pictures is not in the arrangement within each scene but in the arrangement of shots in relation to one another. In becoming art, the motion pictures came to depend—as art does—on arrangement, and the arrangement on which the motion pictures primarily depend is that of the pictures themselves. Although Méliès' films show a trace of this kind of arrangement, the emphasis is on the combination of photographed objects—the actors and the scenery—an arrangement akin to that of a play produced on the stage. *The Great Train Robbery* is cinematic because the film represents arrangement inherent in the motion-picture medium. Porter discovered that the cinematic method of storytelling is based, not on a series of scenes but on the arrangement of shots. Thus he discovered editing.

4. "Famous Players in Famous Plays"

The *Great Train Robbery* was popular. Heretofore, with the exception of Méliès, producers had exploited the motion pictures primarily as a novelty. By 1903, their films, depicting scenes from real life, vaudeville skits, reenacted bits from plays, etc., were less amazing than they had been on that April evening at Koster & Bial's seven years earlier. But *The Great Train Robbery* was different. Here was a motion picture that created interest by something more than the illusion of motion. In it, the device and the pictures were fused as they had not been before, even in the films of Méliès' arranged scenes. Porter's arrangement was of a different kind. Although in 1903 no one—not even Porter—appreciated the significance of editing, audiences liked *The Great Train Robbery* because it told a story in an exciting way. Other films were rushed into production to capitalize on its success—*An Attack on the Agent, The Car Man's Danger, The Little Train Robbery, A Desperate Encounter.* Porter directed some of these films himself; the Edison Company told him to.

Although Porter directed several hundred other films, he did little toward perfecting the kind of arrangement he had happened on in *The Great Train Robbery.* However, as Lewis Jacobs has pointed out, in *The Ex-Convict* (1904), Porter arranged the scenes to show a contrast between the impoverished home of the hero and the mansion of a manufacturer, and in *The Kleptomaniac* (1905), he not only contrasted the legal treatment accorded a poor woman caught shoplifting with that accorded a wealthy and equally guilty woman but also paralleled the stories of the two women. In *The Dream of a Rarebit Fiend*

58

(1906), he effected trickery through stop-motion photography, double exposure, and other devices in the manner of Méliès but arranged the scenes more in the manner of *The Great Train Robbery* than of *A Trip to the Moon*. But for the most part Porter adhered closely to a formula that had resulted in profitable films. Before editing was to be established as the basis of the art, the motion pictures would have to wait for D. W. Griffith.

If *The Great Train Robbery* did not establish editing, it established the story film. The motion pictures at that time depended less on the novelty of the device and more on the use to which the device was put, and the one-act stories were popular. The motion pictures, as a business, picked up.

No other art is so dependent on business exploitation as that of the motion pictures. The very origin of the motion pictures is commercial—a patented mechanical device—and the development of the art has been advanced and retarded by business expediency. Edison freed his pictures from the little peep-show box, not because he recognized the artistic advantage of a screen, but because he recognized Latham as a competitor. Seven years later, one of Edison's mechanics discovered editing. The resulting popularity of *The Great Train Robbery* and of films patterned after it was an impetus to further business exploitation.

A few months before *The Great Train Robbery* was produced, Harry and Herbert Miles, Cincinnanti photographers who had taken some motion pictures in Alaska, established a film exchange in San Francisco, California. Before that time, producers had sold their films outright to exhibitors. Why not, Harry Miles had reasoned, buy a film for $100.00, rent it to an exhibitor for a week for $50.00 and to another for a second week for $50.00 more, and keep the profits on the rental thereafter? It was about as simple as that. The idea, which was put into practice by Miles and his brother, appealed to certain smalltime businessmen, and film exchanges sprang up throughout the country. By 1907, there were more than one hundred of these establishments. The increasing popularity of films was an impetus to the new business, and the new business was an incentive to the production of films.

In the fall of 1905, John Harris and Harry Davis, who had been engaged in various theatre enterprises, converted a store in Pittsburgh into a place for showing motion pictures. They equipped it with ninety-six chairs discarded from an opera house, a secondhand projector, and, adopting an innovation of Méliès', a piano. Having decided on an admission price of five cents, they called their little house the Nickelodeon (*odeon* being Greek for "small theatre"). The Nickelodeon opened with *The Great Train Robbery*. The receipts on the first day are reported to have been $22.50 and on the second, $76.00. Within two weeks, the theatre became so popular that showings started at eight o'clock in the morning and continued until midnight. The Nickelodeon was soon taking in more than $1000.00 a week. Within a year, almost one hundred nickelodeons were opened in Pittsburgh alone. *Nickelodeon* became a common noun. The nickelodeons, like the film exchanges, increased the demand for films, and the demand was further increased as operators began changing their bills more frequently than once a week. Some houses were soon presenting a new bill daily.

If there was money in renting and exhibiting films, there was also money in making them. Only a small amount of capital was needed to make a film. Although Edison's machines were patented, the principle of the motion-picture camera was known, and various types of cameras were constructed. Some of these, Edison thought, infringed on his patents, and the history of the motion pictures in the first decade of the twentieth century is marked by lawsuits over patent rights. Cameras, however, were somehow obtained, and small one-reel films were turned out. A film, even though it contained half a dozen scenes, could be completed in a day. Roof tops of office buildings served as studios, for makeshift scenery could be arranged in the sunlight—as yet the only source of light for making motion pictures in the United States. Sometimes cameras were set up in city streets and parks and in the country, and scenes were filmed against these realistic backgrounds. Actors received five dollars a day. Producer, director, and cameraman were the same person. In 1906, ten years after the appearance of the vitascope, motion pictures were being made in various parts of the United States. Although there was no motion picture center, such as Hollywood, more pictures were produced in New York City and the surrounding area than in any other locality.

It was about this time that the mercury-vapor lamp became a means of filming by artificial light. The Biograph, the Edison, and the Vitagraph companies accordingly moved indoors. Biograph took over a house on Fourteenth Street, Vitagraph established quarters in Brooklyn, and Edison built a motion-picture factory in the Bronx.

In 1908, competition in the motion-picture business resulted in the formation of the Motion Picture Patents Company, a trust comprising the American producers Biograph, Edison, Essanay, Kalem, Lubin, Selig, and Vitagraph, the distributor George Kleine, and the French firms Méliès and Pathé. Patents were pooled, the members of the trust agreed to pay royalties to Edison for the use of his machines, and an agreement was made with the Eastman Kodak Company whereby Eastman would supply film stock only to the members. The formation of the Patents Company was announced on January 1, 1909. The motion pictures had become big business.

The growth of the motion pictures as a business was greater than their growth as an art. The film companies were still turning out short one-reel pictures hardly more indicative of what the art was to become than *The Great Train Robbery.* Even though short stories, epic poems, plays, and operas were now being adapted to the screen, the scope of the adaptations was limited to the length of a reel of film, that is, to about one thousand feet, or twelve minutes' running time.[1] Furthermore, the producers were making money with one-reel films, and they saw no reason to change an established and profitable practice. In 1909, J. Stuart Blackton directed a five-reel film, *The Life of Moses,* for Vitagraph, but the company released it a reel at a time, one reel a week, beginning in January, 1910. Later in 1910, Vita-

[1] Twelve minutes—as Terry Ramsaye points out—became the standard length for a film because, during the early history of the motion pictures, films were booked into vaudeville theatres as turns, and the length of a vaudeville turn was twelve minutes.

graph produced a three-reel version of *Uncle Tom's Cabin,* but it too was released in single reels. However, the next year, when Griffith made a two-reel adaptation of Tennyson's *Enoch Arden* and the film was released in separate reels, popular demand of the nickelodeon patrons resulted in the two reels' being screened in one showing. *Enoch Arden* is thus the first American film longer than one reel.

The telling impetus toward the so-called feature-length film, however, was to come from Europe. Up to this time, European films had not advanced the art of the motion pictures any farther than had those made in the United States. But in France and Italy, producers had at least begun to make films longer than 1000 feet, first in two reels and then in three and four. In 1912, Louis Mercanton, a Paris theatre director, made a four-reel film that was to have far-reaching consequences.

That spring, Sarah Bernhardt, recognized internationally as the greatest actress of her time, had appeared in Paris in the historical play *Queen Elizabeth,* by Emile Moreau. Although *Queen Elizabeth* failed and was withdrawn after a few performances, Mercanton asked Mme Bernhardt to let him film it. Bernhardt had already appeared in the motion pictures as early as 1900, when she was filmed in the dueling scene from *Hamlet,* and later she had starred in a film version of *La Tosca.* In 1912, actors far less renowned than the divine Sarah disdained the motion pictures, but her attitude was different. In the first place, Mercanton's offer gave her an opportunity to recoup some of the thousands of francs lost through the failure of *Queen Elizabeth* on the stage. Besides, appreciating the transience of the actor's art, Bernhardt used to say that the motion pictures were her one chance for immortality. She not only consented to appear before Mercanton's camera but also, it is said, made the screen adaptation of the play. *Queen Elizabeth* was consequently produced as a film.

Queen Elizabeth tells of the legendary affair between Elizabeth I, queen of England, and Robert Devereux, earl of Essex. According to the story, the interception of a ring, which Elizabeth had given Essex with instructions to return it when he needed her help, resulted in the carrying out of his death sentence for treason. The melodrama in the legend appealed to Moreau, and he fashioned the action of his play upon it. To complicate the situation and to motivate the interception of the ring, Moreau has Essex in love, not with Elizabeth, but with the Countess of Nottingham, and he has the Earl of Nottingham discover the Countess in the arms of Essex and thereupon not only instigate the charge of treason but intercept the ring to prevent the death sentence's being revoked. Abetted by Lord Bacon, Nottingham is successful, and Elizabeth, who learns the truth too late, dies of grief.

In presenting the play on the screen, Bernhardt had to reckon with the fact that, whereas a play tells its story primarily by dialogue, a motion picture relies primarily on pictures. The solution to this problem was to present as much of the film action as possible in pantomime and augment the pantomime with explanatory titles. Obviously, all of the dialogue could not be represented unless the titles were inordinately long and numerous, in fact, unless all of the dialogue in the script of Moreau's play were printed on the film. Consequently, details had to be deleted or at least compressed. For example, in the play there is a lengthy scene in which the Countess of Nottingham confesses to Elizabeth the truth about the interception of the ring, Elizabeth prompting the story from her bit by bit. In the film, the confession scene is summarized in a title and pantomimed in less than two minutes. In the play, the Countess is in a semi-dying condition at the time she confesses, and she dies the same hour as the Queen does. In the film, the deletion of minor incidents spares not only her life but her health.

While recognizing the limitations of the screen, Bernhardt must have been impressed with an advantage that the screen has over the stage. As an actress, she was naturally familiar with the problem of scenery in the theatre. Even if she had not written plays, as in fact she had, she knew that it is incumbent on the playwright to tell his story with as few changes of scenery as are consistent with dramatic effectiveness. On the screen, however, scene shifting is no problem at all.

Taking advantage of this difference in scenery, Bernhardt arranged the playing of the film in twenty-three scenes and, reckoning with the difference in dialogue, depended on about as many subtitles. The continuity which evolved may be indicated as follows:

Subtitle: The Queen, anxiously awaiting news of the Spanish Armada, is struck by the enthusiasm and noble bearing of Earl Essex, who alone is confident of success. Drake arrives and announces the total defeat of the Spaniards.
SCENE 1: A pavilion.

Subtitle: Essex, who has become the Queen's favorite, is present at a performance of *The Merry Wives of Windsor* and presents Shakespeare to the Queen.
SCENE 2: A room in the palace, a stage at left.

Subtitle: The fortuneteller.
SCENE 3: A courtyard. The fortuneteller is conducted into the palace.

Subtitle: The fortuneteller predicts an unhappy future for the Queen and tells Essex that he will die on the scaffold.
SCENE 4: Same as Scene 2.

Subtitle: The Queen, greatly upset by the forecast, places her ring on Essex' finger and tells him should he ever be in trouble, on his returning it she will save him however great his fault may be.
(SCENE 4 resumes.)

Subtitle: The Countess of Nottingham, who loves Essex, cannot conceal her grief on hearing the prophecy.
SCENE 5: A throne room.

Subtitle: Departure of Essex for Ireland as Lieutenant General.
(SCENE 5 resumes.)

Subtitle: Essex bids the Countess farewell.
SCENE 6: A hall. Essex enters upstage, comes forward, and goes through a curtained doorway at the right.

SCENE 7: The Countess' apartment.

Subtitle: The Earl of Nottingham discovers his wife in the arms of Essex.

64

SCENE 8: The hall again. Nottingham enters upstage, comes down to the doorway, pushes the curtain aside, draws back startled, and walks in.

SCENE 9: The Countess' apartment. Nottingham enters in the background but is unnoticed by the Countess and Essex.

Subtitle: Nottingham swears vengeance on Essex and confides his plans to Lord Bacon, the bitter enemy of Essex.

SCENE 10: The hall again. Nottingham watches Essex leave the Countess' apartment. Bacon enters, and he and Nottingham converse.

Subtitle: Nottingham and Bacon write the Queen an anonymous letter accusing Essex of treason.

SCENE 11: A room.

SCENE 12: Another room. Bacon enters, puts the letter on the table, and goes out. The Queen enters with attendants, sees the letter, and reads it. Essex is announced and enters. The others leave him alone with the Queen. The Countess enters with a lady in waiting. The lady and the Queen go out, leaving Essex with the Countess.

Subtitle: The Queen discovers Lord Essex is unfaithful to her. She believes the anonymous letter and orders his arrest.
(SCENE 12 resumes.)
The Queen re-enters as Essex is embracing the Countess. A guard of soldiers is summoned and Essex is conducted out.

Subtitle: Essex is taken to Westminster to be tried. The Queen, desiring to save Essex, sends for the Countess of Nottingham to persuade Essex to return her ring as a sign of submission.

SCENE 13: Another room. Through a large opening upstage Essex, the executioner, guards, and others are seen passing in procession, the Queen watching from the room. The Queen speaks to a lady in waiting, and the lady goes out.

SCENE 14: The Countess' apartment. The lady enters and speaks to the Countess. The lady and the Countess go out.

SCENE 15: The room of Scene 13 again. The lady announces the Countess and withdraws. As the Queen and the Countess converse, Bacon enters downstage and eavesdrops.

Subtitle: Bacon informs Nottingham of the Queen's intentions.
SCENE 16: A room, archways separating downstage area from a hallway upstage.

Subtitle: Yielding to the entreaties of the Countess, Essex gives her the ring.
SCENE 17: The room of Scene 16, but the camera has been moved to the left. The procession again. Essex leaves the procession and comes forward to the Countess.

Subtitle: Nottingham prevents his wife from returning the ring and throws it in the Thames.
SCENE 18: A hall. Nottingham meets the Countess, takes the ring from her, and throws it out the window.

Subtitle: Elizabeth signs Essex' death warrant, believing him to be too proud to ask for clemency.
SCENE 19: The room of Scene 13.

Subtitle: The execution.
SCENE 20: A courtyard, scaffold in the center. Essex mounts the scaffold. As the executioner raises his axe, the scene ends.

Subtitle: The Queen views the body of Essex and discovers that the ring is missing.
SCENE 21: A pillared vault, Essex' body on bier in foreground.

Subtitle: Queen Elizabeth forces the horrible truth from the Countess. "May God forgive you. I never will!"
SCENE 22: A room.

Subtitle: After the death of her lover, Queen Elizabeth never had another happy moment and gradually faded away. The death of Queen Elizabeth.
SCENE 23: The throne room. The Queen, in the presence of the court, dies standing up and falls forward in front of the throne.

Subtitle: *Sic transit gloria mundi.*

Since the purpose of *Queen Elizabeth* was to present a world-renowned actress on the stage, the film is highly suggestive of the theatre—as though Mercanton had set up the camera in the orchestra of the Théâtre Sarah Bernhardt and the play had been enacted behind the proscenium. Except for a slight pan shot in Scene 2 and again in Scene 18, the camera remains stationary. All of the shots are long shots, and the acting is directed toward the camera. The sets and the furniture are arranged as they would be on the stage, and the audience seems to view the scenes across the footlights. This illusion is created even before the first scene, for accompanying the credit titles are individual shots of the four leading players in stagelike poses —Mme Bernhardt and Mme Romaine actually bowing to the camera. The spectator is reminded of the theatre even after the last scene, for a shot is appended to present Bernhardt taking a curtain call.

No previous film had been more carefully staged. The scenery is theatrical, even the outdoor scenes being more suggestive of the theatre than of reality. However, the film takes advantage of the possibility of more frequent changes of scene and greater variety and elaborateness of sets than would be practicable in a theatre. The sets make concessions to the period represented, as exemplified in the parquetry floors, the flagstone paving, the mullioned windows, the pillars, the arches, and other architectural details.

In comparing *Queen Elizabeth* with modern films, one must take into account not only the difference between acting for the stage and acting for the screen but also the stage conventions of the theatre in which Bernhardt had been brought up. Although from the beginning of her career she had revolted against acting in the manner of the theatre of the grand style, this style is evidenced in the plays in which she appeared. One of the characteristics of the style is the star system, whereby the star is more important than not only the play but also the rest of the cast. Playwrights wrote plays as vehicles for particular stars. In this kind of play, the star is given built-up entrances, big scenes, and the center of attention throughout. Scenes are written so that the star makes an entrance after the scene has begun and leaves the stage before the scene is over. In the production of the play, the manner is accentuated by stage groupings, timing, etc. In *Queen Elizabeth,* Bernhardt makes her first entrance after the courtiers have grouped themselves to receive her, and the scene does not end until she is triumphantly borne out by her attendants. Her entrance in the scene in which Elizabeth views the body of Essex is particularly theatrical. At the beginning of the scene, attention is drawn from Essex lying on the bier, in the foreground, to a door surmounted by an arched grille, in the background. Attention is drawn to the door by a light from behind, silhouetting the grille. Then the door opens, revealing a lighted passage, and a guard enters. The guard stations himself to one side. The attention of the spectator having been thus directed, Bernhardt makes her entrance. This is not the method of the motion pictures but of the theatre—of the theatre of the grand style.

This kind of theatre was also characterized by spectacle. Shakespeare's plays, for example, as produced in the nineteenth century, were expanded to include elaborate processions and scenic effects for their own sake. In *Queen Elizabeth,* there is a suggestion of this type of spectacle in the procession in which Essex is taken to Westminster. In Scene 13, the procession passes slowly across the background as Elizabeth watches. In Scene 17, it appears again, halting as Essex leaves it to speak to the Countess and then, as he joins it, moving on. The play within the play is spectacle almost for its own sake. If there is any other reason for its being included, it is that since a scene is needed to represent Essex' having become the Queen's favorite and since Shakespeare is said to have written *The Merry Wives of Windsor* because Elizabeth wanted to see Falstaff in love, it would be appropriate to have Elizabeth and Essex watching a performance of the play.

It is pathetically ironic that Bernhardt considered the motion pictures her one chance for immortality, for her fame as an actress depended more than anything else on her voice. According to May Agate, the French poet Théodore de Banville said of Bernhardt, "The Muse of Poetry itself. A secret instinct moves her. She recites verse as the nightingale sings, as the wind sighs, as water murmurs." In her later years, after she had suffered the amputation of her leg and as a result played only while sitting or, as in *Camille,* lying down, she held audiences by virtue of her voice alone. Thus the silence of the screen was no small barrier for her to reckon with in *Queen Elizabeth*. It is as though she had been struck dumb or as though she knew that she was playing to a stone-deaf audience. She compensates for our deafness by exaggerating facial expression and gesture and by inserting a few subtitles. The compensation is generally successful, although here and there the pantomime is unfortunately overdone. It is infelicitous, for example, in the scene in which Elizabeth caresses the dead Essex, particularly since we are all too conscious of what, as the preceding scene ended, was about to happen to Essex' head on the scaffold. Bernhardt plays the death scene standing up, as she did in the play. May Agate, who appeared in the play with her, says:

> Even in her last throes of suffering she made no appeal to pity. There was no truck with the pedants; she died standing up, falling forward onto a mass of cushions, not writhing, senile, amongst them as is recorded historically. It was a great piece of acting, and if the play had been called *La Reine X* the French would have lapped it up as they did her Lucrece.

Whereas, in the manner of the theatre of the grand style, this bit of acting was effective on the stage, it seems less so on the silent screen, at least today. On the other hand, we have become so accustomed to talking pictures that we do not take into account the great handicap under which Bernhardt was working. And so we laugh at some of the scenes in *Queen Elizabeth*.

But Bernhardt was a great actress and, if we would appreciate the difference in time and technique, we would be less condescending toward her performance in this film. We would recognize, for example, that her gestures, although necessarily broad, are purposeful and complete. They are exaggerated, but they are never awkward. We would notice the way she uses her hands. May Agate recalls Bernhardt's having told her, "Never, under any circumstances, allow both your hands to drop to your sides, unless you want deliberately to convey despondency." Miss Agate adds, "I never remember seeing Madame Sarah even once adopt the attitude she condemned. Usually one hand would be fingering a necklace or holding a flower, the other would be half-spread, palm downwards away from the body, never flaccid but tensed and ready for action, as befits a mind which is working."

We should also remember that in 1912, when *Queen Elizabeth* was filmed, Bernhardt could hardly walk, and then only by leaning on someone's arm. Seven years earlier, in an accident in a Rio de Janeiro theatre, she had seriously injured her knee. She was playing in *La Tosca,* in which her part as Floria called for her to fling herself into space from a battlement. On that particular evening, the padding placed behind the set to break her fall had somehow been pushed aside, and in her leap she struck her right knee violently on the bare floor. She never recovered from the injury; in fact, her condition worsened, and in 1915 her leg was amputated. By 1912, it was necessary that stage sets and positions of other actors be arranged so that she would not have to take more than two steps alone. Louis Verneuil, who later was to write plays for Bernhardt to appear in without walking at all, attests that "she was so prodigiously clever, with so much skill and grace at the same time, that nobody in the audience could suspect the incredible effort she had to make in order to seem as if she were walking in normal fashion." As she makes her first entrance in *Queen Elizabeth,* she grasps the back of a conveniently placed chair, but inconspicuously; in fact, her step seems almost vigorous. At the conclusion of the scene she is carried off on a portable bench. At the beginning of Scene 2 she is already seated, and she makes her exit on the arm of Lou Tellegen, as Essex. In only four other scenes does she walk, and in these she relies for support on members of the cast. If it is ironic that she of the golden voice depended on the silent screen for immortality, so it is pathetic that, having made her debut in the motion pictures in the dueling scene from *Hamlet,* she was now forced by lameness to resort to these subterfuges in *Queen Elizabeth.* But subterfuge is part of the actress' art, and Bernhardt was an actress.

All, however, is not subterfuge. In the first place, she had chosen a part in which agility of movement would not have been necessary anyway. At the time Essex was beheaded, Elizabeth

70

was sixty-seven years old. In 1912, that was Bernhardt's age—not apparent, however, in the film. She seems younger, for her vivacity of expression, vigor of gesture, and erectness of posture more than compensate for her not moving about on the stage. In fact, playing opposite the twenty-nine-year-old Tellegen, she makes their age difference seem even less than that between the aging queen and her young favorite, who was thirty-four when he died.[2] In the scene in which Elizabeth discovers the anonymous letter, Bernhardt makes a complete turn in sitting down. If the turn seems artificial, it is because it accords with the conventions of acting at the time, not because the actress who skillfully executes it is crippled. It is significant that Bernhardt plays the death scene standing up. Whenever her acting in *Queen Elizabeth* seems exaggerated, it should be remembered that she is compensating not only for her infirmity but also for our deafness.

Today *Queen Elizabeth* is condescendingly referred to as only a photographed play—which is essentially what Mercanton intended the film to be. On the other hand, even as a motion picture it is better than its detractors suppose.

It tells its story, as a motion picture should, primarily by pictures. It depends little on dialogue. There are only twenty-two subtitles in the entire film, and of these three are interpolated within scenes, and one is appended as a concluding comment. Consequently, five of the twenty-three scenes which constitute the film are not prefaced by subtitles at all. This economy is effected by arrangement of scenes, that is, inasmuch as each scene is a single shot, by arrangement of shots. And it must be remembered that arrangement of shots is the basis of motion-picture technique.

The five scenes without subtitles are the seventh, the ninth, the twelfth, the fourteenth, and the fifteenth. Scene 6 presents Essex on his way to say farewell to the Countess. Since the subtitle prefacing Scene 6 tells where Essex is going and for what

2 The legend about Elizabeth and Essex has a counterpart in the stories about Bernhardt and her leading man. The marriage of Sarah Bernhardt and Lou Tellegen was reported in 1911—a report, however, which was subsequently denied.

reason, no title prefaces Scene 7, in which the farewell takes place. Similarly, the relationship between Scenes 8 and 9 and that between Scenes 11 and 12 are clear without intervening subtitles. Scenes 14 and 15 are not prefaced by subtitles because the action in them is made clear by Scene 13. Even the dramatic significance of Bacon's eavesdropping in Scene 15 is obvious—no title is necessary to point it out.

Now that sound is an adjunct of the motion pictures and the camera has become comparatively flexible, plays adapted to the screen are thought to be less theatre-like than *Queen Elizabeth*. The sound track permits the adaptation of as much dialogue as the play contains. The camera, moving about freely, gives the spectator the impression that he is not confined to his seat in the theatre but can come closer to the scene, up onto the stage itself, and watch the scene from all sides, even from above and below. Movement of the camera, however, does not make an adapted play essentially less like a play than *Queen Elizabeth*— nor does dialogue spoken on a sound track. On the contrary, a play adapted in only these ways is even more like a play than *Queen Elizabeth* because it talks.

Queen Elizabeth was filmed in England in May of 1912. Meanwhile, in the United States, Edwin S. Porter, who had left Edison three years before, was now the head of Rex, a motion-picture company he had formed with the film distributor William Swanson. (The Rex trade-mark, which Porter designed, was a ring of stars, later to be the trade-mark of Paramount.) Together with Joseph Engel and Adolph Zukor, Porter formed the Engadine Company and bought the American rights to *Queen Elizabeth* for the reputed sum of $35,000. Engel was also a member of Rex, and Zukor, a former Chicago furrier who in 1903 had acquired an interest in a penny arcade and had risen in the motion-picture business through managing Hale's Tours shows and nickelodeons, was now treasurer of the Marcus Loew Enterprises. These men planned, however, not merely to exploit Mercanton's film but to produce films of their own to present, as Zukor phrased it, "famous players in famous plays." Porter would direct these films.

72

The star system had already become an institution in the production of motion pictures. At first, producers had discouraged the identification of their players, fearing that popularity would result in demands for increase in salary, and for a while the public identified screen favorites only epithetically: "The Man with the Sad Eyes," "the Biograph Girl," "Little Mary," etc. In 1910, Carl Laemmle, head of the Independent Motion-Picture Company, reversed this policy and deliberately publicized by a ruse the company's leading actress—previously identified as "the IMP Girl"—as Florence Lawrence. Miss Lawrence thus became the first movie star. When the patent companies refused to follow suit, their players began to go over to the independents. In 1913, Biograph gave in by posting names and pictures of its players. The star system was established.

Even before the prints of *Queen Elizabeth* reached the United States, the Engadine Company gave way to the Famous Players Film Company. Daniel and Charles Frohman, the theatrical producers, brought their prestige to the enterprise, the former by joining the new company and the latter by lending the Lyceum Theatre in New York for the first showing of the film. The *première* of *Queen Elizabeth,* a private matinee on July 12, 1912, was reminiscent of that evening sixteen years before when Edison unveiled his vitascope at Koster & Bial's. Because of Bernhardt's renown as an actress and the Frohmans' prestige as play producers, the event at the Lyceum was even more impressive. The audience at the *première* of *Queen Elizabeth* was made up of literary, theatre, and other artistic folk, and they had come to see a motion picture, not in a nickelodeon or a music hall, but in a staid Broadway theatre. The motion pictures had become respectable.

Queen Elizabeth was popular, and Zukor and his partners were encouraged to go ahead with their own productions of "famous players in famous plays." They had persuaded James O'Neill, Eugene O'Neill's father, to be filmed in *The Count of Monte Cristo*—a romantic play in which he had been touring the United States for years—and production, under Porter's direction, had already begun. Meantime, however, word reached the Famous Players Film Company that Selig, a motion-picture company in Chicago, was about to release a three-reel version of *The Count of Monte Cristo* based directly on Dumas' novel. Even though the filmed play would have been different, Zukor and his partners felt that it would be inauspicious to inaugurate their enterprise with a film on a similar subject with a similar title. Accordingly, they substituted *The Prisoner of Zenda,* which Porter had also begun directing. Like *Queen Elizabeth,* it was in four reels. Thus *The Prisoner of Zenda* (1912), starring James K. Hackett, a former Broadway matinee idol, became the first of the company's own productions of "famous players in famous plays." Then the incomparable Minnie Maddern Fiske consented to be filmed in *Tess of the D'Urbervilles,* in which she had appeared on the stage. Other famous players followed suit, and the trend strengthened the respectability which *Queen Elizabeth* had brought to the motion pictures.

By the same token, the importance of the motion-picture actor was strengthened. Mary Pickford, who had become known, because of her parts in the Biograph films, as Little Mary and the Girl with the Curls and who had just completed a season on Broadway in a play called *A Good Little Devil,* not only was filmed in *A Good Little Devil* for Famous Players in 1913 but also signed a contract with Zukor to become a Famous Players actress. It was then only a step to Charles Chaplin, the prime example of the domination of the actor in the motion pictures.

Queen Elizabeth indeed had far-reaching consequences. But except for encouraging the making of multiple-reel films, it did little to advance the motion pictures as art. The advance was to come in another way and from other quarters, and in those quarters it had already started.

5. Editing

If any film produced by the Edison Company rivals the fame of *The Great Train Robbery,* it is *Rescued from an Eagle's Nest,* for with this one-reeler D. W. Griffith inaugurated his career in the motion pictures. Griffith, who had just completed a road tour as an actor with the Nance O'Neill players and at the end of the season of 1906–1907 found himself in New York, tried to sell some stories he had written for the screen. The Edison people were not interested in his stories, but J. Searle Dawley, a director at the Edison plant, decided that he could use Griffith as an actor. Dawley, who was about to direct a film depicting a child carried away by an eagle and rescued from the eagle's nest on a cliff, hired Griffith to play the part of the woodsman who makes the rescue. The interior scenes for *Rescued from an Eagle's Nest* were shot in the Edison studio, and the exterior scenes on the Palisades of the Hudson River. The cameraman was the company's general mechanic, Edwin S. Porter. Griffith received five dollars a day for the two days that it took to make the film.

Griffith had wanted to be a writer. He used to say that he would rather have written one page of Walt Whitman's *Leaves of Grass* than to have made all the motion pictures ever conceived. Although some of his stories and poems had been published in magazines, he was unable to make a living from his writing and had accordingly taken up acting. Nevertheless, he continued to write. Earlier in that year of 1907, he had received one thousand dollars from James K. Hackett for a play entitled *A Fool and a Girl,* which Hackett produced and which failed. Among other writings, the Edison people had refused Griffith's

75

scenario of Victorien Sardou's *La Tosca*. Griffith is said to have gone to a nickelodeon in Chicago when he was there with a play company the year before and, thinking the little films stupid, had made the adaptation of *La Tosca*. Ironically, his scenario was rejected because it contained too many scenes. Griffith appreciated the possibilities of the motion pictures for greater scope than that imagined by those who were already making films.

Griffith got his start as an actor at the age of twenty-two, when he played supporting roles in the Meffert Stock Company in his home town of Louisville, Kentucky. Having thus acquired a taste for the stage, he spent the next ten years, off and on, in acting and, when he was not acting, supporting himself in various other ways—selling subscriptions to the *Baptist Weekly* and the *Encyclopaedia Britannica,* working for a construction company, shoveling ore in Tonawanda, New York—where he had been stranded when a play he was acting in failed there—picking hops, and working on lumber ships plying the West Coast. He was a member of Ada Gray's troupe, with which he played in *Trilby* and *East Lynne.* He appeared as Abraham Lincoln in *The Ensign,* produced by the Neill Alhambra Stock Company in Chicago. He played in *Fedora* with the Melbourne MacDowell Company and as Sir Francis Drake in Nance O'Neill's production of *Elizabeth, Queen of England.* In 1906, while in Boston acting in *Rosmersholm* and *Magda,* he married the actress Linda Arvidson. Then came the failure of his play and his turning to the motion pictures.

It would not have been surprising if Griffith, whose training had been in the theatre, had used the motion pictures as a device to photograph plays in the manner of Sarah Bernhardt's *Queen Elizabeth.* That, on the contrary, he should have exploited the device in the direction that Porter had indicated in *The Great Train Robbery*—but far beyond anything that Porter had attempted—is not easily explained.

His background, however, explains much of the content of his films. Born on a country place at La Grange, Kentucky, January 23, 1875, he was brought up in a southern home in the years shortly after the Civil War. His father, Jacob Wark Griffith, a physician, had fought in the Mexican War, had served as escort to one of the famous wagon trains to California in 1850, and had been a member of the Kentucky Legislature. He commanded a cavalry company in the Civil War and emerged from the war, having been severely wounded three times, a lieutenant colonel. Known for his booming voice—he was called Roaring Jake Griffith—the Colonel gave public readings of Shakespeare. From him David Wark Griffith learned of a way of life that no longer existed in the South and of "the lost cause." David's older sister used to read aloud to him from the nineteenth-century British poets, and he acquired a taste for this kind of literature. Lewis Jacobs attributes to these writings Griffith's choice of romantic subjects for his films, as well as his choice of actresses to present them—the Mae Marshes, the Mary Pickfords, the Lillian and Dorothy Gishes—counterparts of the girlish, delicate, pretty heroines of Victorian poetry.

At the death of the Colonel, when David Wark was ten years old, the Griffiths were nearly impoverished. When he filmed the postwar Cameron home in *The Birth of a Nation,* Griffith must have had in mind his own social background—a background at odds with deprivation. Mrs. Griffith and the children moved to a small farm and then into Louisville. Here in the city, Griffith had a variety of jobs—in a dry-goods store, in a bookstore, on the Louisville *Courier Journal* and, at least once, at the auditorium as a super in a play. Then in 1897, he began acting with the Meffert Stock Company under the name of Lawrence Griffith.

His initial experience in the motion pictures as an actor in *Rescued from an Eagle's Nest* apparently did not diminish the young man's ambition to be a writer. Failing to sell his stories to the Edison people, Griffith took them down to the Biograph studio on East Fourteenth Street. Biograph bought from him *Old Isaac the Pawnbroker, Ostler Joe* (an adaptation of a poem by George P. Sims), and *At the Crossroads of Life* and produced them as motion pictures in 1908. Griffith acted in *Ostler Joe* and *At the Crossroads of Life* as well as in three other firms that Biograph produced that year—*The Music Mas-*

77

ter, When Knights Were Bold, and *The Stage Rustler.* Then Biograph's general manager, H. N. Marvin, asked him to direct a film. Griffith is said to have demurred on the grounds that, whereas he was receiving five dollars a day as an actor, he might fail as a director, and he was persuaded only when Marvin promised him that if he failed as a director, he might have his acting job back. He never acted again.

The film was called *The Adventures of Dollie.* It is a sentimental and improbable story about a little girl kidnaped by gypsies out of revenge and returned to her parents after a cask in which the gypsies have placed her falls off a wagon into a stream and is found floating in a cove. The cameraman assigned to this one-reel production was Arthur Marvin, H. N. Marvin's brother, and G. W. Bitzer, who had joined the Biograph Company in 1896 as an electrician, assisted. Later, Billy Bitzer became Griffith's cameraman in a partnership that lasted for sixteen years.

The Adventures of Dollie, of which no print is extant, assertedly contained the first flash back in any motion picture. Griffith's stage experience resulted in more care in the selection of the cast than had been the practice in the production of previous films. For the mother of the child, Griffith chose Linda Arvidson—not, he told her, because she was his wife, but because she was a good actress. For the father, he selected a young actor he had happened to see coming out of a booking agency, and thus Arthur Johnson, who had never before acted in a film, began a career which made him a screen star. Charles Inslee, an actor whom Griffith had known on the West Coast, was the leading gypsy. Griffith had told Bitzer that he wanted as a location for the film a swift stream close to a house. The place chosen was Sound Beach, Connecticut, now known as Old Greenwich. Filming was completed on June 18 and 19, 1908, and Griffith's first picture had its *première* on July 14 at Keith and Proctor's Theatre in Union Square, New York.

The Biograph Company was so pleased with *The Adventures of Dollie* that Griffith became the company's director. His second picture, an Indian melodrama called *The Red Man and the Child,* filmed on the Passaic River in New Jersey, was released just two weeks after the *première* of *The Adventures of Dollie.* Before the end of the year, the Biograph Company had released forty-four films, the product of Griffith's first six months as a director. In making one of these, *For Love of Gold,* an adaptation of Jack London's story *Just Meat,* Griffith had Bitzer move the camera close to the actors to catch their expressions and thus obviate a subtitle to explain what the characters are thinking. By prefacing and following this full shot with long shots, Griffith effected a psychological meaning by sheer arrangement of shots. In making *After Many Years* (in the fall of 1908), the first film adaptation of Tennyson's *Enoch Arden,* he had the camera brought up even closer. The resulting close-up he inserted between spatially longer shots. Here he was experimenting—consciously or not —with the same principle Porter had groped toward: that the arrangement of shots is the basis of motion-picture construction. However, Griffith had already gone beyond anything Porter had demonstrated. *After Many Years* also contained a flash back. By now Griffith was innovating so boldly that the studio was concerned. Linda Arvidson has recorded a colloquy that resulted from Griffith's suggestion of a scene showing Annie Lee awaiting her husband's return, the scene to be followed by one of Enoch cast away on a desert island:

> "How can you tell a story jumping about like that? The people won't know what it's about."
> "Well," said Mr. Griffith, "doesn't Dickens write that way?"
> "Yes, but that's Dickens; that's novel writing: that's different."
> "Oh, not so much, these are picture stories: not so different."

During the next year, Griffith continued to turn out films for Biograph and, through his experiments, to establish techniques now taken for granted. He experimented, for example, with lighting. Until that time, lighting in the motion pictures had been only arbitrary, that is, light not represented as orig-

79

inating in a natural source, such as a lamp, a fire, or the sun shining through a window, but cast flatly for the purpose of obtaining a clear picture. In *Edgar Allan Poe,* Griffith effected what is called "Rembrandt lighting," whereby the profile is lighted as in a portrait. In directing *The Politician's Love Story,* which was filmed in Central Park, New York, Griffith had Bitzer photograph into the sun, as Porter had been forced to do when he photographed the yacht race. The film was made in February, and the snow-laden trees of the park were outlined in light. In *A Drunkard's Reformation* and in *Pippa Passes,* Griffith effected natural lighting—the source of light originating or seeming to originate from a natural source. In *A Drunkard's Reformation,* a scene is illuminated by light from a fireplace, and, in *Pippa Passes,* light seems to come from the morning sun.

In that same year of 1909, Griffith made *The Lonely Villa.* This was the first film to contain crosscutting, that is, cutting from one scene to another to show simultaneous action in more than one place. In *The Lonely Villa,* a woman and her children are besieged by burglars. The climax is heightened by a cutting between scenes of the wife and the children and those of the husband rushing to the rescue. The device, which Griffith was to exploit in *The Birth of a Nation* and in *Intolerance,* came to be called the Griffith last-minute rescue.

It was also in this year that he made *A Corner in Wheat,* representing a further development of his use of the shot as the basis of a film. *A Corner in Wheat* is based on Frank Norris' novel *The Pit,* in which Griffith found material for vivid contrasts. The opening shots are of quiet rural scenes, which include an extremely long, or distance, shot in which men sowing a field come toward the camera, turn, and go away from it.[1] After its bucolic introduction, the film cuts to a scene of feverish activity in the office of the wheat king and then to a scene of panic on the wheat exchange. As a result of the corner in wheat, the poor cannot afford the doubled price of bread, but the wheat king becomes all the richer. This contrast Griffith effects by

[1] This and a similar shot at the end, which give the film unity, have been likened by Iris Barry to the paintings of Millet.

showing a still shot of the unemployed being turned away from the baker's and then, after the subtitle "Wined and dined, little thinking of the suffering his genius has afforded," a shot of the wheat king's lavish banquet. It was this type of editing that the Russians were later to perfect as montage.

Early in 1910, Griffith took a company of Biograph players to California, where the previous fall the Selig Company had opened the first motion-picture studio. Griffith was attracted to California not only by the mild weather and sunlight but also by the possibilities in background scenery for his pictures. In *The Thread of Destiny: A Story of the Old Southwest,* the scene is the San Gabriel Mission, which Griffith photographed in detail to incorporate background shots—even apart from the action —in the film. In *Ramona,* he had Bitzer photograph the California countryside from great distances; no film before had included shots of such spatial length.

By 1911, Griffith seemed to consider a career as a motion-picture director a respectable one, for he gave up the name Lawrence Griffith and assumed his own—D. W. Griffith. He had apparently, however, not given up his ambition to be a writer. Even when he made *The Birth of a Nation,* he spoke to Bitzer of making a million dollars and retiring to write. It was in 1911 that he made the two-reel version of *Enoch Arden* which the Biograph Company released a reel at a time but which, at the demand of audiences, was later released as a whole.

The success of this first two-reel American film was an impetus to still longer films. Also an incentive was the success of *Queen Elizabeth* and other foreign films as long and even longer. The Italian *Quo Vadis,* in eight reels, opened in April of 1913 at the Astor Theatre in New York, at an admission price of a dollar, and, after a run of twenty-two weeks, went on to make enormous profits in other cities throughout the country. In 1913, Griffith began work on a four-reel film. It was *Judith of Bethulia,* based on a play by Thomas Bailey Aldrich and adapted by Frank Woods, whom Griffith had encouraged to become a scenario writer and who had written the scenario for the first *Enoch Arden. Judith of Bethulia,* released in 1914, was the last film

Griffith was to direct for Biograph. Its sets anticipated those for the Judean story in *Intolerance.*

Griffith had already left Biograph in the fall of 1913 and joined a new producing company, the Reliance Majestic, for which he directed and supervised the making of films until late the following spring. Then he devoted himself to an independent enterprise which was to result in his first great film, *The Birth of a Nation.*

Early in 1914, Griffith, who had been looking about for material for a motion picture greater than any that had ever been made, learned that Frank Woods had written a scenario based on a novel the Reverend Thomas Dixon, Jr., had written in 1905. It was entitled *The Clansman.* The scenario, in fact, had already been put into production, but it had not been completed. Griffith bought the film rights.

The Clansman is a remarkably undistinguished, biased, and socially objectionable novel about the Reconstruction period in the South after the Civil War. As a basis for his film, Griffith supplemented the story with material from another novel by Dixon—*The Leopard's Spots*—and, as Lewis Jacobs has pointed out, with his own recollections of his father's reminiscences, extended the subject to include the war as well as the period following the war.

To make the film, Griffith allied himself with H. E. Aitken in the formation of the Epoch Producing Corporation. The motion-picture industry in Hollywood not only refused to produce *The Clansman* but also opposed Griffith's efforts to produce and distribute it. The cost is said to have been $110,000—many times the amount which had at that time been spent on any single motion picture. Griffith took complete charge of production, even to the raising of money.

The exterior scenes were shot in Southern California and the interior at the Fine Arts Studio outside Hollywood. Griffith rented large areas of Whittier County for distance shots and for the ride-of-the-Clan sequence. Sherman's March to the Sea was shot in the San Fernando Valley. The hundreds of extra players included Civil War veterans. Griffith also secured horses, artillery pieces, the various other equipment, and the vast amount of properties and costumes the film called for.

After six weeks of rehearsing, shooting began on July 4, 1914. Lillian Gish's account of Griffith's method implies that rehearsing continued even after the shooting began: "We were rarely assigned parts," Miss Gish writes, "and the younger members of the company always rehearsed for the older members when the story was being developed, as all the 'writing' was done by Griffith as he moved groups of characters around. . . . When the story was ready to go before the camera, the older players . . . came forward and acted the parts they had been watching us rehearse for them. . . . Very often we would play episodes without knowing the complete story. . . . Only Griffith knew the continuity of *The Birth of a Nation* in its final form." The actual shooting took nine consecutive weeks, and additional scenes were shot later. Then Griffith spent more than three months in editing.

Early in 1915, the film was completed—twelve reels long, the longest American film that had been made—and on February 8, under the title *The Clansman,* it had its first showing at Clune's Auditorium in Los Angeles. On February 20, it was shown in New York City for the censors and a selected audience. At the showing, Dixon—it is said—shouted to Griffith that the title *The Clansman* was too tame, that it ought to be called *The Birth of a Nation.* The world *première* took place on March 3 at the Liberty Theatre in New York. The film was billed as *The Birth of a Nation.*

Griffith's motion picture remained at the Liberty Theatre for forty-four consecutive weeks, a record not to be broken until 1925, by *The Covered Wagon.* It played twice daily, with all the effects later to be associated with so-called colossals—reserved seats, tickets sold in advance, souvenir programs, costumed ushers, full-orchestra accompaniment, etc. *The Birth of a Nation* went on tour throughout the United States like a play, accompanied by the orchestra and shown at leading theatres; it appeared at La Scala and Drury Lane in London; it toured the Continent; and it was shown in Russia, in China, and in India. By 1930, according to Seymour Stern, *The Birth of a Nation* had been seen by more than one hundred million people and, by 1948, had grossed over forty-eight million dollars—the largest sum brought in by a film up to that time.

In a curtain speech at the *première* in New York, Dixon declared that he "would have allowed none but the son of a Confederate soldier to direct the film version of *The Clansman.*" Because of his upbringing, Griffith would not have appreciated the bias in Dixon's novel. Consequently, *The Birth of a Nation,* which presents the Civil War as resulting only from disagreement about slavery, makes the issue an emotional one and distorts the social implications. Negroes, the film implies, are inferior. The good Negroes are good because they are the faithful servants of their masters. The others, who oppose slavery, are despicable. They are a threat to the white man and must be suppressed. Thus the Ku Klux Klan is justified—and glorified. It is made the salvation of the South. In its salvation of individual characters, the Klan is a *deus ex machina* effected in a Griffith last-minute rescue.

The theme of *The Birth of a Nation* is expressed in one of the titles—"the agony which the South endured that a nation might be born." It is the tragedy of the Civil War. To illustrate the theme, Griffith treats his subject in two main parts—the Civil War and the Reconstruction period—together with a prologue and an epilogue. The Prologue pictures the introduction of slavery into America during the seventeenth century and the rise of the Abolitionist movement in the North during the nineteenth. Part I presents the Civil War from its beginning to the surrender of Lee to Grant at Appomattox and the assassination of Lincoln in Ford's Theatre five days later. Part II, the Reconstruction, shows the exploitation of the Southern Negroes by the carpetbaggers—who, according to one of the titles, would "crush the White South under the heel of the Black South"— and the resulting rise of the Ku Klux Klan. The Epilogue states that "the establishment of the South in its rightful place is the birth of a new nation."

Against this epic background, Griffith presents a double love story—that of Ben Cameron (the Little Colonel), a Southerner,

and Elsie Stoneman, a Northerner, and that of Margaret Cameron, Ben's sister, and Phil Stoneman, Elsie's brother. The mis-
fortunes of the two pairs of lovers are made to parallel the Civil
War and the troubles of the Reconstruction, and their fortunes
the resulting new birth of freedom promised in the Epilogue.
The chief characters and incidents thus not only parallel but also
symbolize the main action of the war.

There are other parallelisms and interrelations. For example, Austin Stoneman, Phil's and Elsie's father, is the counterpart of Thaddeus Stevens, a powerful Republican congress-
man and leader of the carpetbaggers. The fate of little Flora,
the youngest of the Cameron children, results from Austin Stoneman's extending power to the Negroes. Stoneman's action not
only causes bitterness in the South but almost wrecks the two
love affairs.

Griffith's style is characterized by symbolism. There is symbolism in the relation of the love stories to the main story and
in more specific ways. Silas Lynch's cruelty is symbolized in his
mistreatment of animals. The Little Colonel, on the other hand,
fondles birds. Elsie Stoneman embraces a bed post. Early in the
film, there is a close shot of parched corn, the meager food of
the Southern soldiers. Later, there is another close shot of parched
corn in the Cameron kitchen: Peace has been declared, but the
Camerons are still undergoing the hardships of war.

Griffith effects various contrasts. There is, of course, the
basic contrast throughout—the North versus the South. There
are also specific contrasts. Griffith intercuts between the scene
of the young folks at the dance in Piedmont, South Carolina,
and that of the old folks at home. After the title "The North
Victorious," there is a shot—masked in the shape of an arch—
picturing the celebration. Then, introduced by the title "The
Camerons get news of the death of their second son," there follows a shot of this scene, in contrast to that of the rejoicing North.

These contrasts are effective on the screen not only because
of Griffith's treatment but also because of their inherently cinematic quality. Other elements in the story call for more elaboration. To explain, for example, why Margaret Cameron refuses

Phil Stoneman's proposal of marriage, Griffith inserts in the proposal scene a flash back to Margaret's brother, who was killed on the battlefield. When the Little Colonel "relates a series of outrages that have occurred," flash backs take the place of speech. Or, again, an insert of a photograph graphically represents what a character is thinking. Griffith used to say, "You can photograph thought."

Griffith's predilection for the romantic accounts in part for the lack of shading in characterization. The characters in *The Birth of a Nation* are no more subtle than those in *The Clansman,* for which Griffith also had a predilection. It should be remembered, however, not only that *The Birth of a Nation* was produced hardly more than a decade after *The Great Train Robbery* but also that Griffith was working with a silent screen. Film characters, like the screen, were only two dimensional. Complex characterization would have to wait until the screen took on the dimension of sound. The characters in *The Birth of a Nation,* however, are less important than the background. It is the epic background of this film that one remembers.

Griffith turned historian to get his sets as nearly like their originals as possible. This painstaking effort is evidenced in the titles preceding scenes that represent specific historical events, as, for example, Lincoln's signing the proclamation for the first call for volunteers. A footnote to the title prefacing this scene reads: "An Historical Facsimile of the President's Executive Office, after Nicolay and Hay in 'Lincoln, a History.'" Scenes similarly documented include those of Lee's surrender at Appomattox, the assassination of Lincoln in Ford's Theatre, and the riot in Masters Hall. The most spectacular of these reconstructions of actual places is that of Ford's Theatre. Not only is the set which Griffith built for this scene the largest which had ever been built for a film, but a comparison of it with a photograph which Mathew Brady, the Civil War photographer, took just after the event shows Griffith's set to be a replica of the theatre —even to minute details—as it was on the night of April 14, 1865. These are indeed scenes of recreated actuality.

Griffith was meticulous in enacting details of these scenes

in accordance with his research. In the Ford's Theatre sequence, for example, the President's party consists of President and Mrs. Lincoln, a young lady, and a young man in military uniform— in accordance with the fact that the Lincolns took a young army officer and his fiancée to the theatre with them that evening. As the party comes up the stairs leading to the hallway behind the presidential box, the bodyguard closes a door at the back. This is the door through which John Wilkes Booth will make his murderous way later. In the few seconds before the door is closed, one can see, through the doorway, spectators in the gallery watching the play. Now the film cuts to the box, viewed from the auditorium, as the party enters. The box combines the two upper boxes to the right of the stage—again in keeping with the record. For on the morning of that fateful day, the theatre manager removed the partition separating the boxes, in accordance with the custom of thus forming a state box on the occasion of the President's attending a play. That evening the play was Tom Taylor's *Our American Cousin,* starring Laura Keene. Accordingly, Griffith not only intersperses the sequence with shots of the play being performed on the stage but in one of these represents Laura Keene's coming down to the footlights and receiving flowers passed up to her. Watching the play, Lincoln takes his wife's hand in his and, a few seconds before Booth fires the fatal shot, reaches back and draws a shawl about his shoulders—details which not only accord with the record but, in the film, constitute dramatic irony. Whether or not Griffith knew how Booth, after shooting the President, let himself down to the stage, eleven feet below the ledge of the box—in the film Booth leaps from the ledge—he takes into account Booth's catching his spur in the draped flag and thus, in striking the stage, fracturing his leg. Griffith is said to have spent two days of camera work before he was satisfied with the detail concerning the spur.

Griffith is also realistic in scenes having no specific counterpart in history. The Cameron house in Piedmont is not the conventionally pictured Southern mansion of enormous proportions but a rather ordinary house set close to the street.

Brought up in La Grange, Kentucky, Griffith knew what the Cameron house should be like. Here and there he stages a scene with so much realistic detail that some of it goes unnoticed by a spectator seeing the film for the first time—as does, for example, the brief glimpse one can get through the door at the rear of the hallway in Ford's Theatre. In the sequence in which Mrs. Cameron visits her son in the Union hospital, one's attention is centered on the scene around Ben Cameron's bed in the foreground, particularly on the terror-stricken mother when "the Army surgeon tells of a secret influence that has condemned Colonel Cameron to be hanged as a guerilla." Not only is this scene acted against a background of realistic detail— wounded soldiers, hospital attendants going about their duties, etc.—but in the far background, as though to universalize the foreground action, Griffith has a weeping woman being helped out of the ward.

Billy Bitzer obtained a collection of photographs taken by Mathew Brady, and on these he based many of the scenes in *The Birth of a Nation*. Some of the shots, particularly in the battle scenes, are almost reproductions of Brady's pictures. Years later, John Huston was to make similar use of Brady's pictures in filming *The Red Badge of Courage*.

For sheer spectacle, nothing that the motion pictures had ever encompassed equals the scope of *The Birth of a Nation*. Griffith's talent as a director is evidenced no less in his handling of crowd scenes than in getting a minute gesture right. The crowd scenes in *The Birth of a Nation* are many and varied: the dance in Piedmont, the battles, the audience in Ford's Theatre, the riot in Masters Hall, and the climactic ride of the Clan. These scenes involve hundreds of extras. On the other hand, in the scene of Sherman's March to the Sea, Griffith obtains the effect of a crowd by deploying relatively few actors in a way that suggests, without presenting, a marching army.

The lighting of the interior scenes is, for the most part, arbitrary. But no director before Griffith ever obtained lighting effects comparable to those of the night battle scenes in *The Birth of a Nation*. Natural lighting from the bursting of shells

88

providing proper and effective illumination, these scenes constitute the first use of night photography in the motion pictures. The acting in *The Birth of a Nation* seems stilted not only because of its contrast to the realism in the film but also because of its dependence on pantomime. For the most part, the alternative to gestures in a silent film is subtitles, and Griffith used subtitles sparingly. The exaggerated acting of Lillian Gish depicting Elsie Stoneman's embracing the bed post and of certain other scenes, particularly those involving the love stories, is partly attributable to Griffith's sentimental strain. Griffith did not follow a detailed scenario. Having only a rough mental outline of the action, he improvised as he went along. In directing the scene in which Elsie Stoneman visits Ben in the Washington hospital, Griffith noticed that a young studio worker was watching Lillian Gish with a particular expression on his face. He told Bitzer to get that expression onto the film. Assigned the part of the sentry standing guard at the entrance to the ward, the young man interpreted the role so expressively that he all but steals the scene.[2] On the other hand, Griffith would direct with utmost restraint a scene admitting of sentimental possibilities. When Ben Cameron comes home after the war, his mother meets him at the door. But Mrs. Cameron does not appear in the scene. Instead, through the doorway one sees only her arm as it goes around her son's shoulders.

There were more than 1,500 shots in the print of *The Birth of a Nation* at its *première*. As a result of objection to scenes of Negroes amuck in Piedmont, Griffith deleted these scenes, and the number of shots is now 1375. However, no film before had contained even as many as 1375 shots, nor so many different kinds. There are 28 shots in *Queen Elizabeth,* all of the same sort. The shots in *The Birth of a Nation* vary from close shots of objects—such as an eye seen through a small hole in a door, a cotton blossom, a pistol, and parched corn in a pan—to distance shots across great expanses of countryside and stills. Griffith

2 The actor's name is not included in the credit titles. He became known, however, as "the Adoring Sentry." In 1951, his identity was still of enough interest to provoke several letters to *Life* magazine. Lillian Gish remembers him as Freeman.

moves his camera freely, now tilting it to take in the dogs at Dr. Cameron's feet, now panning it to encompass a battlefield, or—as in the ride-of-the-Clan sequence—mounting it on the back of an automobile to precede the riding Clansmen.

In the composition of his pictures, Griffith has a tendency to depend on masks, vignettes, split screens, and other devices rather than on the arrangement of the photographed objects, although *The Birth of a Nation* contains examples of the latter arrangement. In one of the scenes in the cotton-fields sequence, action is photographed across the rails of a fence in the foreground. Another scene is centered between tree trunks. Sherman's marchers are framed by the sides of the valley. A battle scene is revealed gradually, not by an iris-in, but by the clearing away of smoke. A particularly effective shot is that of the Clansmen lined up on horseback side-by-side, the camera aiming down the line.

Now that the making of motion pictures has become a specialized but diversified process, a director is favored if he is permitted to edit his own films. That part of the process is usually assigned to a specialist in editing. But Griffith, who, like Méliès, epitomized the industry which the motion pictures have become, was his own editor. It is difficult to imagine how his films could have been edited otherwise, for not only did he shoot his pictures without a prepared script, but only he knew how the parts were to be fitted together. The greatness of *The Birth of a Nation* depends on the exact order in which the 1375 shots appear on the screen, that is, on editing.

Although Porter discovered the principle of editing, it was Griffith who developed its possibilities far beyond those illustrated, for example, by *The Great Train Robbery*. Porter's editing is limited to shifts in scene and implications of parallel action. There is no editing within the scenes of *The Great Train Robbery* and, except for the single close-up of the bandit, there is no change in the position of the camera. The contents of each scene are presented as unselectively as those in *Queen Elizabeth*. But Griffith came to see that by editing he could control the spectator's attention absolutely and thus give the scenes meaning and subtleties otherwise difficult, if not impossible.

Compare, for example, the scene of the shooting of the passenger in *The Great Train Robbery* with the assassination scene in *The Birth of a Nation*. Porter photographed his scene in a single shot, the camera remaining stationary throughout. There is nothing to identify the passenger who tries to escape except his acting. Before he breaks away from the group lined up along the railroad track and is shot for doing so, he sways back and forth, but his motion is inconspicuous. Because the scene is not edited, no relationship is established, except by acting, between this man and the other passengers. Nor, except by acting, is attention drawn to the bandit who shoots him. But in *The Birth of a Nation*, Griffith edits the assassination scene to make it appear not only more real than the shooting scene in *The Great Train Robbery* but also more meaningful. According to the script prepared by Theodore Huff, Griffith edits the scene as follows:[3]

TITLE:
A gala performance to celebrate the surrender of Lee, attended by the President and staff.
THE YOUNG STONEMANS PRESENT.
An Historical Facsimile of Ford's Theatre as on that night, exact in size and detail with the recorded incidents, after Nicolay and Hay in "Lincoln, a History."   24 ft.

SCENE 444
Iris-in to Circle Bottom of Screen
Elsie and her brother come to seats—speak to acquaintances—
Iris Opens to Full Screen to Long Shot of Theatre (from above one side showing stage 1—orchestra, boxes, gallery, etc.)   18 ft.

3 "The figure at the right of each scene is the footage; it also can be taken as the number of seconds the scene lasts. When scenes were under three feet, they were measured exactly—the figure in parentheses being the number of *frames*. Thus 2 (4) means 2 feet plus 4 frames, or a total of 36 frames. (16 frames per foot-second)"—Preface to the script.

SCENE 445
Semi Close-up of Phil and Elsie
She looks through her opera glasses.   3 ft.

TITLE:
The play: "Our American Cousin," starring Laura Keene.   4 ft.

SCENE 446
As 444
The painted curtain rises—maid dusting table.   7 ft.

SCENE 447
Medium-Long Shot of Stage
Star enters grandly.   3 ft.

SCENE 448
As 446
Star bows to audience's applause.   4½ ft.

SCENE 449
As 445
Elsie with fan—applauds—smiles at brother.   6 ft.

SCENE 450
As 447
Star blows kisses to audience—bows.   3½ ft.

SCENE 451
As 448
Star comes forward to footlights—receives flowers—
applause—   9 ft.

TITLE:
Time, 8:30
The arrival of the President, Mrs. Lincoln, and party.   4½ ft.

SCENE 452
¾ Shot of Stairs Back of Box (Sides Rounded)
Stairs dark and shadowy—guard leads man, two women,
and Lincoln up stairs.   8 ft.

SCENE 453
Medium Shot of Theatre Box
First of party enter.   3 ft.

SCENE 454
As 452
Lincoln hands hat and coat to man—enters box door r.   5 ft.

SCENE 455
As 453
Lincoln comes forward in box.   4½ ft.

SCENE 456
Semi Close-Up of Phil and Elsie
They see Lincoln—applaud—rise.   6 ft.

SCENE 457
Long Shot of Theatre
Audience standing up, cheering.   2½ ft.

SCENE 458
As 453
Lincoln bows.   2 (6)

SCENE 459
As 457
Audience cheering.   2½ ft.

SCENE 460
As 458
Lincoln and party sit down.   6½ ft.

TITLE:
Mr. Lincoln's personal bodyguard takes his post outside the Presidential box.   6 ft.

SCENE 461
¾ Shot of Hall Back of Box (Corners Rounded)
Guard enters—sits in chair in front of box door.   10½ ft.

SCENE 462
As 459
Audience still standing—play tries to go on—   4 ft.

SCENE 463
As 460
The box—President and Mrs. Lincoln bowing.   8 ft.

SCENE 464
Medium-Long Shot of Audience and Box (Corners Soft)
Cheers—waving handkerchiefs.   3 ft.

SCENE 465
Medium Shot of Stage
Old style footlights—painted scenery—people leave stage—couple alone, come forward—spotlight follows them.

9 ft.

TITLE:
To get a view of the play, the bodyguard leaves his post.

SCENE 466
Medium Shot of Hall, Rear of Box (Edges Rounded)
Guard tries to see play.

3½ ft.

SCENE 467
Medium Shot of Stage

3 ft.

SCENE 468
As 466
Guard gets up—opens rear door to gallery.

6½ ft.

SCENE 469
Long shot of Theatre   Iris Up Toward Boxes and Gallery
Guard comes.

3 ft.

SCENE 470
Medium Shot of Gallery (Circle)
The guard seats himself at edge.

4 ft.

TITLE:
Time, 10:13
Act III, scene 2

2 ft.

SCENE 471
Long Shot of Theatre   Iris at Upper Right Corner of Screen
The gallery—man in shadows.

4 ft.

SCENE 472
Semi Close-Up of Phil and Elsie
Watching play—Elsie laughing behind fan—points with fan to man in balcony—asks who he is.

7 ft.

TITLE:
John Wilkes Booth

(14)

SCENE 473
Semi Close-Up of Booth (Circle Iris)
(Napoleon pose) in the shadows of gallery.   2 (2)

SCENE 474
As 472
Elsie is amused by his mysterious appearance—laughs
behind fan—looks at him thru opera glasses.   6 ft.

SCENE 475
As 473
Booth waiting.   2 (3)

SCENE 476
*Medium-Long Shot of Gallery and Audience (Sides
Rounded)*
Booth waiting.   5½ ft.

SCENE 477
As 475
Booth waiting.   4 ft.

SCENE 478
Medium Shot of Stage Play
Comedy line—man waves arms.   3½ ft.

SCENE 479
Medium Shot of Lincoln's Box
They laugh—Lincoln feels draught—reaches for shawl. 6½ ft.

SCENE 480
As 477
Booth watches.   3 ft.

SCENE 481
As 479
The box—Lincoln drawing shawl around shoulders.   5½ ft.

SCENE 482
Long Shot of Theatre As 471   Iris Opens
Booth goes to box door.   5 ft.

SCENE 483
Medium Shot (Circle)
Guard in gallery—Booth opens door behind him.   1 (7)

SCENE 484
Medium Shot of Hall Back of Box (Corners Softened)
Heavy shadows—Booth enters softly—closes and locks door—peeks thru keyhole at box door—stands up majestically—pulls out pistol—tosses head back—actor-like— 12½ ft.

SCENE 485
Close-Up of Pistol (Circle Vignette)
He cocks it. 3 ft.

SCENE 486
As 484
Booth comes forward—opens door to box—enters. 9 ft.

SCENE 487
The Box As 479
Booth creeps in behind Lincoln. 4½ ft.

SCENE 488
The Play As 478
The comic chases woman out—cheers. 4 ft.

SCENE 489
Medium Shot of Box
Lincoln is shot—Booth jumps from left side of box. 4½ ft.

SCENE 490
Long Shot of Theatre
Booth jumps on stage—shouts. 2½ ft.

TITLE:
"Sic semper tyrannis!" 2 ft.

SCENE 491
Medium Shot of Booth on Stage
Holds arms out—limps back quickly. 3 ft.

SCENE 492
Medium Shot of Box
Lincoln slumped down—Mrs. Lincoln calls for help. 2 (6)

SCENE 493
Semi Close-Up of Phil and Elsie
They hardly realize what has happened—rise— 4½ ft.

Ford's Theatre Sequence in *The Birth of a Nation*
Directed by D. W. Griffith for Epoch Producing Corp. in 1915.

D. W. Griffith Directing *Intolerance*
for Wark Producing Corp. in 1916

G. W. Bitzer is at the camera; Mae Marsh and Miriam Cooper
are in the car. "Griffith seems to have depended on the inspiration of the moment for much of the direction."

SCENE 494
Long Shot of Theatre
Audience standing up in turmoil—Elsie in foreground
faints—Phil supports her—   4 ft.

SCENE 495
As 492
Man climbs up into box to Lincoln's aid.   5 ft.

SCENE 496
Medium-Long Shot of Theatre and Boxes
Audience agitated.   3½ ft.

SCENE 497
Long Shot of Excited Throng
Phil and Elsie leave. *Fade-Out*   11½ ft.

SCENE 498
Medium Shot of Box
They carry Lincoln out. *Fade-Out*   10½ ft.

If the scene were done like Porter's, there would be only
a single shot, or two at the most, to show parallel action in the
passage outside the President's box. However, by breaking the
scene down into fifty-five shots, Griffith obtains effects that would
not be possible in one or two long shots. He establishes a relationship between Lincoln and Booth—showing Lincoln's un-
consciousness of danger and Booth's intention; between Lincoln
and the play—showing where Lincoln's attention is directed;
between the bodyguard and the play—showing why the bodyguard leaves his post; and even between Lincoln and the audience in Ford's Theatre, particularly Elsie and Ben—showing
that the audience too is unconscious of the terrible deed about
to be committed. Griffith emphasizes Booth's murderous intention by the close shot of the revolver. He interpolates shots of the
stage not only to indicate where all of the characters except
Booth are centering their attention but also to create suspense.
This suspense is heightened by having Elsie direct Ben's attention to the balcony at the side of the box, and then cutting to
Booth—his first appearance in the film: will anything come of
his thus being noticed? These and other details, such as Lin-

97

coln's premonitory gesture of drawing the shawl over his shoulders, would be ineffective if done in the manner of *The Great Train Robbery.*

Editing is effected in various other ways. In *The Birth of a Nation,* Griffith not only cuts scenes before they are ended but also juxtaposes long, medium, and close shots—thus obtaining variety in the spatial length of the shots. He also varies the temporal length—the length of time a shot remains on the screen—and the objects which the shots contain. Any sequence in *The Birth of a Nation* illustrates this variety. An excellent sequence to study is that of the climax, which involves a typical Griffith last-minute rescue—or rather two rescues. It represents simultaneous action, not just in two different places, but in several—an office, a room adjoining the office, a street, the exterior and the interior of a cabin, and various parts of the countryside. It illustrates variety in the temporal length of the shots and variety in the objects photographed. Griffith tends to begin a sequence with a temporally long shot and decrease the temporal length as the sequence progresses. This pattern, modified by a variety in the spatial length, gives the film its rhythm.

The very nature of editing admits of effects which are not artistically possible in any other medium of storytelling. One of these is crosscutting. In the Ford Theatre sequence, for example, Griffith cuts from the auditorium to the passageway behind the President's box to show simultaneous action in both places. In this sequence the places happen to be close together. But crosscutting permits as easily the presentation of action happening simultaneously in places widely separated, as in the ride-of-the-Clan sequence. On the other hand, shots may be juxtaposed merely to show contrast, as in the cutting between scenes of battle and those of the Camerons at home. Editing is not limited, however, to the way in which the shots are arranged— each sequence beginning with a title and a fade-in (or an iris-in) and closing with a fade-out (or an iris-out).

Whereas Méliès, having discovered the dissolve, incorporated it in his films primarily as part of the trickery, Griffith adopted the dissolve as a linking device, a cinematic transition.

A particularly effective dissolve in *The Birth of a Nation* is that in the Masters Hall sequence. The sequence opens with a still, an interior scene of the hall, a subtitle having identified it as the original building. Then the photograph dissolves to Griffith's replica of the hall occupied by the actors. In linking the scenes, the dissolve establishes historical authenticity.

The iris is also a linking device. The effect of an iris-in or an iris-out is now achieved in the developing room as part of the editing process. In Griffith's time, however, the shutter on the lens of the camera was manipulated to decrease the spatial limits of a scene by a contracting circle or increase the limits by an expanding one. In *The Birth of a Nation*, Griffith uses both the iris-in and the iris-out freely. The iris-out is particularly effective in the scene in which the mother and the children are huddled on the side of the valley. As the iris opens, more and more of the scene is revealed until one sees, in the valley below, the cause of the terror. The iris-out links effect with cause. It is comparable to the panning of the camera in *The Great Train Robbery* to reveal what the robbers are running toward. The iris-in has another implication: by gradually enlarging the image on the screen, it directs the attention of the observer. One does not notice everything simultaneously. If the scene opened with the marchers in the valley and the woman and children on the hillside, the connection between the two groups would not be conveyed to every spectator, or at least not to every spectator at the same time. The Masters Hall sequence is concluded by an iris-out to the upper right-hand corner of the frame to draw attention from the whole scene—the Negroes on the floor and the whites in the gallery—to only the gallery part of the scene.

The fade is used somewhat similarly, except that the fade tends to be used only to begin or end a sequence. It is comparable to a curtain which opens or closes a scene on the stage.

Griffith sometimes blacks out part of the screen for particular effect. Shots of the riding Clansmen are masked in elliptical shape to emphasize horizontal extent. A round mask frames the shot entitled "the masked batteries." This device, called a mask, or iris, is still used in the motion pictures, as, for example, in

99

the shape of a keyhole or of field glasses to establish a particular point of view. Griffith frames some of his shots in vignette. Originally meaning a running ornament of vine leaves, a vignette (from *vigne,* vine) is a photograph which shades off gradually into the surrounding ground. Thus in the motion pictures a similarly shaded shot is also called a vignette. Griffith frames flash backs in vignette as if thus making a distinction between present and past. He does not, however, limit the vignette to flash backs. A vignette, for example, frames a distant shot of the besieged cabin, which is thereby made prominent by separation from its natural surroundings.

The composition of a shot may be effected by editing in another way. During the March-to-the-Sea sequence, the screen appears to be cut diagonally in two, the scene of the burning of Atlanta occupying the upper triangle and that of the marchers the lower. This device, called the split screen, Griffith uses again in the Epilogue.

Although titles are not inherent in the cinematic method— the first films had no titles—Griffith incorporates them variously and effectively in *The Birth of a Nation.* There are continuity titles, that is, titles to link scenes or indicate action to follow. Griffith effects irony by following the title "War's Peace" with stills of the corpse-strewn battlefield. Then there are subtitles, which indicate dialogue, but Griffith depends on these sparingly. Margaret Cameron's refusal of Phil Stoneman, as pointed out, is represented thus to obviate subtitles. The Grim-Reaping episode, introduced by Lynch's saying, "See, my people fill the streets," and constituting sixty-six shots, contains only two other subtitles.

Whatever the purpose of editing—to emphasize a particular detail, to increase suspense, to recall the past, to symbolize, to effect irony, to represent speech, or to "photograph thought"— the result must be clear to the observer. Editing must not be obvious, but it must not be obtuse. The observer should be impressed by the result rather than by the way the result is obtained. Even though successive shots may have been photographed days apart and in widely separated places, their arrangement can merge them into a coherent effect, and it is this effect which Griffith gets in his film.

Griffith made *The Birth of a Nation* before sound became an adjunct to the screen. But almost from the beginning, music had been an accompaniment to the motion pictures. When the Lumière films were exhibited in New York in 1896, they were screened to a piano accompaniment. Méliès had a special score composed for *A Trip to the Moon*. Camille Saint-Saëns wrote his *Opus 128*, for strings, piano, and harmonium, expressly to accompany the first showing of *The Assassination of the Duc de Guise* in Paris in 1908. By 1915, scores had been composed for other films. But most films were screened to the accompaniment of whatever tunes the pianists chose, the piano being the standard musical instrument in motion-picture houses. There was an attempt, however, to match the mood of a film: lively music was played during lively scenes, solemn music during sad ones. Music publishing houses printed music to accord with various kinds of scenes. A book of sheet music for the motion-picture pianist would be indexed somewhat as follows:

Aeroplane
Band
Battle
Birds
Calls
Chase
Chatter
Children
Chimes
Dances

A piece of music entitled "Hurry No. 2" was intended "for scenes of great excitement, duels, fights, etc." Many of the tunes incorporated classical music. It was not Griffith's intention, however, to permit *The Birth of a Nation* to be screened to haphazard accompaniment. He and Joseph Carl Briel composed a score for a full orchestra. Griffith had studied music, and Briel was a composer and orchestra leader. Seymour Stern describes the music for *The Birth of a Nation* as follows:

> The orchestral score as a whole was not original, consisting as it did of folk-tunes and symphonic selections. Some notable examples of the latter were *In the Hall of the Mountain King,* from the *Peer Gynt* Suite (played during the "evacuation of Atlanta" scenes); strains from the *Ride of the Valkyrie,* mingled with *Dixie* and also with other Wagnerian and other dramatic music (for the ride of the Clansmen); and innumerable fragments or mixed strains from Beethoven, Liszt, Rossini, Verdi, Tschaikovsky and other composers. However, the score did contain a number of original themes and tunes, especially composed by Griffith and Briel for the film, and of these, several have long since become famous: namely, a theme expressing barbarism, insolence and menace, played during the film-prologue, in the scenes depicting the introduction of Negro slavery into colonial America, and more especially during Part II, in virtually all scenes depicting the rise to power of the Negroes, after the Civil War; a somewhat related tune, expressing insolence, sadism and villany, played during the scenes featuring the Hon. Austin Stoneman, or his protégé, Silas Lynch; the love-theme music for the romantic "business" between the Little Colonel and Elsie Stoneman— (radio rights to the use of this motif were acquired by the comedians "Amos and Andy," who used it for years over the air as the opening bars of a musical introduction to their programme);—and, most famous of all, that weird blend of reed-whistles and horn-blasts, the Clan call, composed by Joseph Carl Briel, and played during the scenes showing the birth of the Ku Klux Klan, the summoning of the Clans and the ride of the Clansmen.

Griffith worked with Briel and the orchestra to get the music just right. The orchestra was synchronized with bugle calls, the galloping of horses, dance scenes, etc. to imitate sounds implied in the pictures. The music was also made to comment. And in connection with some of the scenes it became evocative. The score was thus a part of the editing, and the orchestra which played it traveled with the film when it went about the country. Years later, Griffith told Otis L. Guernsey, Jr., of the *New York Herald Tribune*:

The only pure art, if pure art exists, is music, and the sound pictures can't use it to best advantage. No sound track will reproduce the true melodic interrelation of instruments in an orchestra. We used to take films on tour with an orchestra to play the score, and we'd charge as much for admission as a regular legitimate road show. The music was very important— I can remember rehearsing a whole day to make the instruments give just the right sort of hysterical laugh for a scene in *Broken Blossoms.*

The Birth of a Nation is an exciting film to watch. No other treatment of this ambitious theme equals it. Making allowances for the unfortunate bias in Griffith's interpretation of history, one can enjoy the film for its immensity of scope, the construction of its narrative, and its spectacular scenes. Even the sentimental love story does not seriously distract from the realistic background on which it is imposed. Never had the motion-picture camera been used more boldly or with more variety, nor had there ever been such an effective use of close shots, close-ups, distance shots, and camera movement. But *The Birth of a Nation* is most fascinating for its editing. Griffith boldly cuts scenes before they are ended to transport the spectator at once in time and space. He juxtaposes long, medium, and close shots and varies the shots spatially and temporally while effecting variety in the objects of his camera. Nothing approaching it had ever been accomplished on the screen before. Woodrow Wilson said that *The Birth of a Nation* "is like writing history with lightning." The greatness of the film is all the more impressive because it was almost independent of anything the art had produced. Until Griffith made *The Birth of a Nation,* the motion pictures had not got far beyond *The Great Train Robbery.*

The Birth of a Nation raised a furor. Griffith was accused of libeling ten million Americans. The National Association for the Advancement of Colored People, together with various individuals, including President Eliot of Harvard University, Oswald Garrison Villard, editor of the *Nation,* and Jane Addams of Hull House, protested. Riots broke out in some of the cities where the film was screened. Griffith answered the attacks by citing documentary evidence in support of the controversial scenes and by publishing a pamphlet entitled *The Rise and Fall of Free Speech in America*. His final answer was his film *Intolerance*.

Before *The Birth of a Nation* was released, Griffith had started work on a film which was to have been called *The Mother and the Law*. It was based in part on the report of the Federal Industrial Commission concerning the killing of nineteen employees of a chemical plant during a strike and in part on the Stielow murder case, prominent in the news of the time. Having become involved in the controversy over *The Birth of a Nation*, Griffith decided not to release *The Mother and the Law* by itself but to work it into a larger film that would have intolerance as the theme. Accordingly, he added to *The Mother and the Law* three other stories which purport to show intolerance in three other periods in history. Intolerance, Griffith says in the film, is the motivation of tyrants, groups and individuals, uplifters in all ages everywhere. It is the cause of persecution, torture, and war. Its only counterforce is love. The subtitle "Love's Struggle throughout the Ages" appeared on the program when the film was originally shown.

After the introductory titles, which announce that the "play," as the film is called, is made up of four separate stories, laid in different periods of history, and that the play turns from one story to another as the theme unfolds, the modern story—originally *The Mother and the Law*—begins. "In a western city," as the first title in the story states, "we find certain ambitious ladies banded together for the uplift of humanity." The uplifters persuade Miss Jenkins, spinster sister of a wealthy manufacturer, to contribute to their cause. Miss Jenkins obtains the money from her brother, who, in self-compensation, reduces the wages of his employees. Thus is caused a strike which results not only in the deaths of some of the workers, who are mowed down by the militia, but in the meeting and then the marriage of the Boy and the Dear One, as the hero and heroine are sentimentally called. Jenkins' injustice, however, has put the Boy in an evil environment, and he has become the victim of the Musketeer of the Slums. Now, in attempting to free himself of the Musketeer, he is sent to prison for a theft he has not committed, and the uplifters take away Dear One's baby. Released from prison, the Boy is again charged with a crime of which he is innocent—of murdering the Musketeer—and is sentenced to be hanged. Through the efforts of Dear One, however, he is proved innocent and saved from the gallows at the last minute.

The second story, the least developed of the four, opens in Judea in A.D. 27. In it the Crucifixion of Jesus is shown to be instigated by the Pharisees and other intolerant groups.

The massacre of the Huguenots in France on St. Bartholomew's Day, 1572, the subject of the third story, is made the result of religious intolerance. Catherine de Médici persuades her son Charles IX to order the massacre, reminding him of the massacre of the Catholics by the Protestants at Nîmes. As a result, Brown Eyes, the heroine, is killed in spite of the hero's attempt at a last-minute rescue.

In the Babylonian story, intolerance is depicted as the cause of Belshazzar's downfall in 539 B.C. The priests of Bel, intolerant of Belshazzar's worship of Ishtar, goddess of love, betray Belshazzar to Cyrus. Again an attempt at a last-minute rescue fails when the Mountain Girl warns Belshazzar too late that Cyrus is leading his army against the city.

The four stories, which are told simultaneously, are united by a symbol, that of a woman rocking a cradle. Repeatedly during the film, particularly when cutting from one story to another, Griffith inserts, in a vignette, this symbol of the cradle, suggested by Walt Whitman's lines in *Leaves of Grass*:

> *Out of the cradle endlessly rocking,*
>
> * * *
>
> *I, chanter of pains and joys, uniter of here and hereafter,*
>
> * * *
>
> *A reminiscence sing.*

Griffith paraphrases Whitman for a title:

> "Today as yesterday, endlessly rocking, ever bringing the same human passions, the same joys and sorrows."

The woman rocks, unaware of the Three Fates in the background.

Like *The Birth of a Nation, Intolerance* has a symbolic epilogue. Images of "cannon and prison bars wrought in the fires of intolerance" dissolve into "flowery fields," the cross in soft focus appears on a split screen, and the film ends with the cradle-rocking scene.

Intolerance is also like *The Birth of a Nation* in its sentimentality. The epithets "Little Dear One," "Brown Eyes," "the Kindly Heart," "the Friendless One," etc. are in keeping with Griffith's oversimplification of character. On the other hand, there are bits of crude realism, as in the cutting off of the Persian soldier's head—reminiscent of the kinetoscope film, *The Execution of Mary Queen of Scots*—and in details of the massacre of the Huguenots.

The style is characteristically Griffith's. There is the studiedly developed suspense, not only in individual incidents, such as Charles IX's hesitancy in signing the fatal decree and the uncertainty over the outcome of the Boy's trial, but in the events leading up to the climaxes: Will Latour cross the city in time to save Brown Eyes from the mercenaries? Will the Mountain Girl reach Babylon in time to save Belshazzar from the Persians? Will Dear One reach the governor, and then the prison, in time to save the Boy from the gallows? The suspense in the climaxes is developed, of course, by the Griffith last-minute rescue, although in only one of the stories is the rescue accomplished.

There are not only the obvious comparisons among the four stories in *Intolerance,* which, in fact, Griffith called "A Drama of Comparisons," but also comparisons and contrasts in details. As a result the film admits of considerable irony, a favorite figure of Griffith's. There are, for example, the two trials, the one in the Judean story and the one in the modern. The uplifters are the modern counterparts of the Pharisees. There is irony in the episode of the strike at Jenkins' plant: the reformers, led by the industrialist's sister, go to the workers' homes to keep the workers from sin; the militia, called out by the industrialist, shoots the workers to keep the workers from striking. Here the ironic parallelism extends even to details:

"the reformers" vs. *"the militia"*
"led by" vs. *"called out by"*
"the industrialist's sister" vs. *"the industrialist"*
"go to the worker's home" vs. *"shoots the workers"*
"to keep the workers from sin" vs. *"to keep the workers from "striking"*

After the workers have been shot down, the camera, panning across the dead and wounded in the street, takes in a billboard on which is written the legend "The Same Today as Yesterday." It is said that this legend on a billboard, which Griffith saw from a train window as he was on his way from California to New York for the *première* of *The Birth of a Nation,* gave him the idea for *Intolerance.* "What a wonderful man, the Admiral Caligny, if he only thought as *we do!"* a courtier of Charles IX whispers to another courtier. "What a wonderful king, if he only thought as *we do!"* a Huguenot whispers to another Huguenot. The scene in which the uplifters take away Dear One's baby is concluded by the Scriptural injunction quoted as a title: "Suffer little children to come unto me." The possibilities of the motion pictures for effecting contrast through instantaneous transference from one scene to another were an outlet for Griffith's sense of irony. The parallel shots in *A Corner in Wheat—* the poor people at the baker's unable to buy bread and the lavish banquet of the wheat king—anticipated similar ironic contrasts in *Intolerance,* as, for example, the lavishness of the Jenkins' home contrasted with the simplicity of Dear One's, or "Babylon's greatest noble" luxuriously served wine at Belshazzar's feast contrasted with the Mountain Girl milking a goat in the tenement district to obtain a drink for herself.

Symbolism, another favorite figure of Griffith's, is as pronounced in *Intolerance* as in *The Birth of a Nation.* There is the familiar use of animals to represent attitudes and traits of people, or the symbol may be an inanimate object: Cyrus' sword, for example, seen in a close shot. There is symbolism in the backgrounds to the titles to each of the stories: the fleur-de-lys, the book *Intolerance,* the stone tablets, etc. And there is, of course, symbolism in the cradle-rocking shots. More cinematic as a symbol is the long shot of the industrialist sitting alone in his office, his dominance emphasized by the bare foreground. Years later, in *A Place in the Sun,* George Stevens was to call for a similar shot of the hero sitting alone in the office of his industrialist uncle.

Griffith worked even less from a script in making *Intolerance* than in *The Birth of a Nation.* The scenario for the film was entirely his own, but it existed only in his notes, which he destroyed before filming began. He seems to have depended on the inspiration of the moment for much of the direction. The actors were ignorant not only of the whole plan of the film but even of the plots of the stories in which they appeared.

Intolerance is not only more spectacular than *The Birth of a Nation* but also more spectacular than any film that had been made previously, and in some ways its spectacle has not since been equaled. It calls for four great settings differing widely in time and place and for the many sets needed for each of them. Whereas today such effects as these are more often than not obtained by models and process shots, Griffith built all of his sets full-size. The walls of Babylon were erected on a 254 acre plot near the present juncture of Hollywood Boulevard and Sunset Boulevard in Hollywood, ancient Jerusalem rose on a site several miles away, and sixteenth-century Paris fifteen miles away at Inceville. The Pacific Electric Railway laid tracks to connect Babylon with its main line and with that of the Southern Pacific to bring in supplies and equipment. Billy Bitzer, in a letter to Seymour Stern, recounts the building of the sets:

> Imagine laying out what were to be the mammoth, stupendous sets for "Intolerance," without sketches, plans or blueprints at the beginning. . . . Mr. Griffith, "Huck" Wortman and myself would have a pow-wow as to how the sun might be, its approximate arc-position months hence—and that was the beginning of a set for "Intolerance," to which, as it progressed

and became a fifty-foot-high structure, a hundred or more feet long. Mr. Griffith kept continually adding. So that eventually these walls and towers soared to a height of well over a hundred and fifty feet, although at the beginning their foundations were intended only for a fifty-foot height. Huck had to continually reinforce their bases for the ever-increasing height, which perturbed Huck a whole lot, and also shot my light-direction plans all to pieces.

In addition to the casts of characters for each of the four stories, thousands of extras appeared in the film. According to Seymour Stern, 4000 players were included in a single shot in the scene of Belshazzar's feast, 8000 in Cyrus' armies, 5000 in the attack on the great gate of Imgur-Bel, 3500 in the Judean story, 1000 in the modern story, and 16,000 in the scene of the Persians' advance on Babylon—"the largest mob-scene and greatest single mass-shot ever staged for any film." According to Bitzer and Griffith, the total number of players in *Intolerance* was 60,000.

The cost of the film was about $2,000,000. It is said that $650,000 was spent on Belshazzar's feast and related scenes. In 1955, it was estimated that if *Intolerance* were remade, it would have cost more than $30,000,000. Thus it is relatively the most expensive film in the history of the motion pictures.

As they were for *The Birth of a Nation,* all exterior shots were taken outdoors. Even the beam of light falling on Lillian Gish and the cradle came from the sun through a hole in the roof of the otherwise darkened set. The subtitle introducing Part II of the film is "A Sun Play of the Ages."

The original print of *Intolerance* was tinted: blue for the Judean story, sepia for the French, gray-green for the Babylonian, and amber for the modern. Night scenes were blue, sunny exteriors yellow, and night battle scenes red.

The acting is comparable to that in *The Birth of a Nation.* It is as sentimental and as realistic. Lillian Gish has said that Griffith took Robert Harron and Mae Marsh to the death house in San Quentin Prison before they filmed the last scenes of *Intolerance.* In the Judean story, the acting gives the sequences

109

dignity by studiedly slow movement. In the French story, Josephine Crowell, who played the kindly Mrs. Cameron in *The Birth of a Nation,* effects credible malevolence as Catherine de Médici. Mae Marsh's acting as the anxious wife in the trial scene has been said to be even more expressive because Miss Marsh did not know the outcome of the trial.

In variety of shots, no other film has equaled *Intolerance.* From its space-filling distance shot of the Persian Army to a close shot of the sword of the Mighty Man of Valor, from a view of Belshazzar's feast as the observer looks down onto the court far below to close-ups of the feasters, it contains shots of varying distances and angles. There are close shots of Margery Wilson's eyes and of just the lower part of Miriam Cooper's face. To introduce the feast sequence, the camera shoots the court from a distance and from above. This kind of shot is called an establishing shot, that is, a shot which establishes the whereabouts of a scene or the relationship of details to be subsequently shown in closer shots. After thus introducing the sequence, the camera comes down toward the court and then tracks up the steps. In the attack on Babylon, the camera moves perpendicularly up the side of the great wall. In the modern story, it tilts up the wall of the Musketeer's room. For the pursuit-of-the-train sequence, it was mounted on an automobile, as it had been for photographing the ride of the Clan in *The Birth of a Nation.*

Griffith gives careful attention to the composition of his shots. The camera in the modern story is directed across the row of prone soldiers, their guns pointed in parallel lines, and makes a composition comparable to that of the line of mounted Clansmen in *The Birth of a Nation.* This pattern was to be followed later in the shot of the sailboat masts in *Potemkin* and in that of the bows of the English archers in *Henry V.* The white of candles in the Huguenot home and of the headdresses of the Huguenot women contrasts strikingly with the dark background. Architectural features of the sets frame shots in the Babylonian scenes. For example, when the high priest of Bel looks down on the city he is planning to betray, Griffith relates the character and the object of the character's attention by placing the camera to photograph the priest in the foreground and Babylon, framed by an opening in a wall, in the background. The opening thus at once serves the purpose of a mask and is an inherent part of the scene. In another shot, the great wall of Babylon splits the screen in half. In the Judean story, a shot is framed by the arch of a gate.

Intolerance is important primarily for its editing. As in *The Birth of a Nation,* Griffith makes use of crosscuts, flash backs, fades, irises, dissolves, etc. Catherine de Médici says, "Remember, gentlemen, when hundreds of our faith perished at the hands of the Huguenots," whereupon a flash back depicts what is to be remembered. A flash back photographs the thoughts of the Friendless One as she is about to shoot the Musketeer. In the trial scene, a flash back gives the Boy's reply to the evidence against him. The iris is used, as in *The Birth of a Nation,* to open and close sequences. An iris-in on the great gate of Imgur-Bel introduces the Babylonian story. Comparing this use of the iris-in with its use in introducing Sherman's March-to-the-Sea sequence in *The Birth of a Nation,* Seymour Stern writes that "the camera retreats through the ages and time rolls backward." A fade-out followed by a fade-in denotes a lapse of time in the scene in which Dear One and the Boy are praying. The dissolve links the scene of the empty headquarters of the uplifters to a similar scene of the headquarters occupied, as in the two comparable shots of Masters Hall in *The Birth of a Nation.* A dissolve makes a transition from a long to a medium shot of the uplifters, from a medium to a close shot of an alcohol still, and from a shot of the bell tower of St. Germain to that of a single bell. There are also dissolves in the Epilogue. Griffith sought composition not only in the arrangement of photographed objects but also by editing. There is, for example, the masked shot of the Persian warrior falling from the wall, the shot blacked out at the sides to emphasize height. Processing gives the shot of the onrushing Persians a menacingly dark sky for a background.

The famous shots of Mae Marsh's hands in the courtroom scenes are alternated with shots of the Judge and of the Boy to depict the wife's anguish. Griffith was the first to appreciate the close shot as particularly cinematic—a means of emphasizing something already shown and of directing attention to it as the stage cannot. Any one of the sequences illustrates how editing guides the attention of the audience precisely as the director wishes. The scene in the death chamber in the modern story is made up of shots varying in spatial and temporal length, in angle, and in subject—of the knives cutting ropes, of the guards' faces, of the Boy in his cell, of the trap falling. This is the method of a film, not of a play. It effects its purpose in a way that no other medium can. It is purely cinematic.

Titles are used much as they are in *The Birth of a Nation,* that is, to describe action to follow, to comment, to indicate dialogue, etc. As in *The Birth of a Nation,* footnotes to titles document references to historic fact. Continuity titles are superimposed on backgrounds suggestive, as pointed out, of the four stories. Titles underline Griffith's theme: "Brown Eyes and her family ignorant of the web intolerance is weaving around them," "Cyrus repeats the world-old prayer to kill, kill, kill, and to God be the glory world without end," "Intolerance burning and slaying," and "Returning to our story of today we find Miss Jenkins aligning herself with the Pharisees." In the final sequences, the titles are few. Relationships between situations having been established, explanatory titles are not necessary.

If it was necessary to establish the fact that the unit of motion-picture construction is not, as in *Queen Elizabeth,* the scene but the shot, *The Birth of a Nation* accomplished this. *Intolerance* expanded the use of editing, particularly in the presentation of simultaneous action. Griffith crosscuts not only within each of his four stories but from one story to another. At the beginning of the film he spends several consecutive minutes in getting each story under way—seven minutes on the modern story, four on the Judean, five on the French and, after a return for three minutes to the modern story, nine on the Babylonian. As he progresses, he cuts more and more frequently from one story to another. Toward the end of the film some of these cuts are lightning-like. In the climax, some of the shots are only one-fifth of one second in duration.

Werner Krauss and Conrad Veidt in *The Cabinet of Dr. Caligari*
Directed by Robert Wiene for Decla-Bioscop in 1919.

"Expressionism in this film is primarily a matter of staging. Not only are light and shadow painted on the sets, but the sets are deliberately distorted in perspective."

Gibson Gowland as McTeague in *Greed*
Directed by Erich von Stroheim for the Goldwyn Co. in 1923.

"Many shots in the film are studied arrangements of actors, furniture, and even wall decorations. In the murder scene, the doorway, draped in Christmas tinsel, ironically frames McTeague."

Although Griffith did not plan *Intolerance* or give it that title until he had made the modern story as *The Mother and the Law*, the modern story is the basis of the film. Each of the other stories is related to it. It not only introduces—and ends—the film but is the only story that Griffith returns to before he has introduced all of the others; that is, after beginning the third story, the French, he returns to the modern story before beginning the Babylonian. Furthermore, he devotes more of his film to the modern story than to any of the others. Ironically, however, only in an incidental way can its theme be considered intolerance at all. It is significant that the modern story had been a separate film with a conventional happy ending before Griffith decided to combine it with three other stories also purporting to be based on the same theme. Even if the ending were not happy, the story would not be primarily one of intolerance. The uplifters are intolerant, but they are only links in chains of circumstance. By securing Miss Jenkins' money, they indirectly cause the strike, and the strike indirectly causes the Boy to get into trouble. Later, the uplifters take away Dear One's baby, but the baby is of so little importance that Griffith does not have it returned to its mother at the end of the story.

Neither is the Babylonian story, the second longest and most spectacular of the four and the *raison d'être* of the film, any more strongly based on intolerance than the modern story. Because the priests are jealous of Ishtar, they betray Belshazzar to Cyrus. But even if the priests' jealousy were intolerance, it is not the cause of the war but only, indirectly, of Belshazzar's losing the war. However, one does not really care which side wins. As Julian Johnson has observed, it is just a great show.

The weaving together of the four stories does not then produce the effect that Griffith intended. Nor does the cradle-rocking symbol overcome this weakness. The symbol is only a literary one, depending on the accompanying paraphrase of lines in *Leaves of Grass* for its meaning. As John Howard Lawson points out, nothing happens to the woman rocking the cradle. She is still only a literary symbol at the end of the film.

The greatness of *Intolerance* does not lie in its theme or

in its spectacle, for the greatness of a motion picture cannot depend merely on the photographed objects. Its greatness is in Griffith's execution of his plan. He appreciated, as no one else had, that in the motion pictures, immeasurably more than in any other medium, there are means of compressing time, place, and action. He effects this compression in *The Birth of a Nation*. *Intolerance,* says Terry Ramsaye, was "the first and only film fugue." Its weaknesses, including the four separate stories told as one, make it one of the monstrosities of the motion pictures, but the bold use of cinematic techniques by which they are told overcomes the weaknesses by greatness.

Intolerance had its *première* at the Liberty Theatre in New York on August 5, 1916. Because of the fame of *The Birth of a Nation,* the interest in the gigantic sets Griffith had built in California, and the announcements in the New York newspapers of "D. W. Griffith's Colossal Spectacle," the opening attracted even more attention and a larger crowd than had the earlier picture. Griffith had spent two months editing 300,000 feet of film. The released print, 13,000 feet long, took almost three and one-half hours to screen, not including two intermissions.[4]

As they had for *The Birth of a Nation,* Briel and Griffith composed a special orchestral score incorporating familiar music and played by the orchestra of the Metropolitan Opera House. The music was varied as well as familiar—Beethoven's *Minuet in G* for the peaceful scene in the Huguenot home before the massacre, Handel's *Largo* for the scene in which Jesus is scorned by the Pharisees, "In the Good Old Summer Time" for a day at Coney Island, etc. The film provides opportunity for considerable use of imitative music, such as bugle calls, bells, and gongs, as well as accompaniment to the various dance scenes.

In its first four weeks at the Liberty Theatre, *Intolerance* drew larger audiences than *The Birth of a Nation* had during the same length of time, but attendance fell off thereafter, and the run at the Liberty was concluded after twenty-two weeks.

[4] Deletions, attributable primarily to censorship, have since reduced the length of this time. The print distributed by the Museum of Modern Art Film Library has a running time of about 170 minutes.

Financially, *Intolerance* was a failure. Although after the New York run the film toured the United States and Europe, Griffith never recouped the vast sums of money—from the profits of *The Birth of a Nation*—he had poured into the production of it. The cause for the failure is said to have been that audiences were baffled by the rapid crosscutting among the four stories. Actually, however, Griffith introduces and develops the stories so clearly that the increased rate of cutting as the film nears its end can hardly hide the meaning. If the meaning is hidden, it is in the stories themselves, not in the way in which they are told. But movie audiences are not so much interested in the way stories are told as in stories. Here Griffith failed them.

But if Griffith had never made another film, his fame as the greatest of all motion-picture directors would still be secure. For greater even than the films which he made was his revelation of the possibilities of the art of the motion pictures. He continued to make films until after the introduction of sound, his most famous ones, in addition to *The Birth of a Nation* and *Intolerance,* being *Hearts of the World* (1918), *Broken Blossoms* (1919), *Way Down East* (1920), *Orphans of the Storm* (1921), *America* (1924), *Lady of the Pavements* (1929), and *Abraham Lincoln* (1930). But, like Méliès, Griffith was ignored in his later years by the industry for which he had done more than anyone else. He died, almost forgotten, in a hotel room in Hollywood on July 23, 1948. As if in atonement for neglect of their master, motion-picture people gathered for his funeral and testified to his greatness. No one, however, has evaluated his work more aptly than a fellow director, René Clair: "Nothing essential has been added to the art of the motion picture since Griffith."

6. Expressionism

 B ecause of Dickson, Edison, and other Americans, the motion-picture machine originated in the United States and because of Porter and Griffith, the art of the motion pictures too, but the evolution of the motion pictures has been international. In Germany, for instance, as early as 1898, five years before Porter made *The Great Train Robbery,* a film called *Excursion* evidenced the rudiments of editing. *Excursion* is a short film picturing some bicycle riders, but unlike films of the time on comparable subjects—traffic scenes, waves breaking, trains approaching, etc.—*Excursion* is composed of several shots: a long shot of bicycles in the distance, a closer shot of bicycles winding along a road, a shot of the riders' faces, a shot of the cyclists' legs in motion, and finally the cyclists in full shot. But the Germans did not continue to contribute to the rise of the art; instead they copied.

At the time of World War I, however, they struck out in an interesting direction. Some of the young Germans working in experimental theatres—directors, actors, scene designers—started experimenting in the motion pictures. The form which their work took was expressionism. Of all the German expressionistic films, the most famous is *The Cabinet of Dr. Caligari,* directed by Robert Wiene and produced in 1919.

This film originated in the experiences of its scenarists, Hans Janowitz and Carl Mayer. At a fair in Hamburg in 1913, Janowitz, a young Czech, observed quite closely the suspicious actions of a shadowy figure in a park on the Holstenwall. The next day, Janowitz read in the newspaper of a murder at the fair. Attending the funeral of the victim, he suddenly had the sensation of having discovered the murderer. After the war, Janowitz met Mayer in Berlin and told him of his experience. Mayer, who had been an infantry officer in the German Army and had come out of the war a pacifist, told Janowitz of having become embittered against a military psychiatrist who had examined him. The two discussed the possibility of making a film based on Janowitz' experience at Hamburg and Mayer's experience with the psychiatrist. Then one evening at a fair in Berlin, they visited a side show in which a hypnotized strong man foretold the future. The collaborators now had their story. The title was the result of Mayer's happening on the name *Caligari* in looking through *Unknown Letters of Stendhal*.

The subject of their scenario is a mountebank, Dr. Caligari, who comes to a North German town called Holstenwall and obtains a permit to operate a concession at a fair. Ostensibly, Caligari's show is the exhibition of a somnambulist, Cesare, who answers questions about the future, but actually Caligari uses Cesare as an agent for committing murders. Finally detected by a student named Francis, whose friend Alan was one of Caligari's victims and whose fiancée, Jane, was kidnaped by Cesare, Caligari seeks refuge in an insane asylum. Pursuing him there, Francis discovers that the superintendent of the asylum and Caligari are the same person. With the assistance of members of the asylum staff, Francis finds in the director's office a book about an eighteenth-century homicidal showman named Caligari whose agent is Cesare. Faced with the evidence that he has been emulating the original Caligari, the mountebank becomes violent and is placed in a strait jacket.

In undertaking the direction of the film, Robert Wiene put Janowitz' and Mayer's story into a frame so that it is told by Francis as an inmate of the insane asylum. As the film opens, Francis and a fellow inmate are sitting on a bench in the garden of the asylum. Jane, who is also an inmate, passes by. "What she and I have experienced," Francis says, "is yet more remarkable than the story you have told me. I will tell you." As Francis goes on, "In Holstenwall, where I was born . . . ," there are an iris-out on the asylum scene and an iris-in on a picture of Holstenwall, and Janowitz' and Mayer's story begins. Correspondingly, at the end of the story, when Caligari has been put into the strait jacket, the scene becomes the garden again. Francis is saying to his fellow inmate, "Today he is a raving madman chained to his cell." Francis and his companion then get up and walk into the courtyard of the asylum. Meeting Caligari there, Francis becomes hysterical and is overpowered by attendants, who carry him into the same room where Caligari was restrained. After examining Francis, Caligari announces, "At last I recognize his mania. He believes me to be the mythical Caligari. Astonishing! But I think I know how to cure him now." Thus the film ends.

It is said that at the time *The Cabinet of Dr. Caligari* was made, the studio was limited in its quota of electric power and that it was therefore decided to obtain lighting effects by painting light and shadow on the scenery. This expressionistic distortion in the film accords with the theory that expressionism in the German drama was partly due to the scarcity of materials for stage production after the war. Similarly, montage originated, about the same time, as a result of the scarcity of film stock in Russia. Wiene had chosen three scene designers to do the sets for *The Cabinet of Dr. Caligari*—Hermann Warm, Walter Röhrig, and Walter Reimann—and it was Warm's suggestion to paint light and shadows instead of representing them realistically. *The Cabinet of Dr. Caligari* evidences not only this distortion of reality but other manifestations of expressionism too.

Expressionism results from the attempt of the artist to express meaning beyond reality. The result is a studied distortion. In expressionistic drama, which developed as an art form in Germany at the end of World War I, the resulting distortion is manifested in various ways: type—or even abstract—characters, kaleidoscopic sequence, unrealistic dialogue, frank use of the aside and the soliloquy, monodrama, symbolism, telescopic characterization, etc. The staging of expressionistic plays calls for a corresponding distortion which takes the form of expression of the medium of the stage itself: scenery and properties painted on backdrops, abstract settings, arbitrary lighting, vaudeville-like use of spotlights, robot-like stage movement and gesture, the extension of the acting area to include the auditorium as well as the stage, etc.

Some of these manifestations are evident in *The Cabinet of Dr. Caligari*. Not only are light and shadow painted on the sets, but the sets are deliberately distorted in perspective—in keeping with the madman's imagination. The shadows are painted to fall unnaturally. The opening scene of the story within the frame —the town of Holstenwall—is a painted one. The town clerk's desk and chair are unnaturally high to symbolize authority and to dwarf Caligari. There is sharp contrast between Cesare's black, tight-fitting costume and Jane's white, flowing gown to emphasize the girl's helplessness. Caligari's make-up gives the impression of having been carelessly applied. The acting itself is distorted, particularly that of Werner Krauss as Dr. Caligari and of Conrad Veidt as Cesare. As Cesare attempts to escape, Veidt's body seems to lean against the wall as if, as Siegfried Kracauer observes, the wall exuded him. The titles and subtitles, in the original print of the film, were represented in crooked letters.

Although expressionism in *The Cabinet of Dr. Caligari* is primarily a matter of staging, there are expressionistic elements in the story itself. For example, telescopic characterization is represented in the identity of Caligari with the superintendent of the asylum. Thus both characters are portrayed in the film by only one actor. In keeping with another expressionistic manifestation, all of the characters are types. The content is also expressionistic in its suggestion of the monodrama. Told in a frame, the story is that of one individual, the madman Francis.[1]

For all its stagelike methods, *The Cabinet of Dr. Caligari* has certain cinematic elements. Although most of the scenes are in medium shots, comparable to the method of *Queen Elizabeth*, there are cuts to close-ups and even close shots. Occasion-

[1] In his book *From Caligari to Hitler*, Kracauer makes the point that in representing the story of Caligari as told by a madman, Wiene changes the meaning, that whereas in Janowitz' and Mayer's original scenario madness is shown to be inherent in authority, in the revised version authority is glorified, and its antagonist is mad. The film, Kracauer concludes, thus mirrors the eagerness of the Germans, after the war, to withdraw into a shell.

ally the camera moves, as, for example, in a tracking shot of the faces of the men in the asylum office examining Caligari's book. There is crosscutting between Cesare and Jane when Cesare approaches Jane's house and between Caligari and Francis when Francis, having become suspicious of Caligari, is investigating him. There is a flash back to show Cesare's having been admitted to the asylum. The story within the frame is, in fact, a flash back too. In making the transition from the frame to the story, Wiene cuts several times between Francis telling the story to his fellow inmate and the beginning of the story itself. Some of the transitions here, as in other parts of the film, are effected by the iris-out and the iris-in. "In Holstenwall, where I was born," reads the subtitle. An iris-out on Francis is then followed by an iris-in on a scene of the painted town on the hill. In an iris-out on Caligari, the circle contracts to the black stripes on the back of Caligari's light-colored gloves. The iris is used freely throughout.

The reason that *The Cabinet of Dr. Caligari* has had little effect on the development of motion-picture art is that the conspicuous characteristic of the film—expressionism—is almost entirely a matter of staging. Expressionism in *The Cabinet of Dr. Caligari* is effected no more cinematically than are the "arranged scenes" of *A Trip to the Moon*. For example, although there is expressionistic symbolism in the height of the town clerk's desk and chair, the effect is obtained as it would be in the production of a play on the stage: the camera merely photographs the scene. Similarly, the other elements of expressionism in the film are effected not by the camera but by the scene designers. Although the camera offers possibilities for distortion of reality quite as much as stagecraft does, if not more, Wiene chose to effect expressionism in the film as though the camera were only a recording instrument. *The Cabinet of Dr. Caligari* is famous for its expressionism, but the expressionism in *The Cabinet of Dr. Caligari* is of the theatre. The film implies the motion pictures primarily as a machine.

7. Naturalism

When in 1923 Erich von Stroheim was engaged by the Goldwyn Company to make a film version of Frank Norris' novel *McTeague,* the assignment seemed appropriate. Von Stroheim had demonstrated, in films he had already made, new possibilities in the art of the motion pictures, particularly in the realistic treatment of material. In this respect he is comparable to Eugene O'Neill, who at the time was similarly contributing to the art of the drama. Von Stroheim, it was assumed, would appreciate the naturalistic *McTeague* and, as a gifted director, translate it properly into cinematic terms. The Goldwyn Company failed, however, to take sufficiently into account the fact that von Stroheim, again like O'Neill, was an artist who refused to be bound by the conventions of his art. Thus the producers were dismayed at the film version which von Stroheim made of *McTeague*—the colossal motion picture *Greed.*

Von Stroheim had a career as varied as Griffith's. He was born in Vienna, Austria, in 1885. A graduate of the Imperial and Royal Military Academy, he served as second and first lieutenant in the Austrian Army. Then, in 1909, he came to the United States, where his diversity of occupations, accounting at least in part for the realism which he was to effect in his films, included being a peddler of flypaper, a dishwasher, a railroad section hand, a book agent, a deputy sheriff, a lifeguard, a riding master, a vaudeville actor, and a private in the New York National Guard. His first appearance on the screen was as a Negro in *The Birth of a Nation.* When Griffith made *Intolerance,* von Stroheim not only acted the Second Pharisee but served as "assistant director," a position which has been described as that of a glorified property man. Later, because of his army experience, he became Griffith's "military advisor." During World War I, he was a familiar figure in current films—including Griffith's *Hearts of the World*—as the brutal German officer. Monocled, stiff-necked, and aggressively unpleasant in these roles, he exploited the epithet "the Man You Love to Hate." He died in a Paris suburb in 1957.

Von Stroheim's versatility in the motion pictures is in the tradition of Méliès and Griffith. His first film, *Blind Husbands*, which he directed in 1918, was based on a scenario by von Stroheim; the settings were by von Stroheim; and—for, unlike Griffith, he did not give up acting when he became a director—the leading character in it was played by von Stroheim. *Blind Husbands*, called the first American film with a sophisticated approach to sex, not only manifested von Stroheim's feeling for comedy of manners but also anticipated the flair for realism which was to culminate in *Greed*. Included among the credit titles for *Foolish Wives* (1921) are the following: "Original story and screenplay by von Stroheim," "Directed by von Stroheim," "Settings and design: von Stroheim," "Count Wladislas Karamzin . . . Erich von Stroheim."

Because of his insistence on realism, von Stroheim acquired a reputation for extravagance and arrogant independence. His Stanislavski-like concern for authentic detail made the production of his films expensive. For the hotel scenes of *Foolish Wives*, he set up a complete electric bell system, not even seen. Said to have cost $1,000,000, the film grossed only $800,000. In 1922, when he was directing *The Merry-Go-Round*, he was replaced by another director, the reason being not only his daring treatment of the story but also his extravagance. In directing *The Merry-Go-Round*, a satire on the old royal family of Austria, von Stroheim reputedly had the soldiers' underwear marked with coats of arms and spent $10,000 on medals for the army. It is reported that he used up 200,000 feet of film on *The Wedding March* (1927), made in two parts—"The Wedding March" (fourteen reels) and "The Honeymoon" (ten reels). Von Stroheim was so incensed that his two-part work had been given to someone else to cut that he refused to have the second part released in the United States. *The Wedding March,* for which he had written not only the continuity but also the original story and which is marked by his cynicism and irony, has been described as his profoundest work, not excepting *Greed.*

While von Stroheim came to represent the artist refusing to compromise with Hollywood commercialism, his producers encouraged the spreading of reports about the master's lavishing time and money in the making of films. He admitted that after the mutilation of *Greed,* which was also drastically cut after he had completed it, he abandoned his ideals. "I have had to quit realism entirely," he declared. "When you ask me why . . . I am not ashamed to tell you the true reason: only because I do not want my family to starve."

Von Stroheim's last connection with the motion pictures was as actor rather than director. In Hollywood during World War II, he assumed again his German-officer parts—now the arrogant Nazi. Then he returned to Paris, which had been his home for several years, and appeared in French films, including his own adaptation of August Strindberg's play *The Dance of Death.* In 1950, he was the butler in the Hollywood-made film *Sunset Boulevard,* an ironic story of a motion-picture actress who cannot accept the fact that she is no longer glamorous. There is irony of a different kind when in the concluding scene the butler, for the sake of humoring the now deranged actress, pretends that he is directing her in a new picture, for von Stroheim's great contribution to the motion pictures is as a director, although he made hardly more than a dozen films. Of these, the greatest is *Greed.*

The technique of *Greed* shows the influence of Griffith. As Griffith's assistant, von Stroheim had learned, for example, the cinematic values in the varying distances of the camera from the photographed objects. *Greed* contains Griffith-like close-ups, even of the McTeague cat. There are close shots comparable to those in *The Birth of a Nation* and *Intolerance*: of McTeague's feet as he walks along the hall, of McTeague's feet—together with the mule's—wearily treading the dry, cracked floor of Death

Valley, of Marcus Schouler's clenched fist during the wedding ceremony, of the rattlesnake, of the gila monsters, and of inanimate objects, such as part of the ore crushers, a jackknife, and a watch fob. Movement of the camera in *Greed* is no less effective than Griffith's, as, for example, in the tracking away from the wedding group as it breaks up and in a panning which emphasizes the vastness of Death Valley. The shots are carefully composed. In many of them, for all the naturalism, there is a studied arrangement of actors, furniture, and even wall decorations. In the murder scene, the doorway, draped in Christmas tinsel, ironically frames McTeague. In another scene, the white of Trina's apron and of McTeague's coat stands out against the otherwise dark costumes and dark background in a composition suggestive of that of the white and black contrast in the scene in the Huguenot home in *Intolerance*.

In its editing, *Greed* is no less Griffith-like. Crosscutting during the murder sequence not only effects dramatic irony but suddenly relates the immediate and horrible action to the everyday world, with which the murderer will sooner or later have to reckon. The crosscutting in the climax is in the manner of the Griffith last-minute rescue. Also suggestive of Griffith are some of the contrasting and parallel shots, of Marcus getting "four bits" from McTeague and Trina counting her hoarded wealth, of Trina fondling the gold coins and the mottled arms reaching down into the treasure chest, of the empty canteen and the gold coins spilled out on the ground, etc. In its transitions, *Greed* represents von Stroheim's having learned from Griffith the effective use of the dissolve, the fade, and the iris.

For all his flamboyance, von Stroheim is a serious artist, and he was never more serious than when he made *Greed*. Evidence of his seriousness is the dedication of the film to his mother. It was not out of mere pique that he refused to see *Greed* after the producers took it out of his hands and had it cut. Having adapted *McTeague* to the screen as he believed a novel should be adapted, he considered the deletions a violence both to his film and to his theory. Years later, he told Peter Noble:

124

I had always been against cutting great chunks out of a novel to fit it into screen time. Some of the world's masterpieces have been hacked in this way to make a film director's holiday, but I always believed in putting a novel *completely* on the screen just as it was originally written.

This is what he tried to do when the Goldwyn Company gave him carte blanche in 1923. To accomplish his purpose, he filmed *McTeague* not just chapter by chapter but almost paragraph by paragraph.

Filming a novel in this way would, obviously, result in a picture much too long. There is, however, nothing in the cinematic method of storytelling that determines how long a motion picture should be. On the other hand, a motion picture implies an audience seated in a theatre to see the picture at one sitting or, at most, at one sitting with intermissions, as Griffith arranged for *The Birth of a Nation* and *Intolerance*. In this respect a motion picture is comparable to a play. In *Alice Sit-by-the-Fire,* James Barrie, who was a novelist as well as a playwright, makes a distinction between a novel and a play:

> In a play we must tell little that is not revealed by the spoken words; you must ferret out all you want to know from them, although of course now and then you may whisper a conjecture in brackets; there is no weather even in plays except in melodrama; the novelist can have sixteen chapters about the hero's grandparents, but there can be very little rummaging in the past for us; we are expected merely to present our characters as they toe the mark; then the handkerchief falls, and off they go.

Here Barrie the playwright is pointing out, in a Barriesque stage direction, the limitations which the stage imposes on the drama. A play is shorter than a novel because an audience can be expected to be attentive in a theatre for only a limited time, and it has been established that this time is about two hours. Since a film likewise depends on holding the attention of an audience in a theatre, films are no longer than plays; they are, in fact, usually shorter, one reason being that a movie audience expects

to see not only the feature film but several shorter films as well—
a newsreel, an animated cartoon, a travelogue, etc. Furthermore,
the shorter the main film, the more showings may be fitted into
a day and thus the more money taken in at the box office. It is
not aesthetics, but economics, that has determined that a film
should be ninety minutes long.

Von Stroheim's method of filming *McTeague* resulted in a
motion picture not only longer than ninety minutes but longer
than *Intolerance*. Exactly how long it was has not been established. The original print has been either inaccessibly stored
away or destroyed, and reports differ as to its length, the esti-
mates varying from 18 to 150 reels. According to Lewis Jacobs,
whose figure is 42 reels, *Greed* would have taken ten hours to
screen. At this rate, 150 reels would represent thirty-five hours.
Even allowing for variation in the length of a reel, *Greed* was a
long film. The Goldwyn Company turned the print over to a
studio worker, who edited it mainly by cutting out chunks and
bridging gaps here and there by titles. Although the film was
thus cut down to its present length of 11 reels, or two and one-
half hours, enough of the original film remains to illustrate what
von Stroheim meant by "putting a novel *completely* on the screen
just as it was originally written."

How close he came to his purpose cannot be estimated precisely, since all of the evidence is not available. However, *Greed*
was not, nor could it have been, *McTeague* "*completely* on the
screen just as it was originally written." That it was not is evidenced by von Stroheim's own changes, apparent even in the
extant version, and that it could not have been is patent, for
the mediums of novel and film are different.

In the first place, von Stroheim changes the historical period
of *McTeague*. He represents the story as commencing in 1908,
whereas Norris began writing *McTeague* in 1892 or 1893 and
completed it by 1898. Von Stroheim's purpose was apparently
to bring the outcome of the story down more nearly to the time
Greed was filmed—1923. Inasmuch as *Greed* includes actual shots
of San Francisco streets and environs, von Stroheim may have
decided on this change for the sake of verisimilitude, but in mak-

126

ing the change, he sacrificed absolute verisimilitude to the novel and thus compromised his theory.

Whereas Norris begins the novel by presenting the hero already established as a dentist, *Greed* opens with McTeague as a young man working in the gold mine. In the novel, the gold-mine episode is introduced indirectly and only briefly. Sitting in his dental chair in that scene with which the novel begins, McTeague is reminded, by the tunes he is playing on his concertina, of his life ten years earlier. In the film, these recollections are presented directly—not in flash backs, as they would have been if von Stroheim had put the novel on the screen just as it was originally written. This change to an earlier point of attack is significant, for it is characteristic of films to begin their stories at the beginning. *Greed* begins with an iris-in on the title "The Big Dipper Gold Mine, 1908, Placer County, California." For about ten minutes—in contrast to hardly more than two hundred words that Norris devotes to this part—the film presents McTeague's early life before it brings McTeague up to the point in the story at which the novel begins. Like most films, *Greed*, therefore, requires no exposition.

Greed deviates from *McTeague* in the presentation of events near the climax. Chapter 21, which narrates McTeague's flight across Death Valley, ends as follows:

> He tramped forward a little farther, then paused at length in a hollow between two breaks, resolving to make camp there.
> Suddenly there was a shout.
> "Hands up. By damn, I got the drop on you!"
> McTeague looked up.
> It was Marcus.

The first part of Chapter 22, the concluding chapter of the novel, tells of Marcus' joining the posse to track down McTeague, of the rest of the posse's giving up, and of Marcus' going on alone. One-third of the way through the chapter, the action is brought up as follows to the point at which the preceding chapter ends:

> "If he ain't got water with um," he said to himself as he

pushed on, "if he ain't got water with um, by damn! I'll be in a bad way. I will, for a fact."

*   *   *   *

At Marcus' shout McTeague looked up.

This is the novelistic method of representing simultaneous action. However, Griffith having shown how the motion pictures can present action so that it seems more nearly simultaneous, von Stroheim rearranges the order of these incidents. The flight-and-pursuit sequence opens with a continuity title "McTeague had been missing from San Francisco for weeks when—." There follows an insert of a poster announcing a reward of a hundred dollars for the capture of "John 'Doc' McTeague." Then after a medium-long shot of a crowd, in Western outfits, looking at the poster, there is a close-up of an individual in the crowd: it is Marcus. After a few more shots to emphasize Marcus' connection with the crowd and the interest in the poster, there is another continuity title—"The fugitive." The next shots are of a valley and of McTeague leading his mule. The film now cuts back to Marcus and his associates. It is night. A brief sequence shows Marcus joining the posse to track down McTeague. Again there is a continuity title—"That night desolation lay around Mac." A series of shots pictures the fugitive, unnerved, firing at imaginary pursuers and then throwing his rifle away. Again the film cuts back to Marcus, who is starting out with the posse. This cut is made without a continuity title, for now the relationship between the two lines of action has been established. The sequence continues in this manner for fifteen minutes, during which time it crosscuts seventeen times between the pursuer and the pursued, before the lines of action are united in Marcus' catching up with McTeague.

Mortimer Adler says that, when a novel is adapted to the screen, "it must be contracted in the direction of dramatic magnitude [by which he means the limited number of characters and incidents in a play as contrasted with the larger number in a novel] but expanded with respect to dramatic detail [i.e., the amount of detail in the development of single incidents]."

The present version of *Greed,* for example, leaves out Old Grannis and Miss Baker and, as a result, incidents in connection with them. Maria appears only briefly; Zerkow is left out entirely and, accordingly, the affair involving him and Maria. McTeague's actions after the murder are considerably curtailed, are limited, in fact, to the last stages of the flight across Death Valley. This kind of deletion contracts the scope of a novel toward that of a play, which has even fewer characters and episodes than a film.

Von Stroheim would not agree, however, that when a novel is adapted to the screen, "it must be contracted in the direction of dramatic magnitude." He intended that his film should have the epic magnitude of Norris' novel. Its unprecedented length implies that it did. The contractions in *Greed,* it must be remembered, are not von Stroheim's.

On the other hand, *Greed* illustrates Adler's corollary to the dictum about expansion: A novel adapted to the screen "must be expanded with respect to dramatic detail." These expansions in *Greed* are von Stroheim's. Whereas in *McTeague* Norris only briefly refers to certain episodes in the hero's life, in *Greed* von Stroheim presents them directly and in detail. There is, for example, the episode which leads to McTeague's becoming a dentist. Norris narrates it in two sentences:

> Two or three years later a travelling dentist visited the mine and put up his tent near the bunk-house. He was more or less of a charlatan, but he fired Mrs. McTeague's ambition, and young McTeague went away with him to learn his profession.

In *Greed,* the two sentences are expanded into twenty-eight shots, taking almost four minutes of screen time. The expansion of the five words "he fired Mrs. McTeague's ambition" illustrates the difference between the novelistic and the cinematic method of storytelling. A continuity title announces what is to be depicted: "Filled with the one idea of having her son enter a profession and rise in life . . . the chance came at last to Mother McTeague." The shots in the rest of the sequence are as follows:

> *Fade-in to Medium-Long Shot*: A crowd in front of a mining shack.

129

Sign on shack: MIKE'S SALOON.

Medium Shot: The crowd surrounding the dentist and the dental chair, in which is seated a Chinaman.

Medium-Close Shot: The patient in the chair. McTeague standing at right. The dentist extracts a tooth and holds it up for the crowd to see.

Full Shot: Mrs. McTeague watching.

Medium-Close Shot: McTeague.

Close-Up: Mrs. McTeague.

Long Shot: The whole scene.

Medium-Close Shot: McTeague.

Close-Up: Mrs. McTeague.

Medium Shot: The patient leaning over and spitting. The dentist, in his long white coat, standing beside him.

Dissolve to the same scene except that McTeague, in a black frock coat, is in the dentist's place. The patient stands up, reaches into his pocket for a coin, and pays McTeague.

Dissolve to the preceding scene. The Chinaman pays the dentist.

Close-Up: Mrs. McTeague.

Medium Shot: The crowd around the chair. *Fade-Out*.

The adaptation of novel to screen involves, however, more than expansion. In describing the wedding of Trina and McTeague, Norris writes:

> Then Trina and the dentist were married. The guests stood in constrained attitudes, looking furtively out of the corners of their eyes. Mr. Sieppe never moved a muscle; Mrs. Sieppe cried into her handkerchief all the time. At the melodeon Selina played "Call Me Thine Own," very softly, the tremolo stop pulled out. She looked over her shoulder from time to time. Between the pauses of the music one could hear the low tones of the minister, the responses of the participants, and the suppressed sounds of Mrs. Sieppe's weeping. Outside the noises of

the street rose to the windows in muffled undertones, a cable car rumbled past, a newsboy went by chanting the evening papers; from somewhere in the building itself came a persistent noise of sawing.

The predominant image in that passage is sound: the sounds in the room itself, the sounds from the street and, finally, a sound from somewhere in the building—"a persistent noise of sawing." Without specifically naming it, Norris is implying that, in spite of the immediate concern of the characters with a momentous event, the everyday world is going on just the same, and in "a persistent noise of sawing" he is implying a premonition of discord in this marriage.

When von Stroheim made *Greed,* sound was not yet an adjunct of the screen. How then would he express in pictures the idea Norris expresses in the noise of the sawing? A similar problem arose when *What Price Glory?* was filmed three years later— that of representing on a silent screen the sounds of battle. The problem in *What Price Glory?* is solved by a title which reads: "Deafening roar of guns . . . shrieks of shells." Von Stroheim's solution is different. Recognizing that the street noises and the sawing are symbolic, von Stroheim changes the audio symbols into a visual one. During the wedding scene, he points his camera over the shoulders of the bridal couple and past the face of the minister to the window. Through the window is seen, passing in the street outside, a funeral procession.

Most of the changes resulting from the translation of novel to film might be expected of an appreciative and imaginative director. A pupil of Griffith's, von Stroheim should have made more of these changes than he did. He was misled by his zeal to put *McTeague* completely on the screen.

The naturalists said that they were trying to write the truth. A prefatory title to *Greed* is, significantly, a quotation from Frank Norris:

> I never trucked. I never took off the hat to fashion and held it out for pennies. By God, I told them the truth. They liked it, or they didn't like it. What had that to do with me? I knew it for the truth then, and I know it for the truth now.

In its naturalistic motivation, von Stroheim's film is true to Norris' novel. Man, according to the naturalists, is the product of his heredity and his environment. In keeping with this sociological approach, *McTeague* is a story of disintegration of character. McTeague's downfall is partly caused by fate—fate, for example, that he meets and marries Trina, whose character is also weak. A continuity title in *Greed* reads: "First, chance had brought them together. Now mysterious instincts as ungovernable as the winds of heaven were uniting them." Since Norris implies that his hero's heredity is also responsible, von Stroheim, paraphrasing a passage in the novel, inserts this subtitle: "But below the fine fabric bred of his mother ran the foul stream of hereditary evil, a taint given him by his father."[1] Fate is against the characters. There is always the chance that they may escape, but there is also the chance that they may not.

The film is also faithful to the naturalism of the novel in its detailed picture of working-class life in California at the turn of the century. The neighborhood in which McTeague lives on Polk Street in San Francisco is photographed with documentary-like realism. Von Stroheim is no less realistic in his picture of the dental parlors and McTeague at work in them than Norris, who is said to have studied *A Textbook of Operative Dentistry* to get McTeague's dental procedures just right. The wedding feast is filmed in scrupulous accord with Norris' description. Vividly recording the mores of a people at a particular time and place, *Greed* is no less a sociological document than *McTeague*.

The tendency of the naturalists to emphasize drabness of environment characterizes *Greed* as much as it does *McTeague*. The film by no means glamorizes. Von Stroheim even outdoes Norris in drabness. In the courtship scene in the novel, Trina and McTeague sit on the roadbed of the railroad along the muddy shores of San Francisco Bay. In the film, they perch on the concrete causeway over the sewer outlet, Trina having suggested, as set forth in a subtitle, "Let's go over and sit on the sewer." The scene of the marriage proposal, the little railway

---

[1] It is the only reference to McTeague's father in the present version of *Greed*. He appeared in von Stroheim's original film.

132

station to which the couple returns in the rain, could not have been represented on the screen less romantically.

As a naturalist, Norris would have been delighted with the faithfulness of von Stroheim's film to the slice-of-life treatment implicit in his novel. Von Stroheim went to actual locations described in *McTeague* to film his scenes—the San Francisco streets, San Francisco Bay, Death Valley, etc. He even had an expensive set built to represent a San Francisco street because of the alterations which time had made in the real street.[2] The drearily realistic butcher shop, together with the fat butcher in his bloody apron, the saloon, the dental parlors, the Cliff House, with its player piano—everything looks authentic. The camera again and again focuses on naturalistic detail: the cracked washbowl—unemptied—and the bed—unmade—in the McTeague flat, the patch on the face of the man who announces that Trina has won the lottery, Marcus' picking his ear—and his nose—the ragged bandages on Trina's fingers, and August Sieppe's agonized fidgeting after the theatre.

Greed shows von Stroheim appreciative of another naturalistic trait of *McTeague*—irony. The introduction of the funeral procession into the wedding ceremony is a departure in fact from the novel but not in ironic spirit. Norris' irony is even heightened by the visual images in the film, as, for example, Trina's gold pieces in contrast to the personal appearance of the McTeagues and to their surroundings, the Christmas setting for the grisly murder—no less grisly for being presented only indirectly—and the coins spread out on the floor of Death Valley as Marcus says, "We are all dead men."

Romanticism is, paradoxically, a characteristic of naturalism, and the romantic elements in *McTeague* appear as well in *Greed*. The heroine's winning five thousand dollars in a lottery and becoming a miser, the revenge motive which leads the villain into the desert after the hero, and the melodramatic ending are presented in detail and emphasized by subtitles.

[2] However, an observant critic, Rodney Ackland, points out an anachronism: Whereas the cast is costumed according to the time of the story, the passers-by in the San Francisco street scenes wear clothes of the time the film was made.

Von Stroheim makes quite as much of another paradoxical characteristic of naturalism—symbolism—as Norris does. Many of the symbols are inherent in the naturalistic elements of the story. There is, for example, the rain. *Greed* is not a picture of sunny California. Rain interrupts the courtship scene, and rain makes the scene of the marriage proposal even drearier. Looking for symbolism in a work of art is precarious, for one may find symbols the artist was not conscious of. On the other hand, it is more than probable that symbolism is intended in details such as the tear in the photograph of the bridal couple and in the express train's roaring by as McTeague embraces Trina. Here and there von Stroheim introduces symbols of his own—the canary's fluttering in the cage as McTeague contemplates the anesthetized Trina, the cat's leaping at the canary as McTeague reads the forbidding letter, the cat's eye winking when Marcus tells the McTeagues that he is going away, etc. If *Greed* seems to depend on symbolism even more than *McTeague,* it is because von Stroheim attempts to represent, by visual images, passages which he could not otherwise represent so readily on the silent screen, as, for example, the funeral procession which he substitutes for the noise of sawing. That some of his symbols involve animals may be ascribed to von Stroheim's having been a pupil of Griffith's. It is significant that in the first scene of the film McTeague fondles a bird and that, in the last, he frees the canary from its cage. The gold-colored objects in *McTeague*— the huge tooth, the bird cage, the ore, the coins—not only appear in *Greed* but in the original print of the film were tinted yellow. The use of concrete objects as symbols is also reminiscent of Griffith. The unrealistic shot of the mottled arms reaching down into the treasure chest is as obvious a symbol as the cradle-rocking shot in *Intolerance.*

The theme of *Greed* is that of *McTeague.* It is pointed up in incident after incident and underlined by titles. The film, like the novel, shows the effect of greed not only on the hero but on the other two main characters. Greed causes the death of each of them. The one-word title von Stroheim chose for his film seems to have been inevitable.

But *Greed* is an anomoly. The way in which it is true to *McTeague* is at once its flaw and its virtue. Von Stroheim's theory of completeness in the transference of a novel to the screen resulted in a film monstrosity. The significance of *Greed*, however, is not so much in the extent to which von Stroheim compromised—in the extent to which he translated novelistic terms into cinematic ones—original and interesting as these translations may be, as in the extent to which he actually succeeded in his purpose. His success was only partial, but he made a more nearly literal transcription of a novel than is represented by any other film. The literalness, however, is not due entirely to his purpose; it is due also to the very nature of the motion pictures, that is, their inherent reality. A film can be more realistic than a novel. By the same token it can be more naturalistic. Norris said that he told "the truth," by which he meant the whole truth, for naturalism implies completeness. Von Stroheim made *Greed* not only as naturalistic as *McTeague* but more so. Utilizing Griffith's techniques when they served his purpose, von Stroheim demonstrated in *Greed* possibilities of the screen for meaningful content. *Greed* violates the rules, but it is one of the most powerful films that the art of the motion pictures has produced.

8. Montage

Sergei Eisenstein's approach to the motion pictures was, like Méliès', through the theatre. When Méliès first saw the Lumière films, he realized that the *Cinématographe* was a means of expanding his performances of magic at the Théâtre Robert-Houdin. Eisenstein, also a theatre director, saw in the motion pictures not just a means of expanding stage performances but a means of expression far beyond anything the stage could effect.

Although the films of Eisenstein and those of Méliès could hardly be more different, there is a similarity in the backgrounds and early inclinations of these famous directors. Sergei Mikhailovich Eisenstein was born on January 23, 1898 in Riga, Latvia. His father, of Jewish descent, was an engineer for the city of Riga; his mother was a Russian lady of independent means. At an early age, Eisenstein showed an aptitude for drawing and for a while attended a school of fine arts. But his father, intolerant of art, particularly as a vocation, wanted Sergei Mikhailovich to be an engineer. Although young Eisenstein enrolled in the Institute of Civil Engineering at the University in St. Petersburg, he chose a course within engineering leading, he said, "not to mechanical, technical fields but to one closely allied to art—to architecture." Then the Russian Revolution broke out, and Eisenstein, having left the university to join the Army of Workers and Peasants, contributed his artistic skill to the cause by decorating military supply trains with banners and posters satirizing the old regime and glorifying the Revolution. When in 1920 the Bolshevik Government was established, he joined the Proletkult Theatre as a scene painter, but soon he was designing

136

the complete production of plays. When he was only twenty-four years old, he became the director of the Proletkult. It would seem that here were evidences of another Méliès—the prosperous middle-class background, the early inclination to art, particularly drawing, the parental intolerance of art as a means of livelihood and the wish that the son would follow the father's practical profession, the compliance—at first—but the eventual revolt in favor of the earlier bent, the satiric spirit expressed in caricature for political propaganda, the attraction to the theatre, and the attainment, at a youthful age, of a theatre directorship.

Here, however, the similarity ends. Méliès adapted the motion pictures to the confines of the stage. Eisenstein, who found the stage too confining, seized on the motion pictures as a means of breaking the confines entirely.

By the time Eisenstein saw Griffith's films, he had definite ideas about the difference between a play and a production of the play on a stage. "A written play," he said, "belongs to literature, and those who are interested only in its content should read it in the privacy of their rooms." The stage, he contended on the other hand, "belongs to the performers, for whom the play is merely, or, at most, a stenciled material on which their art is embroidered." He held that the director's function is to co-ordinate their efforts. Eisenstein used to say that he wished he could dispense with actors and use puppets instead. At the Proletkult, he made the stage a circus-like arena, the audience on three sides. Indeed, his production of *The Wise Man* at the Proletkult in 1923 was more circus-like than theatre-like. In her biography of Eisenstein, Marie Seton refers to Eisenstein's stage at the Proletkult as "acrobatic." Her description of the production of *The Wise Man* implies not only the extent to which Eisenstein had broken with theatre convention but also a groping toward the kind of editing which was to characterize his films —montage:

> The stage properties were unique. The floor of the arena was covered with a soft carpet, as necessary physical protection for the actors. Attached to the ceiling was the high trapeze. Scattered about for easy use were rings, horizontal poles, vault-

ing horses, slack wire, and other instruments used as the con-
tiguous extension of a stage gesture. Thus, the actors, commencing a line of dialogue with relative dramatic formality, ended
with a gymnastic twist. In place of the dramatically formalized
expression of rage as hitherto employed in the theatre (even
in the Meyerhold Theatre), the climax of the rage became the
lightning flash of a somersault; while exaltation found expression in a *salto-mortale,* and lyricism in a delicate pirouette along
a tightrope.

When he saw *Intolerance,* Eisenstein realized that the motion
pictures offered possibilities far greater than those hemmed in
by the puny scope of the stage, even of his acrobatic stage, and
that he had found the way to resolve his problem.

Eisenstein set about seriously studying the motion pictures.
Boris Ingster, who was one of his associates, says that during
the day Eisenstein studied motion-picture photography and at
night attended the only motion-picture theatre in Moscow showing American films. "We joined him behind the screen," says
Ingster, "because none of us could afford to pay our way into the
theatre night after night, and fortunately the friendly manager
permitted the young film enthusiasts to watch the show from
the vantage point of Eisenstein—a vantage point that gave one
a rather distorted view of the proceedings." Eisenstein was impressed by the editing, but he saw something more in editing
than, for example, the linking of scenes to effect flash backs or
crosscutting. He saw that, through joining together strips of film,
it would be possible to link scenes different not just in time and
space but in content as well. Then he evolved his theory of
montage.

Montage is said to have originated in Russia as a result of
a shortage of film stock. Soviet film directors found that they
could join pieces of film, only a few frames in length, and obtain
effects not inherent in the individual pieces. It will be remembered that Porter made parts of *The Life of an American Fireman* from bits of film he found in the Edison factory. The Soviet
directors, however, obtained their effects from joining unrelated
shots—a theory that Eisenstein perfected, as Griffith had perfected Porter's.

138

Eisenstein came to realize that unrelated shots might be combined to imply something other than merely the sum of the concepts of the shots. He explains his theory in his books *The Film Sense* and *Film Form*. Citing a passage in Pushkin's *Pultava,* he says that "the poet magically causes the image of nocturnal flight to rise before the reader in all its picturesque and emotional possibilities":

> But no one knew just how or when
> She vanished. A lone fisherman
> In that night heard the clack of horses' hoofs,
> Cossack speech and a woman's whisper.

Eisenstein points out that there are three shots in this passage: (1) clack of horses' hoofs, (2) Cossack speech, and (3) a woman's whisper, and that these three representations—they are sounds—are combined to evoke an emotional experience in the reader. To these three sound pictures, Eisenstein observes, Pushkin adds a visual picture, which has the effect of a full stop. It is a close shot:

> And eight horseshoes had left their traces
> Over the meadow morning dew.

Eisenstein's point is that Pushkin gives the reader more than the information that Marya has vanished—he has, in fact, said as much in the first line and a half—that by combining the objective images he gives the reader the *experience* of vanishing and that he does so by montage.

Eisenstein likens montage to the trope, that is, he says, quoting *The Shorter Oxford English Dictionary,* "a figure of speech which consists in the use of a word or phrase in a sense other than that which is proper to it," and he cites "a *sharp* wit (normally, a *sharp* sword)" as an example. Although of course montage is editing, it is editing of a particular kind. "To the parallelism and alternating close-ups of America," Eisenstein writes in reference to editing in American films, "we offer the contrast of uniting these in fusion, the montage trope." He points out that Griffith's films do not contain "this type of montage construction," that although Griffith's close-ups create atmosphere and outline traits of character and although the close-ups of the chaser and the chased speed up the tempo of the chase, "Griffith at all times remains on a level of *representation* and *objectivity* and nowhere does he try through the *juxtaposition* of shots to shape *import* and *image*." He observes that in *Intolerance* Griffith attempted montage. But, he says, citing Griffith's description of *Intolerance* as "a drama of comparisons," that is all it remains— a drama of comparisons. And he explains why the attempt to unite the four stories by the cradle-rocking shot is unsuccessful: Griffith had been inspired to translate the lines of Walt Whitman, "not in the structure, nor in the *harmonic recurrence of montage expressiveness,* but in *an isolated picture,* with the result that the cradle could not possibly be *abstracted into an image of eternally reborn epochs* and remained inevitably simply a *lifelike cradle,* calling forth derision, surprise or vexation in the spectator."

Akin to Eisenstein's conception of montage is the device in films whereby an interpolation of a shot of a speeding train, or of only the driving wheels, indicates a journey, or that of the hands of a clock rapidly turning, leaves being torn from a calendar, or a succession of shots of the same scene in different seasons of the year indicates passage of time. This kind of interpolation, or, as it is called, Hollywood montage, conveys only fact. True montage, on the other hand, implies, as Eisenstein says, "a juxtaposition of shots to shape import and image."

Montage implies that the way the film is built up, that is, the arrangement of the shots, is as important as, if not more important than, the content of the shots. Eisenstein, like Griffith, directed the taking of the pictures in a series of scenes bearing little similarity to the form the pictures would take in the completed film. The most important work in the making of *The Birth of a Nation* and, particularly of *Potemkin* was not in photographing the scenes but in breaking them down and rearranging the pieces according to an artistic plan. In 1930 Eisenstein went to Mexico to make a film that he was going to call *Que Viva Mexico!* Because of a misunderstanding with Upton

Sinclair, who was financing the undertaking, Eisenstein was not permitted to complete the film. Instead it was taken out of his hands, edited by some one else, and released as *Thunder Over Mexico*. But the film is ineffective because the editor did not know how Eisenstein had planned to cut the scenes into pieces and arrange the shots.

Eisenstein elaborated his theory of montage. It is significant that the passage he cites from Pushkin involves images of sound, because even before sound became an established adjunct to the screen, Eisenstein was already explaining how montage could be applied to sound in relation to pictures. In his books he distinguishes nine kinds of montage, including what he calls "chromophonic," or color-sound, montage. In an essay published in 1929 he discusses two kinds of montage he incorporated in *Potemkin*: rhythmic montage and tonal montage.

In rhythmic montage, he explains, "formal tension by acceleration is obtained . . . by shortening the pieces not only in accordance with the fundamental plan, but also by violating this plan." Contending that "the most affective violation is by the introduction of material more intense in an easily distinguished tempo," he cites the Odessa-steps sequence in *Potemkin*:

> In this the rhythmic drum of the soldiers' feet as they descend the steps violates all *metrical* demands. Unsynchronized with the beat of the cutting, this drumming comes in *off-beat* each time, and the shot itself is entirely different in its solution with each of these appearances. The final pull of tension is supplied by the transfer from the rhythm of the descending feet to another rhythm—a new kind of downward movement— the next intensity level of the same activity—the baby-carriage rolling down the steps. The carriage functions as a directly progressing accelerator of the advancing feet. The stepping descent passes into a rolling descent.

Whereas in rhythmic montage, Eisenstein says, "it is movement within the frame that impels the montage movement from frame to frame," in tonal montage, movement "embraces *all affects* of the montage piece. [Tonal montage] is based on the characteristic *emotional sound* of the piece—of its dominant.

The general *tone* of the piece." A typical use of tonal montage would be, he says, "working with the combinations of varying degrees of soft focus or varying degrees of 'shrillness,' " and he cites as an example the fog sequence in *Potemkin,* that part of the film in which the harbor is photographed through the fog:

> Here the montage was based exclusively on the emotional "sound" of the pieces—on rhythmic vibrations that do not affect spatial alterations. In this example it is interesting that, alongside the basic tonal dominant, a secondary, accessory *rhythmic* dominant is also operating. This links the tonal construction of the scene with the tradition of rhythmic montage, the furthest development of which is tonal montage. And, like rhythmic montage, this is also a special variation of metric montage.
>
> This secondary dominant is expressed in barely perceptible changing movements: the agitation of the water; the slight rocking of the anchored vessels and buoys; the slowly ascending vapor; the sea-gulls settling gently onto the water.

Appreciating the screen as a powerful means of propaganda, the Soviets nationalized the motion-picture industry in 1919. "Of all the arts," declared Lenin, "the most important for us in my opinion is the film." The nationalization of the industry was at once an advantage and a disadvantage to the Russian directors—an advantage in that it freed them from commercialism and allowed them to experiment whether their films made money or not and a disadvantage in that they were expected to make films glorifying the Revolution and the new ideology. Such were the conditions under which Eisenstein set out on his career as a director of motion pictures.

His first film was *Strike,* completed in 1924. *Strike,* which treats of the activities of the Russian working class in the days before the Revolution, is not a story so much as a mood. If there is a hero in *Strike,* it is the masses.

The next year Eisenstein completed *Potemkin,* and then in 1928 he made *October*—or, as the film was entitled outside of Russia, *Ten Days that Shook the World*—to commemorate the tenth anniversary of the October revolution. *October,* like *Strike* and *Potemkin,* has no conventional story. The subject is the flight of Kerensky, the attack on the winter palace, and the victory of Lenin. Again the hero is the masses. That the cast was drawn largely from among the people of Leningrad, where most of the scenes were shot, represents both the experimental and the didactic in Eisenstein's films. To Eisenstein, actors are of the theatre, and the motion pictures should depend upon them as little as possible. The hero being the masses, the masses are appropriately the actors. *October* thus has a documentary-like quality which is characteristic of all of Eisenstein's films.

Before he made *October,* Eisenstein started a film to have been called *The General Line,* but after completing *October,* he reorganized and rephotographed *The General Line* and brought it out in 1929 as *The Old and the New.* Propaganda for collective farming, it depicts the advantages of modern methods and modern machines over primitive agriculture.

By the time he completed his next film, *Alexander Nevsky,* it was 1938. The screen had been talking for a decade, Eisenstein had visited Hollywood and had made his ill-fated expedition into Mexico to film *Que Viva Mexico!* and he had returned to Russia to find himself out of favor with the government. He was accused of being a bourgeois individualist and an artist for art's sake. But either the political climate changed, or it was believed that Eisenstein had, and he was commissioned to make *Alexander Nevsky.* Although *Alexander Nevsky* is a sound film —with a musical score by Sergei Prokofiev—its best parts do not depend on speech, as for example, the charge of the Teutonic knights across the ice of Lake Ladoga. The sequence of the charge of the Teutonic knights is said to have been the inspiration for Laurence Olivier's filming the charge of the French knights in *Henry V.*

Eisenstein's last film was *Ivan the Terrible* (1944), even greater in pictorial quality than *Alexander Nevsky.* Part II of *Ivan the Terrible* (completed in 1946 but not released until 1958), however, was criticized as not following the Party line. But Eisenstein admitted error, and Stalin consented to his making the third part of the film, in which certain sequences from

Part II were to be included. Part III was never completed. On the morning of February 10, 1948 Eisenstein was found dead in his study in Moscow.

The greatest of Eisenstein's films is *The Battleship Potemkin*. Eisenstein had been commissioned to make a film about that earlier, though not successful, Russian revolution of 1905. It was in fact to have been called *1905*. But after shooting scenes in Moscow and St. Petersburg, he was not satisfied with the results. Part of the trouble is said to have been that the weather in the north of Russia was unfavorable for photography. Then Eisenstein's cameraman, Edward Tisse, came back from Odessa with reports of sunshine and the beauty of that city on the Black Sea. He was particularly enthusiastic over the great marble steps leading down to the shore and the curving quay. So Eistenstein changed his base of operations to Odessa. One of the incidents in the 1905 revolution had taken place off Odessa anyway—the mutiny aboard the armored cruiser *Potemkin* during the last days of the Russo-Japanese War. When Eisenstein arrived in Odessa and saw for the first time the great steps leading down to the beach where the Tsarist troops had massacred the citizens, the scene so appealed to his imagination that he decided to discard the work he had already done on *1905* and limit the subject to the mutiny aboard ship and the immediately related events in the city. The original cruiser *Potemkin* had been scrapped, but for the scene of the meeting Eisenstein obtained the use of a ship of the same class—the *Twelve Apostles*. Since the superstructure of the *Twelve Apostles* had been dismantled, Eisenstein had it replaced by a replica of lath and plywood. The other shipboard scenes he shot on the cruiser *Komintern*. Most of the actors in the film were residents of Odessa and sailors of the Russian Navy. Before he began shooting, Eisenstein reconstructed the Odessa incident of twenty years before. He talked to survivors of the massacre. "The only thing I need is contact with the people," Marie Seton quotes him. "How many times I have gone out with a preconceived plan of execution, all thought out, with sketches and drawings, and then, on feeling their nearness, I have changed the idea completely. It is they, in their sponta-

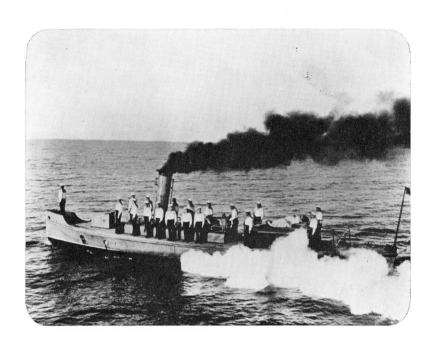

One of the Few Tracking Shots in *The Battleship Potemkin*
Directed by Sergei Eisenstein
for First Studio of Goskino, Moscow, in 1925.

The Ship's Surgeon in *The Battleship Potemkin*

"The doctor with his sharp beard, nearsighted eyes, and near-sighted mind is perfectly epitomized by the pince-nez."—Sergei Eisenstein. Eisenstein deliberately selected his actors to represent types.

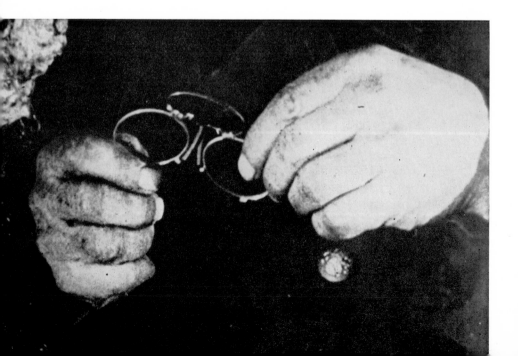

neity, who actually imprint on the film the great tone of reality." The shooting of the scenes at Odessa and on shipboard in the harbor at Sevastopol took only twenty-three days. By the end of 1925 the film was completed and, Eisenstein having changed its title from *1905* to *The Battleship Potemkin,* it had its *première* on January 1, 1926 in Moscow.

Eisenstein builds the film in five parts, each part being indicated by a subtitle. The hundreds of shots from which he composes the parts may be summarized as follows:

PART I. *Men and Maggots.* The night watch aboard the *Potemkin.* . . . The off-duty watch (the crew's quarters). Vakulinchuk haranguing the sailors: "Comrades, the time has come to act." . . . Morning. Shipboard routine. . . . Sailors gathered about a chunk of maggoty meat: "We've had enough garbage to eat." Ship's doctor Smirnov: "The meat is good. No further discussion." . . . The cook preparing the meat. . . . The bowls of steaming soup set on the chain-suspended, swaying tables in the sailors' mess. . . . The sailors buying food from the canteen. . . . The galley. Sailors washing dishes. A sailor examining the motto on a plate: "Give us this day our daily bread."

PART II. *Drama on the Quarterdeck.* A bugler. . . . The crew lining up on deck. Captain Golikov coming on deck. Officers lined up. "Those satisfied with the food . . . two steps forward!" Officers stepping forward. A few members of the crew stepping forward. "All others will hang from the yardarm!" Matyushenko rallies some of the men to the gun turrets. . . . Captain Golikov calling for the marines. Doomed sailors huddled at the edge of the deck. "Cover them with a tarpaulin!" The priest: "Lord, reveal Thyself to the unruly!" Executive Officer Giliarovsky: "At the tarpaulin—Fire!" Vakulinchuk: "Brothers! Do you realize who you are shooting!" Giliarovsky: "Shoot!" The marines lowering their rifles. . . . The crew taking over the ship. Officers thrown overboard. Vakulinchuk killed. . . . His comrades taking Vakulinchuk's body ashore in the ship's tender. . . . Vakulinchuk's body in a tent near the pier.

PART III. *An Appeal from the Dead.* Fog over the harbor. . . . The dead sailor in the tent. . . . Citizens coming to view the body of the fallen hero. "We will remember!" A placard on

Vakulinchuk's body: "For a spoonful of soup." . . . A message from the *Potemkin*: "Death to the oppressors!" . . . The crowd on the great steps watching the *Potemkin*.

PART IV. *The Odessa Steps*. White winged boats flying out to the *Potemkin*. . . . Food being passed aboard. . . . Rejoicing on shore. . . . People on the great steps. Suddenly, the Cossacks. The crowd being mowed down. . . . The brutal military power answered by the guns of the battleship. . . . The headquarters of the generals bombarded.

PART V. *The Meeting of the Squadron*. Night aboard the *Potemkin*. . . . "Landing impossible. The squadron is on its way." The sailors' decision: "With one voice they decide to meet the squadron." . . . Shipboard activity. A bugler: "To battle stations!" . . . Sailors in the engine room. . . . An ammunition hoist. . . . Dials, the indicators moving. . . . a gun manned. . . . Shells handled. . . . "Full speed ahead!" . . . The ship's engines turning. . . . Water flowing past the side. . . . Black smoke from a funnel. . . . The ship's wake. . . . The engines. . . . The wave cast by the bow. . . . Smoke. . . . A ship's gun rising, the muzzle close up. . . . "The enemy is within range!" Signals from the *Potemkin* to the squadron: "Brothers!" The gun lowering. . . . The squadron sailing past. . . . Sailors at the rail cheering. . . . The *Potemkin* coming head on, its bow blacking out the screen.

Typical of Eisenstein, *Potemkin* presents a theme more than a story. The theme, symbolized by the ship, is resistance to oppression. The theme is inherent from the beginning of the film. The first few shots are of water flowing over a jetty and of water breaking over rocks, after which appears the first subtitle, a quotation from Lenin: "Revolution is the only lawful, equal, effectual war. It was in Russia that this war was declared and begun." There is, of course, the story of the mutiny, and the mutiny is led at first by an individual, the sailor Vakulinchuk. But Vakulinchuk is killed, and he too becomes a symbol, round which the people gather and which makes the sailors only the more determined to throw off their oppressors. The hero is no longer Vakulinchuk, except as a symbol. The hero is the masses.

Thus the characters in *Potemkin* are not individualized. Here, in another way, Eisenstein's work is documentary-like. Eisenstein deliberately selected his actors to represent types. He used the word *typage* to describe his selection of a non-actor to play a particular role because the person seemed to him to represent the characteristics the role calls for. Eisenstein's typage is comparable to what in the theatre is called type casting. Eisenstein once explained to Marie Seton how he applied his theory:

> When he wanted to create a character, a street cleaner, for example, he went out into the streets and there observed the characteristics of people who were engaged in cleaning the streets. From the general characteristics he observed, he formed a composite image of a typical street cleaner. Then he searched for the individual who possessed the greatest number of traits observed in the many street cleaners, though he might in fact not be a street cleaner. When he found that person, he considered him as the best and the truest image of the "type."

When he was filming *Potemkin,* he could not find anyone in Odessa who seemed to him to be the type of Smirnov, the ship's surgeon. But when he was in Sevastopol, where he had gone to shoot the shipboard scenes, he recognized in a hotel porter, who had become one of his prop men, the type he had in mind. The actor is nameless, but having seen *Potemkin,* one remembers the perky little doctor. When the doctor is tossed overboard, his glasses catch on one of the ship's lines and hang dangling there. Eisenstein had Tisse make a close shot of the dangling glasses, all the more effective because in an earlier scene the doctor takes his glasses off and uses them as a magnifying lense to examine the controversial meat. Eisenstein said: "The doctor with his sharp beard, nearsighted eyes, and nearsighted mind is perfectly epitomized by the pince-nez in the 1905 style which is held in place, like a fox terrier, by a thin metal chain attached to the ear."

Another unforgettable character is the priest, the ship's chaplain. Eisenstein again had decided exactly what the priest should be like, and he found a gardener who fitted the type. He did not even need make-up. Eisenstein said: "A thirty-year-

147

old actor may be called upon to play an old man of sixty. He may have a few days' or a few hours' rehearsal. But an old man will have had sixty years' rehearsal." When it came to the scene in which the priest is knocked down the companionway, the old gardener demurred. So Eisenstein made himself up as the priest for this scene. The scene was shot by Tisse as the gardener watched and, thus reassured, the old man acted the scene himself. It is possible that when *Potemkin* was edited, the footage of Eisenstein was incorporated in the film. As the priest lies at the foot of the companionway pretending to be dead, he opens one eye and immediately closes it, in an expression said to have been characteristic of Eisenstein. If Eisenstein had not intended to be in the film, it is odd that he should have made himself up just to show the gardener how to fall down stairs.

The documentary quality in *Potemkin* is not in the characters alone. The staging is documentary-like for its background of Odessa and the Black Sea coast. In the scenes at sea, however, there is a lack of reality. Although the film is about a ship, the sea is slighted. The oncoming squadron, for example, is ridiculously close when it is first sighted by the crew of the *Potemkin*. Eisenstein does not have the feeling for the sea that Robert Flaherty does. On the other hand, the harbor scenes are effective —the tender bringing Vakulinchuk's body ashore, the fog, the ships at anchor, and the gulls. Particularly documentary-like are the scenes aboard ship—the sequence of shots, at the beginning of the film, of the crew's quarters, shots of shipboard routine in the sequence before the mutiny and, in the last part of the film, the variety of shots as the *Potemkin* is got under way—the engines beginning to turn, the signal light flashing, the bugler sounding the alarm, and sailors manning the ammunition hoist, handling shells, and loading guns. Interspersed with these are other shots—of the water rushing past the side, of the ship's wake, and of smoke pouring from the funnels.

There is a great variety in the temporal and spatial length of shots and in angles. There are distance shots of the harbor, the Odessa shore, and the quay. There are close shots of a ship's dial, a candelabrum, a life preserver. It is a tendency of the Russian directors not to move the camera, and Eisenstein is no exception. In the scenes on the Odessa steps, however, Eisenstein had a trolley built large enough to hold himself, Tisse, the assistants, and the camera and carry them up and down the side of the steps to photograph the massacre. In making this sequence Eisenstein had a camera attached to a man's waist to photograph the scene as the man falls. There are tracking shots of the tender moving through the harbor and a tilting and panning of the camera to show the people marching on the quay. But otherwise the camera is stationary. Eisenstein had Tisse change lenses instead of moving the camera, saying he did not want to disconcert his inexperienced actors.

Documentary-like as *Potemkin* is, there is hardly a shot in the film that is not studiedly composed. The sailors' hammocks form a variety of geometric patterns. A ship's grating casts a checkered shadow on a sailor's face, emphasized by a close-up. The little boats on their way out to the *Potemkin* are photographed through a colonnade on the shore. The masts of the sailboats tied up at the curving quay fill a scene from foreground to background, suggestive of the composition in the line of the hooded horsemen in *The Birth of a Nation* and anticipating that shot in *Henry V* in which a pattern is formed by the longbows in the hands of the English archers at the Battle of Agincourt. The opening of a tent, through which the camera photographs the harbor, masks the shot triangularly. Two of the *Potemkin's* guns symmetrically frame the deck. The film is brought to a close as the great bow of the ship comes directly head-on until it blacks out the screen.

Eisenstein is a master not only in directing crowd scenes but in moving groups of people in studied composition. For example, he had Tisse set up his camera aboard ship to catch sailors simultaneously running in opposite directions at different levels, a ship's rail forming a dividing line from lower left to upper right in the manner of a split screen. Taking advantage of the steep slope from Odessa down to the shore and of bridges, walls, steps, and other architectural features of the city, Eisenstein moves crowds in more than one direction in individual shots. A line of people moves down an incline from upper right to lower left while another line is crossing the scene from left to right at the bottom. In another shot the pattern of movement represents a line moving from right to left at the top while a second line comes in from center to left at the bottom. One of the lines may represent a curve, or two curves, or three. A crowd moves from lower left toward upper right through the arch of a bridge; joining this line, another group comes in from the left and moves toward lower center; at the same time, a line marches across the bridge from right to left at the top.

But *Potemkin* is important most of all for its montage. Few films depend less on movement of the camera. Few depend as little even on movement within the scene. No other film depends so much on the arrangement of shots. It is said that Eisenstein was converted to the motion pictures by *Intolerance.* Indeed all of *Potemkin* is built up in a way suggestive of the last sequence in *Intolerance,* in which Griffith cuts back and forth not only within each of the four stories but among them. But whereas in *Intolerance* the cutting becomes a tour de force, in *Potemkin* it is effected so smoothly that the story is told without calling attention to the cutting. In *Intolerance,* Griffith does not, as Eisenstein says, "try through the juxtaposition of shots to shape import and image." In *Potemkin,* Eisenstein does try to do just that. As a result he succeeds in effecting montage.

On examination one can see how he does it. Consider, for example, the Prologue. Its two scenes—water flowing over a smooth jetty and splashing up in sheets and water dashing roughly over rocks—are separated into five shots, arranged alternately. They symbolize Lenin's words, quoted as the first subtitle. The scene in the sailors' quarters is built up by thirty-nine separate shots, on the screen an average of four seconds each. (In all of *Queen Elizabeth* there are only twenty-eight shots.) The action in this sequence depends almost entirely, except for five brief titles, on the arrangement of the shots.

One of the famous sequences in *Potemkin* is that in which the shots of the marble lions are interpolated. It occurred to Tisse, who had noticed the statues of the lions decorating the imperial gardens at Alupka, that shots of three of the lions, each in a different position—asleep, awake, and rising—could be made to represent a single lion springing to action. Although at first Eisenstein was not impressed by Tisse's suggestion that they photograph the lions for this purpose, he later acquiesced; he and Tisse went back to Alupka and made the shots. Eisenstein then interpolated them in the sequence of the massacre. He says in *Film Form*, "In the thunder of the *Potemkin's* guns a marble lion leaps up in protest against the bloodshed on the Odessa steps." There is no better example of movement obtained entirely by editing. The shots of the stone lions, arranged in rapid succession—ten frames for the first lion, fourteen for the second, and seventeen for the third—are as motionless as stills.

Montage effects another kind of relationship in the sequence of the mutiny. To show that the Church supports the Tsarist oppression of the common people, Eisenstein cuts from a shot of the officer tapping the hilt of his sword with his finger tips to a shot of the priest tapping his crucifix against the palm of his hand. And to make the implication obvious Eisenstein has the camera brought up close to each of these objects, the sword hilt and the crucifix, in succession.

The shots of the priest and the officer, the crucifix and the sword interrupt the action at a crucial moment. The marines, lined up on deck, have been given the command to fire on the sailors massed under the tarpaulin in the bow. Eisenstein then, as it were, makes time stand still while he digresses to call attention to the affinity of the Church with the Military. He expands time even further by other digressions here. The incident, beginning with the officer's command "Attention!" and continuing until the marines lower their rifles, would in actuality be a matter of but a few seconds, but it lasts on the screen for nearly three minutes. The time is expanded by the interpolation of a series of shots, varying in spatial as well as in temporal length: a medium-close shot of two officers; a close shot of the executive officer; a long shot of the deck, the sea in the background; a medium-close shot of the marines; a long shot of the deck, the turret in the background; a distance shot of the ship on the water; a full shot of the tarpaulin over the sailors; a two-shot of Vakulinchuk and another sailor; a close shot of a life preserver; a long shot of the ship's bow head-on; a close shot of a bugle; etc. The incident is edited in fifty-seven shots. Editing similarly expands time in other parts of the film, particularly in the scene of the massacre on the Odessa steps.

Although Eisenstein seldom resorts to the dissolve, there are several dissolves in *Potemkin*. When Captain Golikov threatens the sailors with hanging, he points up. Then follows a shot of the yardarm as seen from the deck. After several shots of men and officers turning their heads to look—here again time is expanded—the shot of the yardarm is repeated. This then dissolves to a similar shot of the arm, except that now six men are hanging there. Here, of course, Eisenstein is effecting what Griffith meant when he said that "you can photograph thought." Two other dissolves in *Potemkin* are also reminiscent of Griffith. In the sequence in which citizens come to pay their respects to the dead sailor, a long flight of steps extends down the center of the screen, masked on both sides to emphasize height. This scene dissolves to that of the same steps crowded with people descending them. The coming of night aboard ship is implied by a dissolve from a shot of the deck massed with sailors to that of the deck empty. One is reminded of the photograph of the interior of Masters Hall in *The Birth of a Nation* dissolving to the shot of Griffith's replica of the hall occupied by the Negro legislature or of the shot of the empty office in the modern story of *Intolerance* dissolving to that of the office bustling with uplifters.

Potemkin is so cinematic that, watching it, one forgets that it is a silent film. It is, of course, enhanced by musical accompaniment. The original musical score for *Potemkin* was composed by Edmund Meisel, a pioneer in film music. Kurt London records that several European countries which permitted the showing of *Potemkin* forbade Meisel's music to be played with it because the provocative rhythm was liable to incite revolutionary instincts. "The rhythms which mark the departure of the mutinous ship, as the engines begin to move," London observes, "have become famous and have since been imitated countless times."

Although the Meisel score for *Potemkin* has been lost, the music can be approximated, for Arthur Kleiner has composed a score for piano accompaniment based on his recollection of the original. In 1950, the Film Studio of Moscow produced a "sound version" of *Potemkin,* consisting, not of spoken dialogue, but of sound effects and background music by N. Kryukov. Except for a few changes in titles, this version presents Eisenstein's original film intact.

Potemkin is the opposite of *A Trip to the Moon* because of montage. Whereas in Méliès' film the values are primarily in the photographed objects, in Eisenstein's they are primarily in the way the photographs are arranged. Arrangement is the province of the artist. Willa Cather says in "The Novel Démeublé":

> Whatever is felt upon the page without being specifically named there—that, it seems to me, is created. It is the inexplicable presence of the thing not named, of the overtone divined by the ear but not heard by it, the verbal mood, the emotional aura of the fact or the thing or the deed, that gives high quality to the novel or the drama, as well as to poetry itself.

For "page" may be substituted "screen." In *Potemkin,* as in any truly cinematic film, "the inexplicable presence of the thing not named" is effected by arrangement. Griffith established the principle of arrangement in the motion pictures as *editing.* Eisenstein extended it as *montage.*

9. Sound

"It is because the moving picture has perforce to do without the potent appeal of the spoken word that it can never be really a rival of the drama." Thus declared Brander Matthews in 1917. And in 1917 most people would have agreed. Within a decade, however, the premise would no longer hold, for in 1927 the screen began to talk.

From the time the motion-picture machine was invented, attempts had been made to match the pictures with sound. In fact, the idea of motion pictures had first occurred to Edison as that of a device whereby "motion and sound could be recorded and reproduced simultaneously." Edward K. Dickson contended that in 1889, in his experiments which were to lead to the kinetoscope, he had synchronized a phonograph record of his voice with his image projected onto a screen. In 1903, when George Hale presented his Tours-of-the-World films, he accompanied them with train noises. The Lyman Howe travelogues, the successors to Hale's Tours, were screened with a background of a still wider variety of sound effects. And, of course, almost from the beginning a musical accompaniment was considered essential to the screening of motion pictures.

Although in 1906 Eugene Lauste, who had been associated with Dickson at the Edison laboratory and who had assisted the Lathams in building their camera, took out a patent in England for the recording of sound on the film itself, his patent did not attract attention. In 1920 a sound-on-film device was demonstrated by Charles Hoxie in the laboratories of the General Electric Company, and four years later Lee deForest recorded on his phonofilm the musical score for *The Covered Wagon*. But Hollywood was unimpressed, or at least pretended to be. The situation was similar to that in 1895 when Edison refused to convert the kinetoscope into a screen machine. It is reminiscent of the refusal in 1909 of the Motion Picture Patents Company to adopt Charles Urban's cinemacolor and, three years later, of the Patents Company's discouraging the production of films in more than one-reel lengths. And today it is recalled in the attempt of the motion-picture industry to discourage the projection of films by television. In the mid-twenties the big motion-picture companies were making money with silent pictures and did not wish to risk their profits by experimenting with sound.

But one of the companies was not making so much money as some of the others. In 1906 three sons of a Russian immigrant family—Sam, Harry, and Albert Warner—had given up the operation of a bicycle repair shop to open a motion-picture theatre in New Castle, Pennsylvania. Then, following the lead of the Mileses, they set up a film exchange. By 1912 the enterprising Warners, joined now by a younger brother, Jack, were producing motion pictures themselves. Their company, Warner Brothers, prospered, but by the mid-twenties it was outranked by Paramount, Fox, First National, and Metro-Goldwyn. The Warners were willing to try something different. So they tried sound.

In 1925 Warner Brothers signed an agreement with the Western Electric Company to make sound films. The project was called vitaphone, and its first film was *Don Juan,* starring John Barrymore. The actors in *Don Juan* were not audible on the screen, but synchronized with the film was a musical score played by the New York Philharmonic Orchestra. And recorded on film was an introductory speech by Will Hays, head of the Motion Picture Producers and Distributors of America. Thus with the *première* of *Don Juan,* on the evening of August 6, 1926 at the Warner Theatre in New York, sound, in the form of vitaphone, was introduced to the screen. Vitaphone was popular with audiences, and the Warners produced two more films by the same method—*The Better 'Ole* and *When a Man Loves.* There was a slight stir in the industry: in 1927 Fox inaugurated the Movietone Newsreel, which talked, and the major companies united efforts to thwart vitaphone.

Then on October 6, 1927 the Warners presented the first film incorporating spoken dialogue—*The Jazz Singer*. The method of most of *The Jazz Singer* was similar to that of the earlier experiments with vitaphone, that is, background music recorded on the film but dialogue represented by subtitles. In *The Jazz Singer*, however, Al Jolson's voice singing was synchronized with Jolson's image on the screen. Furthermore after one of his songs Jolson was seen, and heard, speaking to Eugenie Besserer. It is said that during the filming Jolson had ad-libbed while the microphone was still on and that the spoken words were left in the edited print at the suggestion of Sam Warner. Whether by chance or plan, motion-picture audiences heard for the first time an actor's voice speaking from the screen in a feature film.

But although *The Jazz Singer* did not at once convince the other companies, some of the exhibitors were impressed enough to equip their theatres with sound, and before the end of the year nine producers were licensed by the Western Electric Company to make sound films. The big companies, however, went on making silent films. Sound, they reasoned, might be just a novelty and, even if it did last, it was not certain that it would replace the silent screen. But in July of 1928 Warners presented *Lights of New York*—the first "all-talking" feature picture.

Warner Brothers had won. Motion-picture theatres all over the country rushed to install sound equipment. Whereas in July of 1928 only 220 theatres in the United States were showing sound pictures, by the end of the year, 1,000 theatres had sound equipment and, by the end of 1929, 4,000. Signs went up on theatre marquees: THIS THEATRE IS WIRED FOR SOUND. Attendance at the motion pictures nearly doubled. Within a year after the release of *Lights of New York* Warners obtained a controlling interest in First National and were on an equal footing with the other major companies.

A few silent films were announced for production in 1930, but only one of them was released. This was *Tabu*, a documentary begun under the direction of Robert Flaherty and Fred Murnau and completed, after Flaherty relinquished his interest, by Murnau alone. It was silent because Murnau, who died in

1931, refused to accept sound as a legitimate adjunct to the screen.

Warners had produced not only *The Jazz Singer* but a revolution in the motion-picture industry. And thus, indirectly, they were to revolutionize the art of the motion pictures itself. In giving the screen a voice, they had made possible an aesthetic use of sound comparable to editing. The artistic linking of sound to pictures, however, was to take time, as the discovery of editing had taken time. Out of the motion-picture machine had evolved the art of the motion pictures. Now, by means of another mechanical device, the art was to be expanded.

Although there were those who, like Eisenstein, appreciated the significance of this new dimension and had, in fact, anticipated it and foreseen some of its possibilities, sound at first was exploited almost for its own sake, like a novelty. The introduction of sound was reminiscent of the introduction of the motion-picture machine, which had also been a novelty. Audiences were fascinated by the vitaphone much as, thirty years before, they had been fascinated by the vitascope. In the early talking films it was enough that the pictures of an actor talking be synchronized with the sound of his voice.

Like the first motion-picture machines, the new device had mechanical limitations. The camera now had to be housed in a soundproof booth to keep the whirring noises of the mechanism from reaching the microphone. Whereas long before 1927 the camera had become flexible, the booth gave it a rigidity comparable to that of Edison's camera in the Black Maria and Méliès' in the studio at Montreuil. As a result the actors were once more confined to a limited playing space, as on a stage. In the early sound films shots are reminiscent of those in *Queen Elizabeth*. In fact, because of the microphone, stage movement was even more contained than in *Queen Elizabeth*. Microphones were hidden under tables, in lamps, in vases, and in other stage props, and an actor had to maneuver himself close to a microphone when it was his turn to speak. The motion pictures were hardly more than a mechanical device again.

If *Lights of New York* was a success, it was because of its novelty. Other "all-talking" films were rushed into production, and the phrase "100% all-talking" lured audiences into theatres in ever increasing numbers. The term "movies" became "talkies," an appropriate epithet because in the new films the microphone overcame the camera.

Producers enticed actors from Broadway, for now the voice was the chief criterion, and not all of the actors who were experienced in appearing in silent films could adapt themselves to the new device. A voice at variance with screen personality, a speech defect, a regional accent, or even just inability to memorize lines lost some of the former screen stars the battle with the microphone. Furthermore, whereas in the silent days the director could make the actor almost entirely dependent upon him, audibly directing every move and gesture, now the actor was more on his own, and stage actors had had experience in this kind of independence.

Producers also turned to Broadway for scripts. Plays, which depend primarily on dialogue, seemed even more suitable for adaptation to the screen than before. They seemed so suitable, in fact, that there was a tendency to photograph them rather than to adapt them. Not only had Brander Matthews' premise been upset, but the rivalry to which Matthews had referred was, ironically, being reduced to mimicry, and the art of the motion pictures to the machine.

The rigidity imposed by the microphone was overcome sooner than the construction and technique of these early sound films implied. By 1930, when Metro-Goldwyn-Mayer produced *Anna Christie,* the camera had been taken out of its immobile booth and encased in a soundproof blimp which could be moved about by a crane or a dolly. There are evidences in *Anna Christie* of the camera's regaining flexibility. For example, as Marthy and Chris make their way along the cobblestone street from the dock to the saloon, the camera tracks with them, and it tracks again in the amusement-park sequence to follow Anna and Mat as they stroll from one part of the park to another. The scene in the amusement-park restaurant is opened by the camera's tracking up to the table where Anna and Mat are seated. In the scene in the back room of the saloon the camera pans to follow the actors as they move about, and the scene on the East River opens as the camera pans and tilts from a distance shot across the bridge to take in the river traffic below. Furthermore there is a variety in the spatial length and angle of shots. On the other hand, this flexibility is not typical of *Anna Christie,* which is less suggestive of freedom from the microphone than of the art of the motion pictures shackled by the motion-picture machine. The introduction of sound set the art back twenty-five years. *Anna Christie* represents it once again groping toward its proper form.

It might be asked why, now that the machine had taken on the dimension of sound, plays should not be reproduced on the screen as literally as the medium permits. Particularly today, when color and stereoscopic film make possible still closer approximation to reality, it would seem that the machine was admirably suited to this purpose. And of course it is. Plays literally recorded are justifiable because wide audiences are thus enabled to see them. For a comparable reason symphonic music is recorded on phonograph records. On the other hand, the more literally a play is reproduced on the screen, the more the motion pictures constitute only a machine.

What then is the proper use of the machine in the adaptation of a play? The answer lies in the difference between the art of the drama and the art of the motion pictures, between a play and a film.

That a play is written to be performed determines what it is like. Because it is written, it implies images suggested by words. Because it is performed, it implies actors who speak the words. Because a performance implies stage settings, it is limited in the number of scenes.[1] And because a performance also implies an audience, it is limited in its length. These characteristics in turn determine others. A play, for example, narrates in the present tense. It does not readily shift to the past except by resorting to exposition. It does not admit of lapse of time unless indicated by a device such as the lowering and raising of the curtain or

[1] Although the comparatively bare stage of the Elizabethan theatre permitted plays of many scenes, even the number of these was limited by the time required to establish the locale of each scene and to get actors on and off stage as well as by other elements of dramatic narration.

the stage lights. It does not naturally present simultaneous happenings in more than one place. It tends to have a late point of attack, antecedent action being presented indirectly. It has few characters in comparison, for example, with those in a novel. It contains comparatively few incidents. And it tends to be objective in point of view.[2]

A film, on the other hand, is limited by only one of these restrictions imposed on the drama, namely, length. In fact, most films are shorter than plays. Because a feature film is usually screened in addition to a newsreel and other shorts and because it is to the advantage of the exhibitors to include as many showings in a day as possible, economics has somehow determined that a film should be ninety minutes long. Because the medium of the motion picture is pictures—and, since 1927, pictures embellished with sound—words are of secondary importance. Scene shifting not occupying time on the screen, a film is comparatively unlimited as to number of scenes. A film shifts easily between the present and the past, and even to the future; it admits of frequent lapses of time; and in it time may be compressed or extended. It can present simultaneous actions in more than one place. The point of attack in a film may be early, since all action is readily presented directly. The greater number of scenes makes possible a correspondingly larger number of characters and incidents. Furthermore, because the motion pictures can photograph thought, a film can be more subjective than a play.

However, if a play were adapted to the screen only by an increase in the number of scenes, characters, and incidents, the resulting film would be too long. Since a film is restricted in its length, something must be deleted in the adaptation. Since a play has few scenes, the scenes are developed in detail, in more detail, for example, than in a novel. What is deleted, then, in the adaptation is some of the detail. Thus it is that when a play is adapted to the screen it is not only expanded but contracted. The expansion gives the screen version the characteristics of a

[2] Exceptions to these generalizations are represented by expressionistic plays or plays incorporating expressionistic devices, which tend to circumvent some of the restrictions imposed by the stage.

The Battleship Potemkin

"Taking advantage of architectural features of the city—Odessa
—Eisenstein moves crowds."

Greta Garbo and George F. Marion in *Anna Christie*
Directed by Clarence Brown for Metro-Goldwyn-Mayer in 1930.

"One cannot help suspecting a microphone in the ship's lantern."

novel: many scenes, characters, and incidents, a wide diversity in time, and early point of attack—or at least a flash-back method to reveal the past—the presentation of parallel action, and subjectivity not germane to the drama. The contraction makes the film less dramatic than the play and, correspondingly, more like a novel, because the deletion of detail implies a corresponding deletion of dialogue, which is the basis of the dramatic method. Mortimer Adler states this principle of expansion and contraction as follows: "If a play be adapted to the screen, it must be expanded in the direction of epic magnitude but contracted with respect to dramatic detail." By "epic magnitude" Adler means the comparatively broad scope of a novel, admitting of many incidents, scenes, and characters, and by "dramatic detail" the detail in the development of a particular incident. As he points out, a novel achieves its magnitude by description and narration, and a play achieves its detail by dialogue. Thus it may be said that when a play is adapted to the screen, it becomes more like a novel than a play, except that whereas a novel effects description and narration by words, a film effects them by pictures. A play adapted to the screen does not, however, become completely like a novel. (Even Erich von Stroheim failed to put a novel "completely on the screen.") It becomes a motion picture.

If a play is to be properly adapted to the screen, that is, if it is to become a film with an aesthetic entity of its own and not a mechanical reproduction, it should be adapted cinematically. It should not be bound by the restrictions imposed by the stage but exploit the freedom implicit in the film by virtue of the flexibility, actual and figurative, of the camera. Only then will the result represent, not the motion-picture machine, but motion-picture art.

The film *Anna Christie,* based on Eugene O'Neill's play and directed by Clarence Brown, represents a groping toward the way a play should be adapted to the screen. To the extent that it is expanded toward epic scope and contracted in dramatic detail, it represents the art. To the extent that it fails to take advantage of the possibilities of the medium—because at the time it was filmed the screen had only recently begun to talk—that is, to the extent that it merely reproduces the play, the extent that it is *not* cinematically expanded and contracted, it represents the motion pictures as a machine.

O'Neill's play is in four acts, calling for three different settings: Act I—Johnny-the-Priest's saloon near the water front, New York City; Act II—the stern of the barge *Simeon Winthrop* at anchor in the outer harbor of Provincetown, Massachusetts; Act III—the cabin of the barge, at dock in Boston; Act IV—the same as Act III. Whereas the play represents the saloon in a single set, the bar on the left, the back room on the right, the film represents it in three sets: the bar, the back room, and the exterior. Furthermore the exterior set includes not only the saloon—alluded to in the film as Johnny-the-Harp's—but the street leading to it from the dock, where the barge is tied up. The play represents the barge in two sets: an exterior (the stern) and an interior (the cabin). The film shows not only both exterior and interior but the barge in various places and from varying distances and angles: at dock, under tow in the East River, in a storm at sea, and at anchor off the Massachusetts coast. Furthermore, as though the camera were mounted on the barge itself, there are scenes of river traffic, the water front, and the New York sky line, of a ship under full sail, and of the shipwrecked sailors approaching on a raft out of the fog. Further expansion of this kind is evidenced by the four separate sets for the amusement-park sequence.

There are only three lapses of time in the play, that is, those between acts. In the film there are nine, effected in various ways. They are effected by continuity titles, of which there are three: "The next morning—the water front of the East River, New York City," "A week later—in tow off New England," and "At anchor in an outer harbor along the Massachusetts coast." Some of the transitions are effected by fade-outs and fade-ins. In the amusement-park sequence they are effected by dissolves. A dissolve together with dialogue effects the transition from the barge to the amusement park. When Anna tells Mat that she will not go ashore with him, the scene dissolves to that of Anna and Mat on the roller coaster. Similarly at the end of the amusement-park sequence, dialogue helps to effect the transition. When Anna says, "I'm tired, Mat, I want to go back to the barge," the scene fades out. The next scene is on the barge. On the other hand, for the first third of the film the action is represented as continuous although there are shifts in scene. The first of these shifts occurs when Marthy and Chris leave the barge to go to Johnny's saloon. By a sequence of three shots—the interior of the cabin, the exterior of the barge, and the dock—and by a tracking of the camera from the dock to the saloon, the action is presented with no break in time. Then by a cutting from the exterior of the saloon to the interior and from bar to back room, back room to bar, etc., the action is continuous until interrupted by the first of the three continuity titles. Later in the film action is similarly represented as continuous in a cutting between the interior and the exterior of the barge.

Whereas in the play Chris is talked about before he comes into the saloon, in the film this exposition is obviated by Chris's being presented directly. Thus in the film the scene at Johnny's does not begin until Chris makes his entrance there. The difference is significant because it represents what should happen when a play is adapted to the screen. It is the difference between the dramatic and the cinematic methods of narration. In the play the method is almost entirely dialogue; in the first part of the film, almost entirely pictures. In the play the dialogue about Chris is important. In the film what Marty and Chris say to each other on the barge and on their way to Johnny's is relatively unimportant. The difference may be indicated as follows:

PLAY	FILM
SCENE: "Johnny-the-Priest's saloon. . . .	SCENE: The cabin of the barge. Marthy and Chris prepare to go ashore.
(THE POSTMAN *enters. . . . He exchanges nods with* JOHNNY *and throws a letter on the bar.*)	SCENE: Exterior of the barge. Marthy and Chris go down the gangplank.
THE POSTMAN: Addressed care of you, Johnny. Know him?	SCENE: The street leading from the dock. The camera follows Marthy and Chris as they make
JOHNNY (*picks up the letter, adjusting his spectacles.* LARRY	

163

comes and peers over his shoulders. JOHNNY *reads very slowly.):* Christopher Christopherson.

THE POSTMAN (*helpfully*): Square-head name.

LARRY: Old Chris—that's who.

JOHNNY: Oh, sure, I was forgetting Chris carried a hell of a name like that. Letters come here for him sometimes before, I remember now. Long time ago, though.

THE POSTMAN: It'll get him all right then?

JOHNNY: Sure thing. He comes here whenever he's in port.

THE POSTMAN (*turning to go*): Sailor, eh?

JOHNNY (*with a grin*): Captain of a coal barge.

THE POSTMAN (*laughing*): Some job! Well, s'long.

JOHNNY: S'long. I'll see he gets it. (THE POSTMAN *goes out. Johnny scrutinizes the letter.*) You got good eyes, Larry. Where's it from?

LARRY (*after a glance*): St. Paul. That'll be in Minnesota, I'm thinkin'. Looks like a woman's writing, too, the old divil!

JOHNNY: He's got a daughter somewheres out West, I think he told me once. (*He puts the letter on the cash register.*) Come to think of it, I ain't seen old Chris in a dog's age. (*Putting his overcoat on, he comes around the*

their way to Johnny-the-Harp's.

SCENE: Fade-in to a closer shot of the saloon door as Marthy and Chris approach it.

SCENE: Another view of the door. Marthy and Chris.

SCENE: The door leading to the back room—camera pointing up at a lighted globe over door—marked LADIES ENTRANCE.

SCENE: Marthy and Chris at the door to the bar.

SCENE: Marthy and Chris at the ladies' entrance. Chris leaves Marthy and walks toward the door to the bar.

SCENE: Interior of Johnny-the-Harp's. Chris enters.

end of the bar.) Guess I'll be get-
tin' home. See you tomorrow.

LARRY: Good-night to ye, boss.
*(As Johnny goes toward the
street door, it is pushed open and*
CHRISTOPHER CHRISTOPHERSON
enters.)

Also cinematic is the addition of the amusement-park sequence, made up of several scenes. The last scene in the sequence
finds Anna and Mat seated at a table in a restaurant. A merry-
go-round revolves in the background, its music blaring a gay
accompaniment to the scene. At this point the dialogue constituting the proposal scene of the play is introduced into the film.
Then, as Anna and Mat are talking, Marthy enters the restaurant and wanders toward their table. When Marthy recognizes
Anna and comes up to speak to her, Anna pretends she does not
know her, but when Mat orders the old woman away, Anna
admits that she does. In the play Marthy appears only in Act I.
In the film she is thus again introduced to represent Anna's
past and point up Anna's dilemma. In denying that she knows
Marthy, Anna attempts to ignore her past, and then, admitting
that she knows her, she acknowledges that her past must be reck-
oned with. The amusement-park sequence thus helps not only
to relieve the staginess of the long scenes in the cabin but to
represent the inner conflict cinematically.

In these ways O'Neill's play is slightly expanded in the direction of epic magnitude. But the expansion fails to compensate
for the contraction. As a result the film tends to be only a cut
version of the play.

Anna Christie does not take full advantage of the flexibility
which the motion pictures had regained by 1930. There is, for
example, only the slightest of crosscutting. In the saloon scenes
the action cuts between the bar and the back room. But this cutting is implied in the play itself, the set for the first act representing two sections, the barroom on one side of the stage and
the back room on the other. Marthy's entrance into the back
room is stage-like; it is effected just as in the play. It is as un-

cinematic as Sarah Bernhardt's in the vault scene in *Queen Elizabeth.*

The construction of the play is not essentially changed in the adaptation. The point of attack is approximately the same. Whereas Anna's past might have been suggested cinematically, it is revealed entirely by dialogue, that is, dramatically. Even the soliloquies are not treated cinematically. They remain soliloquies spoken as they would be on a stage, as though Griffith had never shown that you can photograph thought. Furthermore, with the exceptions pointed out, the scenes are as disjunctive as in the play. The act divisions are, in fact, as apparent in the film as they would be if separated by the lowering and raising of a curtain.

Whereas the acting time of the play is about two hours and a half, the screening time of the film is only ninety minutes. Obviously much of the dialogue was deleted in the adaptation. The deletions, in fact, represent about half of O'Neill's script. Since the slight expansion in the direction of epic magnitude compensates for only a fraction of the deletions, the question arises as to whether the impact on the spectator is not weakened by this discrepancy. There are, for example, nuances in O'Neill's play which are lost in the film. The conflict in *Anna Christie,* as in most of O'Neill's plays, is between the chief character and fate. It is this conflict which implies O'Neill's affinity with Greek, rather than with Elizabethan, tragedy. O'Neill is sensitive to irony in the life of man, and in his plays irony is close to fate. Chris intended good by sending Anna away from the sea, which he considered evil. The sea in *Anna Christie* is not only the symbol of evil; it is the motivation for the action. In the revelation scene, the key scene of the play, O'Neill shows that Anna appreciates the nature of the tragedy. When Chris breaks down at the realization of the consequences of his good intention, Anna says, "Don't bawl about it. There ain't nothing to forgive anyway. It ain't your fault, and it ain't mine, and it ain't his neither. We're all poor nuts, and things happen, and we yust get mixed in wrong, that's all." As Ludwig Lewisohn observed, "in that speech and in that moment the essentials of human tragedy are faultlessly set forth." It is the most important speech in the play, and the most important sentence in the speech is the last. It not only epitomizes the situation but implies the theme of the play itself. But in the adaptation the sentence was left out. It is of course inevitable that a powerful play would suffer by the deletion of half of its text.

Considerable excitement awaited the showing of *Anna Christie* in 1930, not only because it was known that Greta Garbo was to enact O'Neill's tortured heroine, but because it was to be the first film in which audiences would hear Miss Garbo's voice. The film was advertised by the slogan on the billings: GARBO TALKS. Indeed the play had been chosen for the actress, not the actress for the play. In reviewing the film for the *New York Times,* Mordaunt Hall wrote:

> Miss Garbo's voice from the screen is deep toned, somewhat deeper than when one hears her in real life. The low enunciation of her initial lines, with a packed theatre waiting expectantly to hear her first utterance, came somewhat as a surprise yesterday afternoon in the Capitol, for her delivery is almost masculine. And although the low toned voice is not what is expected from the alluring actress, one becomes accustomed to it, for it is a voice undeniably suited to the unfortunate Anna.

Under the title "Greta Garbo Talks" Donald Henderson Clarke reported for the readers of the *New York Times,* two months before they would see the film, how Miss Garbo went about her part in the making of *Anna Christie*—a report which is also a commentary on the making of films at this period in the history of the motion pictures:

> When search for a suitable vehicle for Greta Garbo to make her first appearance in an all-talking film was ended with the selection of Eugene O'Neill's stage play, *Anna Christie* . . . , best information is that the only person at the Metro-Goldwyn-Mayer studio who didn't show anxiety over her official introduction to the microphones was Miss Garbo herself.
>
> While the sets, which include the interior of a coal barge, the interior of an old-fashioned saloon and an amusement spot similar to Coney Island, were being built, Miss Garbo was learn-

ing her lines. And when the day came for Miss Garbo to walk in and speak the lines for the microphones she didn't rehearse a sentence, or even a syllable, to discover how she and the synchronized apparatus got along together. She merely walked into the saloon set, through a door marked "Family Entrance," sat at a table and said to Lee Phelps, who plays Larry, the waiter:

"Gimme a whiskey—ginger ale on the side."

Then, as Phelps turned to go, according to direction from Clarence Brown, she adopted what was indicated in the script as a "winning smile" and added:

"And don't be stingy, Baby."

Mr. Brown, who already had directed Miss Garbo in *Flesh and the Devil* and *A Woman of Affairs,* looked up where behind a sound-proof window Gavin Burns, the voice mixer, had been awaiting Miss Garbo's first words, which came to him through the recording system. Mr. Burns grinned and waved at Mr. Brown and Mr. Brown went ahead with his job of directing, which lasted for 850 feet of film.

Miss Garbo had said she didn't wish to learn her lines by bits, but preferred to reel them off by the scene. The camera magazines carry 1,000 feet of film and the first attack of Miss Garbo on the microphones proves to be a fair sample, because after that most of her scenes ran for about one thousand feet.

Information is that many more persons would have been present at the first talking scene made by Miss Garbo if Miss Garbo had been willing. But she was always a stickler, even in the silent days, for having none but workers around her when she was acting, and no one except those actually engaged in making the picture was on hand when she made her first reel in dialogue.

Miss Garbo had not gone onto the set unprepared for work in a dialogue vehicle, however. She; Charles Bickford, who plays Mat; George F. Marion, who plays Chris; Marie Dressler, who plays Marthy; James T. Mack, who plays Johnny the Priest; and Phelps, as Larry, all had been rehearsed through long hours by Brown in order to clean from the action the overemphasis of pantomime, which was one of the unnoted methods by which silent films got around the lack of speech. Miss Garbo knew her business and her lines backward and forward when she went into the first scene. But her insistence on playing the entire scene through without stop the first time the microphones were working was reported as being more than a trifle unusual.

Anna Christie was considered an ideal vehicle for Miss Garbo because in it her slight Swedish accent would be entirely in keeping with the character she was called on to portray. Those who know Miss Garbo know that she has a trick of wrong accent here and there, which helps make her the more fascinating, perhaps, to her admirers, but which does not make her a perfect model for English diction.

The influence of the stage is evidenced in the sets, particularly those representing interiors, and the rigidity of the camera emphasizes their stage-like quality. With the exception of the barroom, each interior is shot from only one side. Although in the restaurant scene there is a tracking shot up to the table where Anna and Mat are seated and there are close-ups and even a close shot, the camera remains on the same side of the table throughout the scene. This fourth-wall perspective affects the acting. In the scenes in the cabin, for example, a table is the focal point. The actors move around it as on a stage, and no change in camera angle breaks the stage-like effect.

There is a preponderance of medium and medium-close shots. The change in spatial length of the shots is effected for the most part by cutting rather than by movement of the camera. The actors tend to remain stationary when speaking, as though moving would take them out of range of a microphone. In the scenes in the back room of the bar, microphones could be hidden under the tables. And one cannot help suspecting a microphone in the ship's lantern, to which Miss Garbo and George F. Marion keep close proximity as they converse in the stern of the barge.

There is also a tendency to temporally long shots. Brown makes occasional use of close-ups, cutting from one actor to another as each speaks. On the other hand, there are long intervals without these breaks. Thus in another way *Anna Christie* is more suggestive of *Queen Elizabeth* than of *The Birth of a Nation, Greed,* or *Potemkin.*

For the most part the sound effects in the film are those

which might be heard on a stage. There is, however, an exception. As Marthy and Chris walk away from the water front, the mechanical piano, heard through the door of the saloon, to which they are making their way, picks up the music from the phonograph playing on the barge, which they have just left. Here the film seems to be groping toward the creative use of sound. The music, inherent in the content, helps to link the two scenes. The only background music is that at the beginning of the film, to accompany the credit titles, and again at the end.

The play-like form of *Anna Christie* is due largely to the newness of sound. The screen had been talking for less than three years, and audiences were still fascinated by the synchronization of sound with image. A play as a scenario presented this combination ready-made. It is not so surprising that the adaptation of O'Neill's play resembles the original as that, here and there, it differs.

If the motion pictures were ever to rival the drama, they would have to do so on their own terms. If *Anna Christie* is a better film than *Queen Elizabeth,* the reason is not the extent to which it depends on sound but, paradoxically, the extent to which it does not. It is significant that the term "talkies" did not stick. For whereas the drama depends primarily on dialogue, the art of the motion pictures depends primarily on pictures. Sound was to become established as a legitimate adjunct. But its proper use was to be only as an adjunct, supporting the pictures. Although *Anna Christie* represents the art lagging behind the machine, it did not lag long. Fortunately for the motion pictures, the proper use of the new adjunct to the machine was soon established. Evidence of its proper use is the subject of the next chapter.

10. The Creative Use of Sound

The first great motion picture was not made until twenty years after the motion-picture machine was invented. Although *The Birth of a Nation* was filmed with equipment which represented an improvement over the *Cinématographe,* the motion-picture camera had become flexible well before its flexibility was artistically exploited. Now that a device had been invented for recording sound on film, the art once more was to grope its way to the proper use of the machine. The weaknesses of *Anna Christie* are due less to the limitations of the machine than the way the machine was used. But this time the art was not to grope so long. If there was any doubt that Brander Matthews had been mistaken in his pronouncement that the motion pictures could never rival the drama because they lacked the potent appeal of the spoken word, it was dispelled with the production of John Ford's film *The Informer* in 1935, less than eight years after the screen had begun to talk.

In his more than forty years in Hollywood, Ford has directed nearly a hundred films, many of them memorable—including *The Iron Horse* (1924), *Arrowsmith* (1931), *The Lost Patrol* (1934), *The Prisoner of Shark Island* and *Mary of Scotland* (1936), *The Plough and the Stars* (1937), *Stagecoach* and *Drums along the Mohawk* (1939), *The Grapes of Wrath* and *The Long Voyage Home* (1940), *How Green Was My Valley* (1941), *The Battle of Midway* (1942), *The Fugitive* (1947), *The Quiet Man* (1952), and *The Last Hurrah* (1958)—but none is more famous than *The Informer.*

Ford has said that *The Informer,* which he filmed in only three weeks, was "the easiest picture" he ever directed, adding, "No wonder. I had been dreaming of it for five years." Ford, who has that quality of Eisenstein's, a social consciousness, is more concerned than most directors with the worth of a story itself. It is not chance that many of his films are adaptations of works of literary merit. He has declared that a good story is one that tells of real people and real problems—a story that has social meaning. Thus he had been impressed by the cinematic possibilities in Liam O'Flaherty's tragedy of an Irishman involved in the Black and Tan troubles in Dublin in 1922. The background of the story appealed to him too, for although he was born at Cape Elizabeth, Maine (on February 1, 1895), his parents were Irish, his father having come from Galway and his mother from the Aran Islands. Ford is proud of his Irish background and of his real name, Sean O'Feeney, and he has long been a student of Ireland and the Irish people.

As a director Ford is in the tradition of Méliès and Griffith. After attending the public schools in Portland and, for a short time, the University of Maine, he became so much interested in the motion pictures that he went to Hollywood, where his brother, Francis Ford, was already acting and directing. It was 1914. Griffith had not yet completed *The Birth of a Nation*. Ford began his career in the motion pictures as a property man, but he was soon filling in as an extra in westerns, and within a year he was assisting his brother and other directors. In 1917 he became a director himself, under the name of Jack Ford. Although it was ten years before Ford was known outside the industry, the trade papers from the beginning took note of the impact of his films and of his photography. Meanwhile he was learning the new art. Ford has been active in many phases of motion-picture production. When his producers permit, he is his own editor. He has written scripts for some of his own films. He has a keen appreciation of the use of the camera, a care in composition, and a style in cutting.

Although Ford had become established as a director of silent films, he adapted himself, as Griffith somehow did not, to the changed nature of motion-picture art. "I use a minimum of dialogue," he says. "I believe the movies are primarily pictures, so I play them that way. Let the pictures do the talking for you."

Although Ford's conception of the relationship of sound to pictures, thus succinctly stated, is not what Brander Matthews had in mind, it is the only relationship whereby sound can embellish the art without detracting from it. The convincing evidence of the validity of this conception is *The Informer*. In no film up to that time had sound been so considerably more than just a realistic accompaniment to the pictures.

Ford is said to have sneaked *The Informer* over on the producers, who were not fully aware of what he was doing. He had agreed to make the film without salary, taking instead a percentage of the profits. It was what Hollywood would have termed a "B" picture. The whole production cost only $218,000 and took only three weeks to make. It seemed at first as though Ford had miscalculated. For although *The Informer* opened at the Radio City Music Hall in New York (on May 9, 1935), it failed to attract large enough audiences and was withdrawn after only a week. But when it was shown in theatres throughout the country, it suddenly became popular, and its success was assured. The New York film critics voted it the best film of the year. The Academy of Motion Picture Arts and Sciences singled it out for several awards, including one to Ford for the direction, to Dudley Nichols for the adaptation, to Max Steiner for the musical score, and to Victor McLaglen for acting. (McLaglen, who plays the title role in *The Informer,* had been under Ford's direction in previous films, the first one in 1925.) *The Informer* has a place on most lists of "the greatest films of all time."

The Informer is the story of a man's temptation, transgression, fear, remorse, retribution, forgiveness, and death—all within the hours of a foggy Dublin night during the exciting times of the Black and Tan troubles in 1922. Thus it has the unity of a Greek tragedy. A continuity title at the beginning, the only one in the film, reads simply: "A Certain Night in Strife-Torn Dublin—1922." As in O'Flaherty's novel, Gypo Nolan, a befuddled Irish lout, has been expelled from the I. R. O., in the film the reason being dereliction of duty. In need of money, he is tempted by a twenty-pound reward to inform on his friend Francis McPhillip, wanted by the British for the murder of a secretary of the Farmers' Union during a strike. Gypo informs, and Frankie, trying to escape from the Black and Tans, is killed. Now helpless without his more intelligent companion, Gypo becomes panic-stricken and is doomed. The rest of the film presents the course of his downfall, which culminates in his being tracked down by members of the I. R. O. and shot. Dying, he is forgiven by the mother of the man he betrayed.

The Informer illustrates what Ford means when he says, "Let the pictures do the talking for you." Effectively as sound is used in this film, it does not intrude on the pictures. In fact much of its effectiveness is due to its unobtrusiveness. Sound is made dependent on the pictures, not pictures on the sound. In *Anna Christie,* on the contrary, the narration depends heavily on the sound track, depends so much on it that one could follow most of the film without looking at the pictures at all. But remove the pictures from *The Informer,* and much of the sound would be incoherent.

In composing the music for Ford's film, Max Steiner adopted what Oscar Levant has called "the Mickey Mouse technique." A chord of music imitates a door slamming, a few notes the falling of coins onto the floor, a run on a harp the blowing of cigarette smoke. Gypo swaggers along to the accompaniment of a march tune. When he rips the poster from the wall, a run of rough music imitates the rough action. The dandy strikes a match against the lamp post: music imitates the scratching sound. Gypo picks up the dandy and tosses him into the street: music imitates the action. This imitative use of music is what Griffith had in mind when he rehearsed a whole day to make the instruments give just the right sort of hysterical-laugh accompaniment for a scene in the silent film *Broken Blossoms.*

The background music is evocative when Gypo stands looking at the printing on the window of the shipping offices:

£10
to
America

Accompanying this scene are a few bars of "Yankee Doodle."

Much of the music in *The Informer* has a commentarial effect. A money theme runs through the film. The theme is expressed, as William Wooten has pointed out, in four descending notes, usually on a bassoon, against a background of wood winds.

Particularly effective is the music inherent in the action itself. One of the most hauntingly beautiful uses of music in all the motion pictures is the singing of "The Rose of Tralee" to the accompaniment of a violin. The singing contrasts not only with the menacing music played just before it, during the screening of the credit titles, but with the mood of "a certain night in strife-torn Dublin." The contrast underlines a corresponding contrast of visual images as the film intercuts between the slight, sensitive-looking boy singing and the hulking, callous-looking Gypo listening. It is a contrast comparable to another in the scene which follows, when Katie, whose first appearance in the film is Madonna-like, is suddenly, by a flinging back of her shawl and a change of expression, revealed to be callous and coarse. The sentimentality of the ballad and of the situation is relieved, however, by the soldiers' frisking the boy as soon as the song is over. There is ironic contrast in the scene at Aunt Betty's as the raucous company earnestly sings Thomas Moore's Irish melody "Believe Me, If All Those Endearing Young Charms."

Here and there a situation is heightened by the very absence of sound. While the soldiers are flashing their lights into the archway and along the wall against which Frankie is trying to hide, there is silence. A silence preceding a sound gives the sound added effect when, after Gypo has stood nervously—and in silence—in front of the major's desk in the police headquarters, the major snaps, "Yes!" The audience is as startled as Gypo. Conversely, an abrupt secession of sound may point up a situation. Shortly after Gypo has read the poster advertising twenty pounds' reward for information about Frankie, he is standing with Katie in front of the window of the shipping offices contemplating the sign which advertises passage to America for ten pounds. "Ten pounds to America," Katie reads aloud. And then as she adds, "Twenty pounds and the world is ours," the music stops suddenly. It stops suddenly when Gypo is surprised at seeing Frankie and, again, when Bartley's entrance interrupts the noisy scene at Aunt Betty's, and when Gallagher, concluding his enumeration of how Gypo has spent the money, speaks the meaningful words: "That makes just twenty pounds."

"Let the pictures do the talking for you." As the film opens, Gypo comes upon one of the reward posters, bearing Frankie's photograph. While Gypo is looking at the poster, there is superimposed on it a close shot of Gypo and Frankie at a bar singing and laughing together. The next shot is an insert of another poster, followed by a medium-close shot of Gypo looking at it. Gypo pats Frankie's picture admiringly; then, after cautiously looking around, he rips the poster from the wall and throws it down. But as he walks along the street, the poster blows after him. Now he comes upon the little group around the street singer. As Gypo, leaning on the seat of a wagon, stands listening to the song, the crumpled poster blows against his leg. He looks down and, seeing the poster, tries to kick it loose. The singing continues. Gypo dislodges the poster, and it blows away. Then the song ends, the soldiers frisk the singer, and the scene dissolves to that of a street, where Katie is being watched by the dandy. The camera moves back when Katie jerks her shawl down over her shoulders, and the scene takes in the dandy as he approaches her. He strikes a match on the lamp post against which Katie is leaning, lights a cigarette, and blows the smoke into her face. Gypo appears. He picks up the dandy and throws him into the street. Thus, in the first five minutes of the film, there are established the situation on which the plot is to be based, the identity of three of the principal characters, the relationship of Gypo to Frankie and of Gypo to Katie, and the foreboding that Gypo may inform on his friend. And during those important five minutes not a word of dialogue is spoken.

A further relationship of Gypo to Frankie, particularly in regard to the twenty-pound reward, is also established without dialogue. This is not the method of a play, is not, for example, O'Neill's method at the beginning of *Anna Christie* to establish the relationship between Anna and Chris. And it is one of the weaknesses of the film *Anna Christie* that the relationship between these two characters is established by just the same method that it is in the play—dialogue. Ford's method in *The Informer,* however, is entirely cinematic. As Gypo dislodges the poster, the camera, in a medium-close shot, concentrates on it against Gypo's feet and then shows it blowing off to the right. A few minutes later, only that brief scene between Gypo and Katie intervening, the poster appears again, this time blowing on from the right and, also in a medium-close shot, against the feet of someone walking. Hands reach down for the poster, and the camera tilts up to reveal Frankie. In the next shot, as Frankie holds the poster in his hands, the camera points over his shoulder to emphasize what he is looking at: his picture. Then as he crumples up the poster and throws it away, he is startled by the approach of a squad of soldiers and darts into an archway to hide. When the soldiers flash their lights into the archway, one of the lights comes to rest on a poster, and Frankie's picture is spotlighted.

Nothing in this film is extraneous. Even the clocks tell not only time but part of the story. Because *The Informer* presents the almost uninterrupted experiences of a single night, transitions are not effected by fades but by dissolves, the only fades being those at the beginning and the end of the film. One of the transitions is that from the scene in the Black and Tan headquarters to the scene in the McPhillip kitchen. Gypo has informed, and soldiers have been sent out to capture Frankie. As Gypo sits with his back to the camera, looking up at the clock on the wall of the police office, the camera looks up at the clock too. The hands indicate six minutes after six. Then the scene dissolves to one showing another clock, at the left of which is a closed door. In this scene, instead of pointing up at the clock, the camera points down. According to this clock it is sixteen minutes after six. The door slowly opens, and Frankie comes in.

Basing his film on a novel rather than on a play, Ford was at an advantage to begin with. Although either a play or a novel made into a film must be "adapted" to the screen, a novel, for one reason because of its point of view, calls for less adapta-

tion than a play. The subjective point of view is not germane
to the drama, at least not to the modern drama. In early plays
the subjective was effected by the soliloquy. But even the two
short soliloquies in *Anna Christie* are awkward when spoken
from the stage today. In *The Informer* Ford is faithful to the
subjective point of view of O'Flaherty's novel. Griffith showed
how, as he said, you can photograph thought, and in *The Informer* Ford shows how photographing thought can include
the microphone as well as the camera.

In the novel the motivation for Gypo's betrayal of his friend
Frankie is expressed introspectively, O'Flaherty describing what
is going on in Gypo's mind:

> He seemed to be deep in thought but he was not thinking.
> At least there was no concrete idea fixed in his mind. Two
> facts rumbled about in his brain, making that primeval noise,
> which is the beginning of thought and which tired people
> experience when the jaded brain has spun out the last threads
> of its energy. There were two facts in his brain. First, the fact
> of his meeting with McPhillip. Second, the fact of his having
> no money to buy a bed for the night.

It would of course be possible to present these two facts cinematically. But Ford and Nichols decided on a different solution:
they have Gypo inform so that he gets money to take Katie to
America.

The motivation is presented almost as subjectively as in
the novel. When Katie remarks, "Twenty pounds and the world
is ours," Gypo grabs her and asks furiously, "What are ye sayin'
that for?"

"Sayin' what—twenty pounds?"

"What are ye drivin' at?"

"Oh, Gypo, what's the matter with you? Twenty pounds!
Might as well be a million."

As they speak these lines, they are standing in front of the
sign on the window of the shipping offices:

£10
to
America
Information
Within

The dramatic irony is clear, because it has been established that
Gypo has another sign in mind:

£20 Reward
Wanted for Murder
Frankie McPhillip

Furthermore, it has thus been made possible to represent cinematically the reason for Gypo's speechlessness at the sudden appearance of Frankie at Dunboy House. Superimposed over
Frankie, as Gypo stares at him, is a printing from the poster:

£20 Reward

The printing dissolves out, but, after Frankie leaves, it reappears
on the wall. Then follow two equally cinematic shots. They
not only narrate the action from this point of the story up to
Gypo's arrival at police headquarters to inform but, without a
word of dialogue, present Gypo's thoughts. After the poster dissolves out, the whole scene at Dunboy House dissolves to that
of the front of the shipping offices, the camera catching the printing on the window:

£10
to
America

Gypo comes on slowly, stops at the window, and looks in. It is
at this point that the few bars of "Yankee Doodle" are heard.
The next shot is of the window from the inside. Gypo is now
facing the camera. He looks down thoughtfully and rubs his face
with his hands. The scene then dissolves to the exterior of the
police headquarters as Gypo approaches.

Thought is somewhat similarly photographed when Gypo
imagines that the girl at Aunt Betty's is Katie. The girl stands

179

in the corner and Gypo, his back to the camera, in the foreground. As the spectator is thus made to look at the girl from Gypo's point of view, the girl's figure dissolves to that of Katie. Thought is photographed too when Gypo contemplates the ship model in the window of the shipping offices. Gypo's reflection is seen in the glass, and over it—and the model—is superimposed a scene representing Gypo and Katie on the deck of a ship, Katie wearing a bridal gown. Heard on the sound track are a few notes of "The Bridal Chorus."

The addition of sound to the motion pictures increased the possibilities of montage. It is not merely the use of sound to record literal dialogue that has made the screen the rival of the stage but the use of sound, together with pictures, to create what Willa Cather calls "the inexplicable presence of the thing not named." The statement that a film tells its story primarily by pictures has had to be modified to include in "pictures" sound used cinematically, that is, montage. Furthermore "sound" should be taken to mean not only inarticulate sounds but speech used in any nonrepresentational way.

Speech may be used nonrepresentationally by a separation of sound from image and thus photograph thought. As Gypo sits alone in the pub after he has received the money for informing, he whispers to himself, "I've got to have a plan! I've got to have a plan!" Then while the camera remains on Gypo, Frankie's voice is heard:

"Ah, Gypo, I'm your brain. You can't think without me. You're lost. You're lost."

The subjective point of view is effected cinematically in other ways. When Frankie runs into the archway to hide from the patrol, the camera, instead of pointing into the archway to show Frankie hiding there, photographs the scene from within the archway looking out. Thus the spectator is given Frankie's point of view. Frankie's death is also subjectively presented. As Frankie climbs out the window to escape, the camera points down at him and, still farther down, at the soldiers rushing into the yard and hurriedly setting up a machine gun. The soldiers aim the gun up at Frankie and thus at the camera—and the audience. The gun is fired, and the camera, still looking down on Frankie and the soldiers below him, catches, in a medium-close shot, Frankie's hand as it loses its grip and slips slowly over the ledge, the only sound the scratching of Frankie's fingernails. The shooting of Gypo is made subjective in a slightly different way. Gypo emerges from the house, stops, looks toward the foreground frightened and, as Bartley comes on at right, yells, "Bartley!" Then the scene cuts to a medium shot of Bartley looking toward the foreground, gun and hand in pocket. Bartley fires toward the foreground. Gypo is not in the picture at all. The shot is reminiscent of that in *The Great Train Robbery* when the outlaw fires "point-blank at the audience." In each the purpose is the same—to bring the audience into the situation.

Nichols says that he "sought and found a series of symbols to make visual the tragic psychology of the informer." Thus in another way, by an emphasis on the visual, the film is made subjective. The fog itself is subjective, for it represents what Nichols calls the groping primitive mind—the mental fog in which Gypo moves and dies. Instead of handing Gypo the reward money, the major tosses it onto the table. Then, with the tip of a cane, another officer pushes the notes in Gypo's direction. The gestures symbolize contempt. The blind man represents, as Nichols says, the brute conscience. The first time he encounters the blind man, Gypo lurches at him and grabs his throat. When he realizes that he is blind, he lets him go. But the tapping of the blind man's stick follows him. Now just the sound has become a symbol—another effective use of sound separated from image. Later that night Gypo tries to buy off his conscience by giving the blind man two pounds.

The posters not only help to tell the story but symbolize the betrayal. The poster which Gypo tears from the wall follows him. At first he is not aware that it has become lodged against his leg, and, as soon as he is, he tries to kick it away. But it has impressed him, and he visualizes it when he sees Frankie a few minutes later. When he comes out of the police headquarters after receiving the money, he stops and looks at a bare wall:

then there is superimposed on the wall one of the posters. In this poster Frankie's face is scowling. When the poster is burned in the grate, the firelight is reflected on Gypo's face. And when Gypo breaks out of the Bogey Hole, he imagines again that he sees one of the posters. As he looks at the wall of a building, the poster appears. Then as the poster disappears, Gypo clutches at the wall, calling out Frankie's name.

In predicting that the motion pictures would never rival the drama, Brander Matthews implied that if the screen could talk, the rivalry would be based on dramatic terms. But as shown by *Anna Christie* and other films done in the same way, the use of the sound track merely to synchronize sound with image does not represent the art of the motion pictures. It represents only the machine. If *The Informer* errs in being less than realistic, its flaws are not due to its use of sound. No film had shown so widely and so well how sound may be used creatively. *The Informer* represents the motion pictures, which had been set back by the introduction of sound, once more established as art.

11. Documentary Film

Robert Flaherty's film *Nanook of the North,* which had been financed by a fur company, so appealed to the Famous Players Company that Flaherty was sent to the South Pacific to photograph the life of the islanders there as he had the Eskimos in *Nanook.* Flaherty called his South Seas film *Moana of the South Seas,* and in describing it in a review in the *New York Sun* in 1926. John Grierson referred to it as a "documentary"—the first time the word had been used in this way. It comes from *documentaire,* a term by which the French described travel pictures. A travel picture is a documentary in the sense that it implies the camera's shooting on the actual locale. In this sense newsreels are documentaries. In the same sense so were the first films of the Lumières.

A documentary, however, is more than an actual representation of life; it is an interpretation as well. A documentary is like a fictional film in that it is narrative. It is like a travelogue in that it is factual. It is also a unified record with a theme. Grierson calls it "the creative treatment of actuality." Thus it implies the motion pictures not only as a machine but also as art.

Nanook is typical of Flaherty's films in that its subject is outside the pale of what is considered civilization. Like *Man of Aran* and *Moana,* it illustrates Flaherty's concern with man in a comparatively primitive state.

Flaherty's life was itself somewhat of a revolt against civilization. Flaherty was born in 1884 in the little community of Iron Mountain, in the Upper Michigan Peninsula, the son of a mining engineer. He attended the Iron Mountain School, but only when he felt like it and, when he did, likely as not, it is

183

said, would show up at eleven o'clock smoking a cigar. When he was twelve he accompanied his father to the Rainy Lake region of Canada, where the elder Flaherty was manager of a gold mine. The settlement was made up of a rough element—miners, Chippewa Indians, gamblers, and other hangers-on of mining camps. Robert Flaherty's companions were young Chippewas. After two years of this life and a similar one in the heart of the Lake of the Woods country, where his father was next employed, young Flaherty attended Upper Canada College, a fashionable preparatory school in Toronto. He remained there only a little more than a year. Still hoping, however, that he might become formally educated, his parents sent him to the Michigan College of Mines. But he found college life too confining. He took to sleeping in the woods instead of in the dormitory and, when called upon in class, would answer in Chippewa. He was expelled before the end of the year.

He undertook several jobs—working with some Finns in a Michigan copper mine, and then in the gold fields again, and exploring with his father for iron in Canada. He travelled over the northern part of the continent, much of the way with an Indian and by canoe. At Hudson Bay he was told by the Eskimos of some great islands out in the Bay, indicated on the charts as little reefs called the Belcher Group. At this time he was employed by the Canadian Northern Railroad, and he got the backing of one of the officials to explore these islands. On his first attempt his boat was wrecked in a storm, but, on returning to Toronto to report, he was encouraged to try again. In preparation for this expedition he went to Rochester, New York, and bought one of the early Bell and Howell motion-picture cameras so that he could record his discovery.

Back at Hudson Bay he set out on his voyage. He reached the islands and found that the Eskimos had been right. The main island in the group he discovered to be more than seventy-five miles in length. After staying so long on the island exploring that the ship was burned for fuel, he and the crew came back to the mainland in the whaleboat, a journey of ten days through the icy waters of Hudson Bay.

He had shot 70,000 feet of film and, having returned to Toronto, spent several weeks editing it. Then one evening, on completing the editing, he lit a cigarette and threw the match onto the floor. In a flash the film was destroyed. A positive print, however, escaped the fire. Flaherty showed it to the American Geographical Society, to the Explorers' Club, and to his friends. Then he realized how bad it was. It was just a series of disconnected scenes. Flaherty said it was boring.

Flaherty realized that it was bad because it was like a travelogue. He decided that if he went back north where he had lived for ten years and where he knew the people, he could make a film that would be different. It would be a film about a typical Eskimo and his family—a story of their lives during one year. No motion-picture producer was interested, but finally in 1920 Flaherty persuaded the French fur company Revillon Frères to finance it. The subject was to be life in the vicinity of their trading station in northern Canada, and they would use the film for advertising in their competition with the Hudson's Bay Company. The scene of operations was Port Harrison, an outpost on the northeast shore of Hudson Bay. Flaherty took with him two Akeley cameras, which delighted him because of their gyro movement. Flaherty believed that he was a pioneer in the use of the Akeley, which could pan or tilt without a distracting jar or vibration and which he used in making all of his films.

On his arrival at Port Harrison in August of 1920, Flaherty followed what was to be his procedure in making documentaries—he became acquainted with the natives. They were to be his actors. He wanted to know them and he wanted them to know him so that they could work together. He established himself in a fifteen-by-twenty-foot hut, set up his generator, and invited the Eskimos in. His phonograph, which he kept continually going, fascinated them. The leading hunter in the community, an Eskimo named Nanook, meaning "the bear," was so pleased with the phonograph that he tried to eat a Harry Lauder record. When Flaherty told the Eskimos that he had come to live with them for a year to take their pictures, they roared with laughter. And when he showed Nanook some stills he had made of him, Nanook held them upside down, because the only image he had ever seen of himself had been his reflection in pools. Flaherty selected Nanook as the central figure in the film.

At the Eastman Kodak Company Flaherty had been shown how to do his own printing. He would project the day's rushes for the Eskimos so that they could see what was expected of them. Working without script, he allowed incidents that happened in the course of the filming to suggest the way to proceed. Thus his story developed out of the lives of the people and their environment.

The first incident he shot was that of the walrus hunt, led by Nanook. When this sequence was printed, Flaherty invited the Eskimos into the hut to see the rushes, projected onto a Hudson's Bay blanket for a screen. The Eskimos kept looking back at the projector, the source of the light, until suddenly one of them shouted "ivuik," the Eskimo word for *walrus*. Then as the scene showed Nanook and his crew creeping down on the herd and Nanook throwing his harpoon, pandemonium broke loose. Here was a struggle for food, and as the harpoon struck and the impaled walrus dove into the sea, the Eskimos shouted "Hold him!" and "Pull!" and clambered over the chairs to reach the screen and help Nanook with the harpoon line. From then on Nanook was constantly thinking up new hunting scenes to film.

Flaherty followed Nanook with a camera for two months hoping to get a picture of him harpooning a seal through a breathing hole in the ice. Finally a dead seal had to be used for this sequence. Lines were rigged to it under the ice, and a group of Eskimos out of camera range yanked on the lines while Nanook, together with his wife and three children, struggled with the harpoon rope. And this is the scene which Flaherty shot. "One often has to distort a thing," he used to say, "to catch its true spirit."

In his sixteen months in the north country filming *Nanook*, which he completed in 1921, Flaherty himself faced the dangers the Eskimos undergo. On one expedition in search of bear they were caught in a drifter, a northern storm so fierce that the flying snow can choke an Eskimo dog to death. They built an igloo and holed in for eight days. On this same expedition, in which they travelled 600 miles over sea ice, Flaherty nearly starved to death. Two years before his death, in 1951, Flaherty told an interviewer:

> An Eskimo lives with menace. It is always ahead of him, over the next white ridge. A storm may be waiting, the game may be gone. The trip on sea ice may leave him on drifting pans. His dogs are dangerous. Eskimo Huskies are like wolves, of course, and they'll round on children that fall down within reach. The wife of a Northwest Mountie was torn apart and killed one year when I was up there. She just slipped. Indians are the Eskimos' constant enemy. Up to a few years ago, the Indians, who had guns first, used to hunt Eskimos for sport, as we hunt bear or deer. I came across an entry in an old journal at one post: "Party of Indians in canoes passed going north at 11 A.M. today hunting Eskimos." When eventually the Eskimos got guns, the Indians let them alone. In those days, one Eskimo was worth about twenty Indians. I like Eskimos. They were always dependable, helpful, and loyal. Nanook was my friend. He starved to death, you know. It was two years after I finished the movie. His family were hungry, he went after game, and a drifter caught him. I felt terrible about it. Nanook was a great man.

Nanook of the North is an ideal documentary. It is a non-fictional, narrative film about the real world. Flaherty said that his film was to be a story about a man who has fewer resources than any other man in the world, a man whose life is a constant struggle against starvation in a land where nothing grows and where he must depend on what he can kill—all in the bitterest of climates. The theme, then, is that of several of Flaherty's documentaries—the will to live. In documenting the lives of a typical Eskimo and his family during one year, *Nanook* gets its unity and its construction. The story opens in the spring and concludes in the following winter.

The technique of *Nanook* is simple. The film is characterized almost by absence of technique. There is no trick photography. There is no studied composition. There is not a single dissolve. The camera does not even pan unless to enlarge the scope of a scene without cutting. One of the first shots is that of the icy waters of Hudson Bay. The whole scene has an undulating motion as though the camera were in a boat riding the swells—as it undoubtedly was. Although the camera thus moves, the movement results naturally from the circumstances of the filming. It is not made to move just for "effect," but it is effective. The simplicity of Flaherty's technique implies an almost complete dependence on the subject of each shot and the order in which the shots are arranged. Of the part showing Nanook building an igloo, Paul Rotha writes, "The screen has probably no more simply treated, yet brilliantly instructive, sequence." Like no film before it, *Nanook* illustrates a creativeness in a very closeness of the art to the machine.

But it has other creative elements. Flaherty stresses the discovery of the essential human story from within. *Nanook* is no patronizing excursion into a quaint and far-off place. Flaherty is not showing that the Eskimo is different from ourselves, rather that he is like us. Although it is a rare kind of ingenuity, fortitude, and bravery which the chief character in the film possesses, the subject is universal—dependence on oneself.

In *Nanook* the dependence is quite physical—the dependence of man on himself to keep alive. For, as in all of his films, Flaherty is concerned with reality not coated over by the veneer of civilization. Flaherty is not only the father of the documentary but the first director to show how the camera can document nature. His contribution to the art of the motion pictures is comparable to that of Porter, of Griffith, and of Eisenstein.

Although the documentary takes for its subject the real world, the subject is not always nature. *Night Mail,* produced and directed in 1936 by Basil Wright and Harry Watt for the General Post Office Film Unit (of England), records the nightly run of a train from London to Glasgow—the *Postal Special.* Made as a propaganda film for the General Post Office, it is intended to depict the importance of the postal system. But like *Nanook of the North,* an advertisement for a fur company, it is also a documentary.

The theme of *Night Mail* is suggested in one of the lines of the commentary: "All Scotland waits for her." The *Postal Special* is an express which carries no passengers, only mail, and for which all other trains are sidetracked.

The film gets its construction from its subject—the run of the *Special* from the time it leaves Euston Station in London at eight-thirty in the evening until it glides down into the yards at Glasgow the next morning.

Within its construction the directors have selected details about the travelling post office and railroading and made them exciting. And since the purpose of *Night Mail* is to show the importance of the postal system to the people whom it serves, the film depicts the countryside through which the train passes.

Whereas *Nanook of the North* is a film about nature and about man in a primitive state, *Night Mail* has to do with civilization and the familiar. But the directors make the familiar interesting, not only by selecting relevant details and putting them together to tell a story, but by artistically manipulating their camera.

A variety of shots presents the *Postal Special's* being dispatched from the London station, the switchman in the towers speeding it on its way, a passenger train being backed onto a siding to let it pass, the *Postal* stopping at Crewe, the main junction for the Midlands, to take on more mail and change locomotives, the clerks sorting mail in the car, and the mail bags being delivered into trap nets at stations along the way. Humdrum routine is given meaning throughout: the track gang standing by at the approach of the train, the dispatcher at Crewe getting permission to hold the *Postal* four minutes because the connecting train from Holyhead is late, a mail clerk questioning the superviser about the address on a letter.

The film is interspersed with shots of the train: close shots of moving parts of the locomotive—the centers of the driving wheels, a section of a driving rod, the flashing in and out of the piston rod, the wheels of the foretruck—a pan shot of the interior of the cab, the camera picking up now one detail, now another, shots of varying spatial lengths and angles as the camera aims along the side of the speeding cars. There is a shot from the front of the locomotive, the camera pointing down at the track, which rushes under it in a changing pattern as the train passes over a switch. In another shot the camera looks forward from the rear of the tender, over the top of the locomotive, in the manner of that remarkable shot in *The Great Train Robbery* which depicts the attack upon the engineer.

The film is also interspersed with shots of the landscape from the moving train. These range from distant shots of the countryside to a shot of the near horizon, above eye level, as the train passes through a cut.

There are shots from another point of view, that of life along the route from London to Glasgow, for the purpose of the film is to show the importance of the post office to the people it serves. Accordingly early in the film a sequence presents a farmer going out to the railroad track and receiving his newspaper as it is tossed from the passing train. There are scenes of industrial plants along the right of way. There is a pan shot of part of the city of Glasgow. Some of the most beautiful shots in *Night Mail* are those of the train seen from the countryside through which it is passing—from various distances and at various angles. One sees the train from above, as though the camera were mounted on a bridge over the tracks, and from a still higher position, as though the camera were in an airplane. Again, at a distance of a mile or more from the track, the camera pans across the hills until it catches, near the horizon, a moving plume of white smoke. The train not only gives these pictures of the countryside a meaning, by relating the mail to the people, but also adds aesthetically to the composition. A moving train can enhance a landscape.

Suspense is created in the routine business of the delivery of a mail sack from the car to a trap net beside the track as the train speeds past. The directors humanize this incident by pointing up the apprehension of the novice mail clerk responsible for swinging the sack out on the hinged bar at just the right second, and the consequent amusement of his fellow clerks. The incident comprises most of a sequence which presents the de-

190

livery and taking on of other sacks of mail as well. Although the incident is hardly more than a minute and a half in duration, it is made up of fifty-eight shots—an average of less than two seconds to each shot. Griffith showed how the camera can force attention on details, and Eisenstein built up whole sequences on them. This sequence in *Night Mail* is comparable to the method of *Potemkin*.

Particularly interesting about *Night Mail* is what the directors have done with sounds relative to trains and railroading. The comparative quiet in which the track crew works—the only sounds the click of tools on metal and stone, the piping of the foreman's whistle, and the warning call, "Stand by, stand clear" —is broken as the train rounds a curve and comes toward the camera. There are the sounds of wheels on the track—and the sounds are varied by distance and speed—of wheels passing over switch points, of the train whistle. There are railroad-station sounds. As they sort the mail, the clerks converse in that drone which characterizes voices made inarticulate by a more insistent noise, as for example, that of a train heard from inside a car.

There is a spoken commentary, but it is slight and unobtrusive, that is, with the exception of the reciting of W. H. Auden's poem about a train and the letters it brings. The rhythm of the poem is intended to imitate the pulsation of the driving wheels, varying as the train labors up a grade and coasts down the other side:

This is the night mail crossing the border,
Bringing the cheque and the postal order,
Letters for the rich, letters for the poor,
The shop at the corner and the girl next door,
Pulling up Beattock, a steady climb—
The gradient's against her but she's on time.

Past cotton grass and moorland boulder,
Shovelling white steam over her shoulder,
Snorting noisily as she passes
Silent miles of wind-swept grasses;
Birds turn their heads as she approaches,
Stare from the bushes at her blank-faced coaches;

Sheep dogs cannot turn her course,
They slumber on with paws across.
In the farm she passes no one wakes,
But a jug in the bedroom gently shakes.

Dawn freshens, the climb is done.
Down towards Glasgow she descends
Towards the steam tugs, yelping down the glade of cranes
Towards the fields of apparatus, the furnaces
Set on the dark plain like gigantic chessmen.
All Scotland waits for her;
In the dark glens, beside the pale-green sea lochs,
Men long for news.

Letters of thanks, letters from banks,
Letters of joy from the girl and boy,
Receipted bills and invitations
To inspect new stock or visit relations,
And applications for situations,
And timid lovers' declarations,
And gossip, gossip from all the nations,
News circumstantial, news financial,
Letters with holiday snaps to enlarge in,
Letters with faces scrawled on the margin.

Letters from uncles, cousins and aunts,
Letters to Scotland from the South of France,
Letters of condolence to Highlands and Lowlands,
Notes from overseas to the Hebrides;
Written on paper of every hue,
The pink, the violet, the white and the blue,
The chatty, the catty, the boring, adoring,
The cold and official and the heart's outpouring,
Clever, stupid, short and long,
The typed and the printed and the spelt all wrong.

Thousands are still asleep
Dreaming of terrifying monsters
Or a friendly tea beside the band at Cranston's or Crawford's;
Asleep in working Glasgow, alseep in well-set Edinburgh,
Asleep in granite Aberdeen.
They continue their dreams

But shall wake soon and long for letters.
And none will hear the postman's knock
Without a quickening of the heart,
For who can bear to feel himself forgotten?

The way in which the recitation is linked to the pictures has been indicated by Karel Reisz as follows:

		Ft.	fr.
1. Mountain scenery. Nearer dawn. *Camera pans slowly* to reveal a train coming up through the valley.	*(Wind)* COMMENTATOR (VOICE A): *This is the night mail crossing the border, bringing the cheque and the postal order, Letters for the rich, letters for the poor,* (*Slow rhythmic music fades in very gently.*)	24	
2. *LS* Train coming across the valley.	*The shop at the corner and the girl next door, Pulling up Beattock, a steady climb—The gradient's against her but she's on time.* (*Over the last line of commentary music is turned sharply up.*)	11	
3. *MS* Stoker and driver shovelling coal into the boiler.	(*Music continues: harsh, rhythmic; as if in time with the sound of engine pistons.*)	9	7
4. *CS* Boiler gate as shovel of coal enters.	(*Music continues.*)	6	
5. *MS* Stoker and driver. As in 3.	(*Music continues.*)	3	6
6. *CS* Hands on handle of shovel as they swing forward.	(*Music continues.*)	1	14
7. *CS* Engine driver looking on.	(*Music continues.*)	3	3

8. Front of engine, as seen from driver's cabin.

(Music fades down.)
Past cotton grass and moorland boulder, 3 8

9. *LS* Train. *Tracking shot, keeping train locomotive just in frame to the left.*

Shovelling white steam over her shoulder,
Snorting noisily as she passes
Silent miles of wind-swept grasses;
Birds turn their heads— 12 3

10. *CS* Locomotive wheels.

—as she approaches,
Stare from the bushes— 2 12

11. Passing trees, as seen from moving train.

—at her blank-faced coaches; 1 12

12. Front of locomotive; from left side of driver's cabin as the train goes under a bridge.

Sheep dogs cannot turn her course,
They slumber on with paws across. 7 14

13. Looking over engine driver's cabin. *Camera facing* in direction of train's movement.

In the farm she passes no one wakes,
But a jug in the bed-room gently shakes.
(Tempo of music slows down to long calm phrases.) 10 10

14. *Slow panning shot* of clouds at dawn.

(Music continues calm.)
Dawn freshens— 12 2

15. *CS* Driver as he lifts his cap and wipes his brow with a handkerchief.
Dissolve to:

—the climb is done.
(Music continues calm to end of shot 20.) 5 7

16. Engine driver's panel.
Camera pans to left to take in scenery as train speeds by.
Dissolve to:

COMMENTATOR
(VOICE B):
Down towards Glas-gow she descends
Towards the steam tugs, yelping down the

glade of cranes
Towards the fields of
apparatus— 15 5

17. *LS* Furnaces and chimneys.   *—the furnaces*
    Dissolve to: *Set on the dark plain*
    like gigantic chessmen. 6 6

18. *LS* Valley with hills in   *All Scotland waits*
    background.   *for her;* 5 14
    Dissolve to:

19. Cottage in the valley.   *In the dark glens,*
    Dissolve to: *beside the pale-green*
    sea lochs, 3 11

20. Valley with hills in   *Men long for news.* 3 8
    background.

21. *CS* Wheels of engine; fast   COMMENTATOR
    rhythmic motion of pistols.   (VOICE A):
    Letters of thanks, let-
    ters from banks,
    Letters of joy from the
    girl and boy, 4 5

Reisz points out that in the first part of the recitation there are four separate phases as follows:

1. SHOTS 1–13: *"The gradient's against her."* During the first two shots the rhythm is established by the commentary. During shots 3–7 music and accelerated cutting produce the beat. In 8–13 the commentary takes up the beat again.

2. SHOTS 13–15: *"The climb is done."* These shots represent a transition between the climb and the descent. The music, the irregular line *"Dawn freshens, the climb is done"* and Shot 15, that of the engineer wiping his brow, suggests the loosened tension after the climb.

3. SHOTS 15–20: *"All Scotland waits for her."* Here the descriptive commentary calls particular attention to itself, the pictures being subordinated to the verse and the shots linked by dissolves.

4. SHOT 21: *"Letters . . . Letters."* The rapid motion of the piston is matched by the staccato beat of the commentary as the train speeds downhill.

The variations in rhythm, Reisz observes, explain the sense of the sequence. During Shot 21, for example, it is the accelerated rhythm of the verse, rather than the content of the commentary or the pictures, which suggests the downhill speed of the train.

More effective, however, than the recitation of Auden's poem about the letters is the use of the sound track to record the noises peculiar to railroading. As the story of a train, *Night Mail* would be incomplete without sound. And the sounds in it are none the less effective for being literal.

Documentary film does not, however, preclude sound used creatively. In *The River,* which Pare Lorentz made the year after *Night Mail,* sound is creative as well as literal.

Before Pare Lorentz wrote and directed *The River,* he had made a documentary film for the United States Department of Agriculture—*The Plow that Broke the Plains.* This film documents the mistreatment of the lands in the West and the resulting dust storms. *The Plow that Broke the Plains* was successful, and the Department had Lorentz make another one the next year to show how deforestation and other mistreatment of the land in the Mississippi River basin caused millions of dollars of damage by floods. The result was *The River,* similar to *Nanook of the North* in that its subject is man and his conflict with nature, and to *Night Mail* in that its subject is man and his use of civilization.

It is said that when Lorentz saw the Mississippi River, he threw away his scenario: the Mississippi seemed dull to him—just a vast flow of brownish water between flat, uninteresting shores. Then he realized that the subject should not be so much the river as its people; it should be about what they had done to the river and what the river had done to them. Lorentz and his cameraman travelled 26,000 miles, and then, when he thought he had completed the footage, there came the disastrous floods of 1936. So he commandeered space in coast-guard boats and airplanes, and when he was through he had 80,000 feet of film. This he cut down to 2900 feet. He has made of it a beautifully unified epic.

In the Preface to the published text of *The River* Lorentz names three books which he says he found essential to any understanding of the Mississippi: Mark Twain's *Life on the Mississippi*, "still the most accurate book ever written on the subject"; the Mississippi Valley Committee's Report (Department of the Interior, 1934), "the best written government report" Lorentz had ever read; and Lyle Saxon's *Father Mississippi*. Lorentz was soundly prepared to direct *The River*.

The film opens with a titled prologue, which states the subject and implies the theme:

> This is the story of a river;
> A record of the Mississippi:
> Where it comes from, where it goes;
> What it has meant to us . . .
> And what it has cost us.

The story is told chronologically, beginning with the river and its tributaries flowing naturally within their banks—the state of the basin before the land was despoiled. Then are shown the growing of cotton, the impoverishment of the South by the Civil War, lumbering and steel-making and, finally, the results—the denuded land, the floods, the effects of the floods on the land, and the effects on the inhabitants of the valley. An epilogue documents the way in which the Tennessee Valley Authority has started to put the valley together again.

The pictures in *The River* are so beautifully composed that they could almost stand by themselves without a sound track. But the sound track adds immeasurably to them—a blending of natural sounds, a musical score composed by Virgil Thomson and incorporating American folk tunes, and Lorentz' commentary spoken by the actor Thomas Chalmers. The generalizing chapters in John Steinbeck's novel on a corresponding subject—*The Grapes of Wrath*—have been compared to the sound track in *The River* because in each the rhythm pervades the story. Effective use is made of natural sounds merely by repetition. For example, the sounds of the steel mill early in the film are imitated in the frantic whistle of a coast-guard boat later. Even

197

in the commentary there is effective repetition—the names of the tributary rivers recited as the rivers are shown at first and recited again when the rivers are shown in flood. "Black spruce and Norway pine," Chalmer's voice is heard accompanying a shot of a beautiful stand of trees. "Black spruce and Norway pine" recited later is made ironic by the now accompanying shot of a landscape completely denuded except for charred tree trunks and stumps.

The commentary which Lorentz wrote to underline his shots has a different relationship to the shots than Auden's poem has in *Night Mail*. Auden's poem is complete in itself. The pictures of the train are, as Ernest Lindgren points out, not even necessary to illustrate it. For the most part, in fact, the pictures do not illustrate it, except in a general way. The commentary for *The River,* on the other hand, is only a comment on the pictures. The commentary is always *under* the pictures, never, as in *Night Mail, over* them.

Lorentz' text is none the less literary. James Joyce called it the most beautiful prose he had heard in years. If the text is prose—in the published version it is represented as verse—it is poetic prose. In the manner of Walt Whitman and Thomas Wolfe, Lorentz effects much of his poetry by naming great place names of the nation—words which are in themselves poetic:

> From as far West as Idaho,
> Down from the glacier peaks of the Rockies—
> From as far East as New York,
> Down from the turkey ridges of the Alleghenies
> Down from Minnesota, twenty-five hundred miles,
> The Mississippi River runs to the Gulf.
> Carrying every drop of water that flows down two-thirds the
>   continent,
> Carrying every brook and rill, rivulet and creek,
> Carrying all the rivers that run down two-thirds the continent,
> The Mississippi runs to the Gulf of Mexico.
>
> Down the Yellowstone, the Milk, the White and Cheyenne;
> The Cannonball, the Musselshell, the James and the Sioux;
> Down the Judith, the Grand, the Osage, and the Platte,

> The Skunk, the Salt, the Black, and Minnesota;
> Down the Rock, the Illinois, and the Kankakee,
> The Allegheny, the Monongahela, Kanawha, and Muskingum;
> Down the Miami, the Wabash, the Licking and the Green,
> The Cumberland, the Kentucky, and the Tennessee;
> Down the Ouachita, the Wichita, the Red, and Yazoo—
> Down the Missouri three thousand miles from the Rockies;
> Down the Ohio a thousand miles from the Alleghenies;
> Down the Arkansas fifteen hundred miles from the Great
>   Divide;
> Down the Red, a thousand miles from Texas;
> Down the great Valley, twenty-five hundred miles from
>   Minnesota,
> Carrying every rivulet and brook, creek and rill,
> Carrying all the rivers that run down two-thirds the continent—
> The Mississippi runs to the Gulf.

Like *Night Mail, The River* was produced as propaganda. *The River* is the story of our despoiling the Mississippi basin by ruthlessly cutting timber, greedily mining for coal and iron, and unscientifically exploiting the land for cotton. The pictures and the text—in the first person plural—are accusatory:

> We built a hundred cities and a thousand towns—
> But at what a cost!
> We cut the top off the Alleghenies and sent it down the river.
> We cut the top off Minnesota and sent it down the river.
> We cut the top off Wisconsin and sent it down the river.
> We left the mountains and the hills slashed and burned,
> And moved on.

It is also the story of the river's savage retaliation. The purpose of the film is to show how we may repair the damage we have done, how, in fact, we have begun reclaiming the Mississippi by reforesting the burned-over and eroded land, properly cultivating the soil, and building dams in the tributaries. The Epilogue shows the accomplishments of the Tennessee Valley Authority.

But like *Night Mail, The River* is an exemplary documentary in spite of its propaganda. Taking for its subject the natural world—nature and man's misuse of it—*The River* has a theme

—nature's retaliatory power and man's being forced to reckon with it—and a unity—not only the story of a river, where it comes from and where it goes, but also the story of how it was, how it became despoiled, and how it can be restored. Telling this story in pictures embellished by sound—sound incorporated literally and creatively—it is a great documentary, if not the greatest that the art of the motion picture has produced.

12. From Play to Film

Although both the film and the play tell their stories by *presenting* them, the manner of presentation is different. As observed in the adaptation of *Anna Christie,* a film which presents its story in the manner of the original play tends to be only a photograph of the play. To be properly adapted to the screen, a play must give up certain of its dramatic characteristics and assume cinematic ones. How these changes should be made is illustrated by the adaptation of Robert Sherwood's play *Abe Lincoln in Illinois* and Noel Coward's one-act play *Still Life.*

In the supplementary notes to his play *Abe Lincoln in Illinois,* Robert E. Sherwood declares that Lincoln's great achievement was "the solidification of the American ideal." But his play, Sherwood says, is not about Lincoln's achievement but rather about the "solidification of Lincoln himself—a long, uncertain process, effected by influences some of which came from his own reasoning mind, some from his surrounding circumstances, some from sources which we cannot comprehend." It was to be "a play about the development of the extraordinary character of Abraham Lincoln." Observing that a playwright is allowed poetic license when his subject is a character out of history, Sherwood says, "The Cleopatra who actually existed may have borne no resemblance to the Cleopatra of Shakespeare's creation nor to the entirely different one of Shaw's, but no one now cares about that, even in Egypt." In presenting the character of Lincoln, however, Sherwood felt that it was not only obligatory to eschew poetic license but desirable because, he says, Lincoln's life was "a work of art," and "his character needs no romanticizing, no

sentimentalizing, no dramatizing." As Sherwood realized, however, the development of Lincoln's character was not only a much
longer process than that which is usually encompassed within
the limits of dramatic action but a process resulting from more
influences than those operating on a fictitious character in a play.
Since Sherwood proposed to present this process and these influences, the problem was to fit them into a form not readily
adaptable to so broad a scope.

As a result *Abe Lincoln in Illinois* represents twenty-eight
years in the life of the hero, from 1833, shortly after Abe has
arrived in New Salem, a backwoods boy from a cabin home on
the Sangamon River, to 1861, when, on the eve of his fifty-second
birthday, he leaves Springfield for Washington to be inaugurated President of the United States. The incidents which Sherwood has selected as contributing to the development of Lincoln's character during these twenty-eight years are presented
in twelve separate scenes, most of them widely separated in time
and involving varied settings and a large cast of characters. It is
therefore not surprising that *Abe Lincoln in Illinois* has been
criticized as a loosely constructed play.

Actually the play is more compact than this criticism implies. Sherwood points out in his notes that Lincoln's life formed
"a veritable allegory of the growth of the democratic spirit, with
its humble origins, its inward struggles, its seemingly timid policy
of 'live and let live' and 'mind your own business,' its slow
awakening to the dreadful problems, its death at the hands of
a crazed assassin, and its perpetual renewal caused by the perpetual human need for it." In declaring that Lincoln's character
needs no dramatizing, Sherwood means not only that it contains
the materials of drama itself but that its actual development is
dramatic. He finds in the chronology of events as history presents
them to him a conflict, a crisis, a climax, and even a denouement.

Abe Lincoln in Illinois is more than a series of loosely con-
nected scenes depicting incidents in the life of a great national
figure. It is a well-constructed play, dramatically presenting the
"long, uncertain process" by which the hero resolves an inner
conflict and the momentous consequences of his resolving it.

In adapting history to his purpose, Sherwood contracts the process. In spite of the contraction, however, the play remains epical, and it is this epic quality which largely accounts for its successful adaptation to the screen.

A play is not usually epical, tending rather to center on a single point. St. John Hankin described his method of playwriting as follows:

> This is what I do with my plays. I select an episode in the life of one of my characters or of a group of characters when something of importance to their future has to be decided, and I ring up my curtain. Having shown how it was decided and why it was so decided, I ring it down again. The episode is over and with it the play.

An episode, however, is not isolated, and frequently an understanding of it depends on an understanding of previous happenings. These happenings the playwright is therefore obliged to present. He does not, however, always present them directly. Mrs. Fiske used to say, "Ibsen gives us the last hours." By this she meant that an Ibsen play observed the unity of time, antecedent action being presented indirectly and the crisis and the climax coming close together. Although most plays are not so nearly unified as Ibsen's, plays tend to be more nearly unified than, for example, novels, which usually narrate most of their stories directly and thus contain many scenes, incidents, and characters.

To be successfully adapted to the screen a play must give up its characteristic unity. The weakness of the film version of *Anna Christie* lies primarily in its faithfulness to the unity of the play. When Sherwood rewrote *Abe Lincoln in Illinois* for the screen and Grover Jones made the adaptation, they were at an advantage, for the epic story of nearly thirty years in the life of a great national hero is particularly suited to screen terms, in fact, even better suited than to the stage. For whereas in writing the play Sherwood had to compress the story into comparatively few incidents and scenes, in the film he had a medium which by its very nature would enable him to present it with less sacrifice of its broad scope.

203

The film gets some of its epic quality from an earlier point of attack than in the play and from a direct presentation of incidents that in the play are only referred to—incidents that happen before the action of the play begins and incidents that are represented as happening off-stage between or during scenes. Whereas the play begins after Abe has become established in New Salem and is part owner of the store, the film opens with a scene in his earlier home on the Sangamon. In the play Josh Speed tells the Bowling Greens that the first time he ever saw Abe Lincoln was when Abe was piloting the steamboat *Talisman*:

> You remember how she ran into trouble at the dam. I had a valuable load of goods aboard for my father's store, and I was sure that steamboat, goods, and all were a total loss. But Abe got her through. It was a great piece of work.

In the film this incident, somewhat altered, is presented directly. Furthermore it is made the occasion of Abe's first meeting Ann Rutledge. The steamboat *Talisman* becomes in the film a flatboat passing New Salem. The valuable load of goods is pigs. In this version Abe's seamanship is less successful. The prow of the boat drops over the dam, and the cargo is spilled into the stream. Next, Abe is shown chasing a pig through the woods. Making a flying leap, he catches the animal by a hind leg and, as he lies prone, holding the squealing pig, Ann Rutledge enters the scene. In the play Abe has already bested Jack Armstrong in a fight. In the film the fight is presented directly. Action represented as occurring between scenes is further material for the film. For example, Ann Rutledge's death, only referred to in the play, is the occasion in the film for two sequences totaling seven minutes, the first, that of Ann's becoming ill at a dance in connection with the political campaign. The sequence opens with a close shot of a sign:

ABE LINCOLN
Our Candidate to the Assembly

The sign hangs in the background of the dance scene. This sequence is concluded after Ann collapses and is taken home.

After an intervening sequence, in which Abe makes a political speech, the scene shifts to the Rutledge cottage, where the death scene is presented. Other examples of this kind of expansion are Abe's winning the election to the Assembly, the resulting celebration, and a dance at the Edwardses', where Abe is presented to Mary Todd.

Sherwood draws on history itself to expand the scope of his play. For example, Lincoln's part in the Black Hawk War is represented by a scene in which Abe is drilling a company of volunteers. The time between Lincoln's marriage, in 1842, and the Lincoln-Douglas debates, in 1858, is bridged for the most part by Hollywood montage—a series of shots and inserts, linked by dissolves and superimposition. The sequence illustrates a continuity title, superimposed over some of these shots, "And then—years that marked the growth of a man and of a nation": a man swinging a pick, a man digging, men building a fence, a mason laying brick, a street in Springfield and a sign

LINCOLN & HERNDON
COUNSELLORS AT LAW

being nailed up, a telegraph pole rising, a newspaper headline reporting the coming of the telegraph service to the West, a train crossing the prairie, Lincoln speaking in the House of Representatives, and headlines implying a growing dissension between North and South. The montage is concluded by an insert reading

ARMED REBELLION
IN VIRGINIA
John Brown
Leads Insurrection
Against Slaveholders

The insert dissolves to a shot of an arch over a doorway. Across the arch is a sign:

HARPERS FERRY
ENGINE HOUSE

Then follows a sequence presenting the arrest of John Brown.

205

This kind of expansion not only broadens the scope of the play but by bridging gaps in time—as, for instance, the sixteen years between Acts II and III—gives the film a continuity which the play lacks. The film includes all but one of the scenes of the play. But so smoothly are the gaps bridged that the scenes seem less like individual units than uninterrupted parts of a continuous picture. For example, the Hollywood montage referred to does not start abruptly after the scene in which Abe asks Mary to take him back. That scene is concluded by a dissolve to a close shot of a family Bible, which opens to a marriage certificate for Abraham Lincoln and Mary Todd Lincoln. A hand is filling in the date: November 4, 1842. Then as the background music rises, there is a dissolve to a double exposure—a medium-close shot of the man swinging the pick. This shot, superimposed on that of a scene in which a mule team moves toward the foreground, unobtrusively begins the montage.

In the play the first scene after the sixteen-year gap is that of the Lincoln-Douglas debate. In the film the debate scene is more smoothly led up to. After the John Brown scene fades out, there is a fade-in to a scene in which Douglas learns that Lincoln is to run against him for election to the Senate. Announcing that he will go to Springfield, Douglas orders a reception with "a brass band at the station and liquor for all." The next scene is that of Abe and his family sitting for their photograph. The children are restless, and the photographer is having difficulty. Then as the picture is finally about to be taken, a band is heard, and the children rush to the window. A distance shot reveals Douglas arriving at the station. The following scene is that of the debate.

Nor after the debate scene is there an abrupt break, as there is in the play, in which the next scene, that of the committee's waiting on Lincoln in the parlor of the Edwards house in Springfield, is represented as taking place two years later. In the film, shots intervening between these two scenes give the impression of continuous action. At the end of the debate scene there is an insert of shorthand notes. (During the debate the reporters have been shown writing at a table beside the debate platform.)

Then there is a cut to a scene which represents Horace Greeley in his newspaper office reading a news dispatch. He reads aloud the last words of Lincoln's rebuttal: " 'A house divided against itself cannot stand.' This government cannot endure permanently half slave and half free!"

"Lincoln? I've never heard of him," observes one of Greeley's assistants.

"You will," says Greeley, and there begins a sequence of inserts of newspaper headlines.

Then follows a scene in which the politicians are talking about Abe. "Anyway," says one of them, "I ask you gentlemen to look him over," whereupon the scene dissolves to that of the parlor: Abe is awaiting the arrival of the committee.

A dissolve also helps to bridge the gap between two of the interpolated sequences—the flatboat episode and Abe's arrival in New Salem. After the scene in which Abe first meets Ann Rutledge, the film shows the flatboat once more on its way downstream. Abe, at the tiller, is looking longingly in the direction of New Salem, which they are drifting past. Then the camera pans from the boat to the river. This shot, of the rippling water, dissolves to a close shot of a wagon wheel turning. Tilting up, the camera reveals the lettering SPRINGFIELD STAGE on the front part of a stagecoach and, continuing to tilt, Abe seated beside the driver. The stagecoach is entering New Salem.

The debate scene represents another kind of expansion. In the play the debate scene is not only adequate for its purpose but particularly effective. Much of its effectiveness results from Sherwood's resorting to the expressionistic device of bringing the audience into the scene, that is, figuratively extending the stage. The stage becomes the debate platform, the audience becomes the crowd listening to the debate in 1848, and accordingly the actors address this audience. But if presented in the same way on the screen, the scene would be not only incongruous, because of the method of the rest of the film, but uncinematic, because of dependence on dialogue. Accordingly the long speeches in the scene in the play are considerably cut—that is, detail is contracted—and the scene is made to include more than the speakers on the platform—that is, scope is expanded within the scene itself.

These are the kinds of expansion implicit in Adler's dictum that "if a play be adapted to the screen, it must be expanded in the direction of epic magnitude." They represent the tendency of the adapted play to be novel-like because of an increase in the number and variety of scenes, incidents, and characters. The increase implies more dependence on the camera than on the microphone. For whereas the method of the play is dialogue, that of the novel is primarily narration and description. Narration and description, which can be represented pictorially, are, unlike dialogue, the essence of the motion pictures. But Sherwood's play requires nearly three hours for presentation on the stage, and the running time of the film is only 100 minutes, part of which is represented by expansion in scope. It is therefore obvious that a considerable part of the play must have been deleted when it was adapted to the screen. The deletions accord with the principle expressed in the concluding phrase of Adler's dictum: "but contracted with respect to dramatic detail." As illustrated in Chapter IX, contraction with respect to dramatic detail implies deletions in dialogue.

In the adaptation of *Abe Lincoln in Illinois* some of the deletions are more than compensated for by direct presentation of allusions in the play. Most of the deletions, however, are absolute. In the debate scene, for example, each of the two long speeches by Abe and Douglas is considerably cut. The scene in which Abe receives the committee is contracted by a reduction in the number of questions which the members of the committee ask the prospective candidate. The film limits this interview, for the most part, to Barrick's questioning Abe about church-going and to Abe's reply.

All of the contractions, however, are not so simple. One of the most effective in the film involves a substitution for the crisis scene. It is the scene on the prairie—which Sherwood calls "the most completely fictitious" of all the twelve scenes. "Lincoln's astounding metamorphosis from a man of doubt and indecision —even of indifference—to a man of passionate conviction and decisive action," Sherwood points out, "was not accomplished in one stroke, by one magnificent act of God." However, since Sherwood was writing a play, he needed to condense the crisis so that it could be presented dramatically. Accordingly he wrote this scene, in which Abe, impressed by the courage of Seth Gale and his family in braving the dangers of the wilderness to help establish a free territory in Oregon, suddenly realizes his own lack of courage and decides to accept his destiny:

> ABE (*suddenly rises*): You mustn't be scared, Seth. I know I'm a poor one to be telling you that—because I've been scared all my life. But—seeing you now—and thinking of the big thing you've set out to do—well, it's made me feel pretty small. It's made me feel that I've got to do something, too, to keep you and your kind in the United States of America.

Seth's little boy is ill, and Seth has asked Abe to speak a prayer for his recovery. Abe has demurred with the excuse that he "couldn't think of a blessed thing that would be of any comfort." But now that he has accepted his destiny, his negative attitude changes, and the first evidence of the change is his offer to speak the prayer. He prays for the boy but also, indirectly, for himself: "Spare him and give him his father's strength—give us all strength, O God, to do the work that is before us." The substitution is not made because the scene is fictitious but because it is dramatic.

In preparation for the change, the opening scene of the film has Sarah Lincoln say to Abe as he leaves home: "Wherever you go, whatever you do, remember what the Good Book says: 'The world passeth, but he that doeth the will of God abideth forever.'" Also in preparation for the change, the setting of Abe's proposal to Ann Rutledge is not, as in the play, the Rutledge tavern, but the woods near the edge of the clearing, where Abe, having seen Ann leave the tavern, has followed her.

The substitute crisis scene occurs, as in the play, after Abe has broken his engagement to Mary Todd. It shows him, bewildered and perplexed, returning to the now deserted New Salem. He leads his horse down the empty street, past the vacant houses, ties it up in front of the tavern, and goes inside. As he looks out across the clearing, there is a cut to what he sees, or imagines he sees: the figure of Ann Rutledge walking away from the tavern as on that other day. Abe follows the ethereal form across the clearing and into the woods. As he stands by the same tree under which the proposal scene took place, Sarah Lincoln's voice is heard: " 'The world passeth, but he that doeth the will of God abideth forever.' " The scene fades out, and in the next one, fading in, Abe is walking briskly along a Springfield street on his way to call on Mary Todd. Thus without dialogue the film accomplishes in less than three minutes what in the play takes a whole scene.

Sarah Lincoln's voice heard on the sound track while the camera remains on Abe is comparable to the separation of sound from image in *The Informer*. Depending for its meaning, not only on the sound and the image, but also on the two incidents previously inserted, it exemplifies "the inexplicable presence of the thing not named." It is entirely cinematic.

The substituted crisis scene results, of necessity, in a contraction of dramatic detail in the scene in which Abe asks Mary to take him back. In the play the value of the latter scene is that it emphasizes the significance of the scene on the prairie. There is no doubt now that Abe has accepted his destiny. Furthermore it makes clear, as though everyone in the audience would not otherwise get the point, how Abe came to make his fateful decision. "What was it that brought you to this change of heart and mind?" Mary asks him.

> ABE: On the prairie, I met an old friend of mine who was moving West, with his wife and child, in a covered wagon. He asked me to go with him, and I was strongly tempted to do so. (*There is great sadness in his tone—but he seems to collect himself, and turns to her again, speaking with a sort of resignation.*) But then I knew that was not my direction. The way I must go is the way you have always wanted me to go.

Obviously this dialogue had to be deleted from the film, but the cinematic way of presenting the crisis makes the reason for Abe's changed attitude so clear that no substitution is necessary.

Although in the adaptation to the screen, the crisis is altered, the climax—Abe's election to the Presidency—and the denouement—the departure from Illinois—are based on the same facts as the play. The only changes in the climax and the denouement are the expansion and contraction resulting from the cinematic method of storytelling.

When a play is adapted to the screen, each scene is usually represented in more than one shot. After the problem of the microphone had been solved and the camera had once more become flexible, scenes incorporating sound could be built up, as Ford showed in *The Informer,* by as many shots taken from as many different angles and distances as in any scene in *The Birth of a Nation.* Although this change is not essential to the cinematic method, it is peculiar to it. In fact, to avoid it is to effect a tour de force. Alfred Hitchcock filmed *Rope* (1948) ostensibly in a single shot, but he guided the attention of the spectator by a continual movement of the camera. In the production of a play a director depends on grouping of actors and sheer acting ability to force attention. In a play, however, attention cannot be absolute. There is no physical barrier to its wandering. It may be diverted by the idle glance of the spectator. It may be diverted by an actor stealing a scene. The motion-picture director, on the other hand, has absolute control over the spectator's attention.

All of *Abe Lincoln in Illinois* is edited in this way. The first scene is that in which Abe leaves his home on the Sangamon. One can imagine how, if this scene were in Sherwood's original play, it would be done on the stage. In the film its parts are related by cutting and movement of the camera. The first shot is that of an exterior of the cabin. It is an establishing shot. But even this establishing shot has been prepared for by the pictures' forming a background to the credit titles, immediately preceding it, for they too are of pioneer scenes. The film itself begins with a fade-in on the Lincoln cabin. Superimposed large over it are the figures 1831. They fade out, and there is a cut to a closer shot of the cabin—a window, through which Tom Lincoln is looking. It is raining. The next shot is of the interior—a medium shot of Tom as he turns from the window and moves right, the camera panning with him. As Tom walks past the fireplace, the camera centers attention on Abe lying on the floor in front of the fire, reading. Panning still farther right, it reveals Sarah Lincoln. There is a cut to a medium-close shot of Sarah, and then to a medium shot of Abe, Tom standing at the right. Reaching down for a brand to light his pipe, Tom speaks the first words of the film: "It's raining, but you wouldn't notice—your nose everlastin' stuck in some book." Thus in a few brief shots the mood and the situation are established.

Editing can emphasize detailed action or gesture that would be ineffective or even unnoticed on a stage. During the debate Mary and the Lincoln children wave to Abe from a second-story window of a near-by building, and Abe, seated on the platform, acknowledges the greeting. If the scene were done in the same way on the stage, it would be difficult to direct the audience's attention away from the speaker to the window at the proper moment and then immediately from the window to Abe. Furthermore, since Abe is sitting at the back of the platform, the speaker would hide him from part of the audience. And it would be difficult to make this exchange of salutations noticeable and yet not seem impolite under the circumstances and therefore out of character. But in the film the incident is made effective by editing. It is done in four brief shots: of the crowd listening to Ninian Edwards, of Abe glancing up to the left, of the group at the window waving, and of Abe's responding by a slight motion of his hand.

The film is remarkably faithful to the characterization in the play. Although in the adaptation to the screen the characters are deprived of considerable dialogue, this loss is somehow compensated for in the expansion in scope. In the play Sherwood intended to show that "the long uncertain process" in the development of the hero's character was effected, as he said, by influences some of which came from the hero's "own reasoning mind." Because the motion pictures can photograph thought, the method by which the film presents, for example, Abe's resolving the inner conflict is a satisfactory substitute for the crisis scene in the play. The long uncertain process was also effected, Sherwood says, by influences some of which came from the hero's surrounding circumstances, and the circumstances are largely represented by the other characters. Billy Herndon, berating Abe for failure to do his "own great duty," is as much the raisonneur of the film as of the play. And Mary Todd, whose role in the play could be, according to Sherwood, "only that of a symbol of her husband's glorious, tragic destiny," is quite as much this symbol in the film. "And how far do you think you will go with anyone like Abe Lincoln, who is lazy and shiftless and prefers to stop constantly along the way to tell jokes?" Elizabeth Edwards rhetorically asks her sister. But Mary, who is determined to marry Abe, is no less determined that he shall not stop along the way. In one of the transition scenes in the film, that of a party at the Edwards house, Abe is telling a joke to a group of men in the hall. The symbolic effectiveness of the scene is almost entirely pictorial. It does not even matter what the joke is. In fact, Abe does not finish telling it, for at this moment Mary Todd comes up. The camera picks her out in the background, approaching slowly but, the symbol of Abe's destiny, determinedly. And no less determinedly she links her arm in Abe's and leads Abe away.

A particular kind of dramatic irony characterizes Sherwood's play, because from a vantage point in time an audience catches meanings beyond those that the characters can appreciate. "You go into politics, and you may get elected," Abe tells Mentor Graham. "And if you get elected, you've got to go to the city. I don't want none of that." "I'm a conservative, all right," he assures Ninian Edwards, who wants the young postmaster to run for the legislature. "If I go into the legislature, you'd never catch me starting any movement for reform or progress." And there is Elizabeth's rhetorical question, "And how far do you think you will go with any one like Abe Lincoln . . . ?" These examples, depending as they do on dialogue, are of course more germane to the drama than to the motion pictures. But in one of the interpolated scenes in the adaptation, the irony is effected as much by the camera as by the microphone. It occurs when Abe, on his first arrival in New Salem, is sworn in as a clerk in the

213

election. The irony is implicit not only in what is heard—Abe's repeating the oath, "I, Abraham Lincoln, do solemnly swear to uphold the Constitution of the United States of America"—but even more in what is seen—the serious-faced young man in pioneer clothes, right hand upraised—in a medium-close shot with which the scene fades out.

It is not to disparage the fine acting in this film to point out that the acting is of no more than secondary importance, or considerably less importance, for example, than in the production of the play. It may be said in general that the better a film, the less important the actors. For the better the film, the less it depends on the method of the stage. It is conceivable that a film might be made without actors at all. Robert Flaherty's *The Titan* (1950), which has been described as pure cinema, was made in just that way. It should be observed that many of the shots in *Abe Lincoln in Illinois* contain no actors and that many that do, call for no particular acting ability. It is one of the flaws of the film version of *Anna Christie* that it depends as it does—and as it was intended to—on Miss Garbo. Because *Abe Lincoln in Illinois* has been adapted cinematically, the film depends more on the arrangement of shots than on the acting in them. It is of course not to be inferred that acting does not contribute to a film. It contributes if only because the content of the shots is important.

A one-act play is adapted to the screen somewhat differently than a full-length play. For whereas in the adaptation of a full-length play scope is expanded, in the adaptation of a one-act play it is expanded even more. And whereas in the adaptation of the full-length play detail is contracted, in that of a one-act play it is contracted less, if at all. This variation is well illustrated by *Brief Encounter,* adapted from Noel Coward's one-act play *Still Life.*

Noel Coward himself wrote the adaptation. Thus, to begin with, the adapter was at an advantage. A playwright knows more about the lives of his characters than he can present in the brief time of a play, of a one-act play in particular. In giving *Still Life* the scope of his film, Coward drew on this kind of knowledge.

The two main characters in his realistic little play meet by chance in the refreshment room of a railway station, continue to meet, fall in love and finally separate. The action, in five scenes spaced out to represent a year's time, takes place in one setting—the refreshment room with its background of travellers, station attendants, and the activity and noise relative to the arrival and departure of the local trains and the roaring past of the expresses. There are allusions in the play to situations and incidents not directly presented. For example, Laura says, "I'm a respectable married woman with a husband and a home and three children." In the film Laura's home is the focus of the story; Laura's husband, only sketchily described in *Still Life,* is presented directly, and so are the children. In the play allusions such as "an accidental meeting—then a little lunch—then the movies" are the bases for sequences in the film. These sequences result in the creation of additional characters: in *Still Life* there are eleven characters: in *Brief Encounter* there are, not including extras, twenty-one.

Several of the sequences whereby the scope is expanded not only elaborate the abortive love affair but symbolize its frustration. In the play the last meeting of Laura and Alec is interrupted by Laura's gossipy acquaintance, Dolly Messiter. In the film comparable discords mark all of the lovers' meetings. They meet by chance at a cafe, where a ladies' orchestra plays squeakily and loudly, and Laura is embarrassed about the check. They escape from the noise of the cafe and go to the movies. But the organist, playing loudly at the movies, is the cellist from the orchestra at the cafe. They go to the movies again, but it is "a terribly bad picture," and they leave before it is over. They go boating, but Alec does not row well and, in an encounter with a low bridge, falls out of the boat. Alec takes Laura to the Grand Hotel for lunch and orders a bottle of champagne, but Laura is disconcerted because two of her acquaintances have been watching them. They drive out into the country in a little two-seater car, but the sun does not shine and Laura is shivering and "not really happy." They return to Stephen Lynn's flat, but the flat is bare and cold and when Alec tries to make a fire, it only smokes.

"I hope the fire will perk up," says Alec, but Stephen unexpectedly returns, and Laura has to escape through the kitchen.

Inasmuch as *Brief Encounter* is the adaptation of a one-act play, detail is expanded too. Some of the dialogue of the minor characters is deleted in the adaptation because the minor characters are made less important in the film than in the play. But the film includes most of the original dialogue and all but two of the characters. Furthermore, since the additional scenes involve additional dialogue, there is more dialogue in the film than in the play. Whereas *Still Life* can be acted in less than three quarters of an hour, the running time of *Brief Encounter* is an hour and a half.

Like most plays *Still Life* reveals the inner lives of the characters only objectively. The subjective point of view does not lend itself naturally to the drama because plays tell their stories primarily by dialogue. But Griffith showed how the motion pictures can photograph thought, and the addition of sound increased this possibility. In adapting *Still Life* to the screen, Coward put the action of the play into a frame: most of *Brief Encounter* is a presentation of what Laura is thinking. It is of course an extension of the inner monologue, and it is intrinsically cinematic. The story being that of an inner conflict, the film gains from the device of the frame, within which the story is told subjectively.

With the exception of a few brief incidents, the story within the frame is told consistently from Laura's point of view. The film opens with a night scene on the platform of the Milford Junction Station and then cuts to the refreshment room, where Laura and Alec are sitting at a table and where the action is that of the last scene of the play. This frame part of the film continues past the action of *Still Life,* which ends as Laura and Dolly are about to leave the refreshment room. The film goes on to show them leaving the room, taking the train to Ketchworth, arriving at Ketchworth, etc. It continues up to the point where Laura, having returned home, is sewing in the library while her husband, Fred, sits opposite her, working a crossword puzzle. Falling into a reverie, Laura narrates the story of her love affair as though she were expressing her thoughts out loud to Fred. Her voice comes over the sound track, but her lips do not move. As she is heard saying, "It all started on an ordinary day, in the most ordinary place in the world," the scene dissolves to the refreshment room. Laura is seated at one of the tables, and Alec enters, as he does about midway through Scene I of *Still Life*. From here on the action includes that of the play, with the exception of a few incidents involving minor characters. Most of the last scene of the play is represented twice in the film—at the beginning, as part of the frame, and toward the end, as the conclusion to Laura's reverie. The second enactment of the scene, however, continues only to that point at which Laura comes back into the refreshment room, having rushed out to throw herself under the express. At that point there is a return to the frame, with which the film ends.

The frame intrudes at one other point. About midway in the film Laura comes out of her reverie for a moment and realizes that she is at home, seated in the library with her husband. This brief intrusion of reality not only reminds us of the story-within-the-story method of the film but points up the conflict.

Part of the frame itself is presented subjectively. In the first scene on the train Laura is so preoccupied that she does not hear what Dolly is saying. Accordingly Dolly's voice is made to fade away on the sound track and, while the camera pictures Dolly still talking, Laura's voice is heard instead.

The story-within-the-story method is complicated by reveries *within* Laura's reverie. For example, Laura recollects that when she was riding home on the train she imagined herself and Alec "in all sorts of glamorous circumstances." As Laura turns to look out of the window, the camera tracks and pans slowly forward until a back projection of the darkened countryside fills the screen. Laura's face is faintly reflected in the window, and Laura's voice is heard on the sound track: "I stared out of that railway carriage window into the dark and watched the dim trees and the telegraph posts slipping by, and through them I saw Alec and me." Then as the view of the countryside dissolves to that of a ballroom in which Laura and Alec are dancing, the noise of the train recedes and is replaced by music. Again Laura's voice is heard: "Alec and me—perhaps a little younger than we are now." The sound of the train returns and the dancing figures dissolve to the passing countryside. Again the train noise dies away and is replaced by the sound of an orchestra tuning up while the countryside changes to a picture of Laura and Alec in a theatre box. Several more imagined scenes are similarly presented. As the last one dissolves to the passing countryside, Laura's reflection appears on the window too. Then the camera pulls back. The window, which has been one with the screen, is now again only the window, beside which Laura is still sitting. In this sequence the primary reverie is represented by Laura, by Laura's reflection in the window, by the landscape outside, by Laura's voice, and by the sound of the train. The inner reverie is represented by the series of scenes Laura imagines and by the music.

The subjective-within-the-subjective occurs again when Laura recalls that as she was sitting alone in the refreshment room she was preoccupied by what she and Alec had said to each other a few moments before about going back to Stephen's flat. As Laura sits at the table recollecting their conversation, the camera shows her in a medium-close shot. The loudspeaker announces her train. Then as the camera remains on Laura, her voice and Alec's are heard on the sound track:

> LAURA'S VOICE: I really must go home.
> ALEC'S VOICE: I'm going back to the flat.
> LAURA'S VOICE: I must go home now, I really must go home.
> ALEC'S VOICE: I'm going back to the flat.
> LAURA'S VOICE: I'm going home.

The difference between objective and subjective narration is strikingly illustrated by two presentations of the same scene. The last scene in the refreshment room is a re-enactment of the first scene there except that now it is presented, not from an objective point of view, but from Laura's. Laura is now remembering what happened in that earlier scene; so there are differences in the way the scene is filmed. In the first place, the reenacted scene is a condensation of the original one, since Laura does not recollect the scene in every detail. Furthermore, whereas the first time the dialogue is realistic, in the re-enactment it is not. Now Laura's voice is heard on the sound track: "Dolly went on talking, but I wasn't listening to her." Accordingly Dolly's voice is made to fade almost out while Laura's, narrating the scene, is heard above it. In the first scene Laura is not shown rushing out to throw herself under the express, the camera remaining instead on Dolly. Now, however, Laura is seen jumping to her feet, *"and the camera pans with her as she rushes blindly out of the door leading to Number 2 platform."* Here the subjective point of view is effected by distortion of image: *"As the camera pans to the door it goes off level, giving the effect of Laura running uphill."* There is a cut to the platform, and Laura is seen running out of the refreshment room and toward the camera and the tracks. Then follows a shot of the tracks from above. Again the camera is tilted to represent the scene from Laura's point of view. An express roars through the station. The next shot, the camera still tilted, is a close-up of Laura as she sways on the edge of the platform and the lights from the train streak past her face. The roar of the train is deafening. Then as the lights stop flashing and the sound rapidly dies away, the camera slowly returns to horizontal. Laura has resisted the impulse to throw herself under the train.

That the story should be told from Laura's point of view is implied in *Still Life.* For it is Laura, rather than Alec, in whom the conflict is stronger. It is she who finally makes the decision between love and duty. Alec is for compromise. Realizing that there can be no compromise, Laura chooses duty. Accordingly the film presents Laura's family but not Alec's. The only evidence of the effect of the affair on Alec, apart from what he says, is presented in the brief scene between him and his colleague Stephen Lynn. Finding out about the clandestine meeting in his flat, Stephen asks Alec to return the latchkey:

ALEC (*giving him the key*): You're very angry, aren't you?
STEPHEN: No, Alec—not angry—just disappointed.

On the other hand, the several scenes of Laura's home life point up the conflict. For example, after Laura has spent the afternoon with Alec, she returns home to find that her son Bobbie has been knocked down by an automobile on his way home from school and has a slight concussion. Although the doctor assures her that the boy is all right, Laura is unnerved:

> LAURA'S VOICE: I tried not to show it, but I was quite hysterical inside as though the whole thing were my fault—a sort of punishment—an awful sinister warning.

Laura even attempts to tell Fred about having had lunch "with a strange man." But Fred is unconcerned. "He's awfully nice—" Laura says, "he's a doctor."

Abstractedly filling in a word in his crossword puzzle, Fred remarks, "A—very—noble—profession."

The dramatic irony piles up as the scene continues:

> LAURA: I thought perhaps we might ask him over to dine one evening.
> FRED: By all means— (*he looks up*) Who?
> LAURA: Doctor Harvey. The one I was telling you about.
> FRED: Must it be dinner?
> LAURA: You're never at home for lunch.
> FRED: Exactly.

The irony makes Laura laugh almost hysterically, and it only increases when Fred, assuming that she is nervous because of Bobbie's accident, says, "I told you when you came in that it wasn't anything serious—there was no need for you to get into such a state."

Laura's comment is the most ironic in the scene: "No—I see that now—I really do."

The deletion of the only two characters who appear in *Still Life* but not in *Brief Encounter* is in keeping with the change from the objective to the subjective point of view. These characters are minor. One of them is the girl who comes in with a message for Beryl, the assistant at the lunch counter, and the other is the young man who orders coffee and a sandwich. Although in the film Laura and Alec are amused by some of the conversation and by-play of the station people, they are not seriously concerned in Beryl's private affairs. To include in the film, then, the business of the message would involve both a violation of the subjective point of view and an irrelevancy. The young man's ordering coffee and a sandwich interrupts the colloquy between Albert Godby, the ticket taker, and Myrtle Bagot, the manageress of the refreshment room. In the play the progress of Albert's affair with Myrtle is continually checked by the official duties of the participants and restricted by its being carried on in public. This low-comedy affair parodies the affair between Laura and Alec. The parody is kept in the adaptation, but the subjective point of view of the film reduces the importance of the station attendants. Since the young man is not necessary, he is left out.

There is another result of the changed point of view. In the play the station attendants are aware of the affair between Laura and Alec and make allusions to it when the principals are not on the scene. But since, in the film, the story is told from Laura's point of view, this aspect of it is deleted in the adaptation. Also deleted are other bits of dialogue which take place in the station but which Laura would not hear.

The device of the story told within a frame admits readily of cinematic treatment. It is, in effect, the old device of the flash back. The conventional means of bridging the gap between a frame and a story within the frame is the dissolve. In *Brief Encounter,* however, the gap is bridged by more than the dissolve. In the first place, the subjective point of view has been introduced during a scene in the frame at the beginning of the film when Laura's thoughts are expressed out loud on the sound track. But even in this scene, which presents Laura and Dolly in the train compartment, the intrusion of the subjective is effected smoothly by a separation of the visual from the audio image. Dolly's incessant chatter and Laura's nervous condition make the separation of the images seem natural—Dolly's moving lips but no sound from them, Laura's closed lips but Laura's voice. The subjective having thus been established, it does not seem awkward when the images are again separated in the transition from the frame to the story within it. Furthermore the dissolve does not occur at once, but only after Laura's voice has been heard for a minute or so while movement of the camera and cutting keep Laura's speech from seeming stagy. As the library dissolves into the refreshment room, the image of Laura in the library does not fade out with the rest of the scene. Consequently Laura is represented as being at once in the library and in the refreshment room; that is, she is watching herself. Finally, there is the music which comes over the radio. Laura has tuned in on the Rachmaninoff Concerto in C Minor. The music, which lulls her into a reverie, helps to bridge the gap between the frame and the subjective part of the film, not only at this point, but also later when the frame intrudes again, that is, when Laura is roused from her reverie by Fred's calling out to her because the radio has become too loud.

The music serves also as an accompaniment to the reverie itself. It becomes, in effect, the background music to the subjective part of the film. Familiar music originating in the story adds to the realism, as for example, that of the barrel organ, the ladies' orchestra in the restaurant, and the organ in the motion-picture theatre. But the use of familiar music as background music is usually avoided in films because of conflicting associations it would set up in the minds of the audience, the attention of which the director is trying to control. In *Brief Encounter*, however, the Rachmaninoff Concerto is more than background music. Because it has been introduced naturally in the frame, it subtly relates the realistic to the subjective part of the film. The use of the Concerto is also evocative, for as Roger Manvell has pointed out, the heavily emotional music enables the film to get away from the expression of emotion through open words and deeds.

The relation becomes less subtle, but no less effective, when, about midway in the film, Laura is momentarily roused from her reverie:

> *In the foreground of the picture the dim outline of Laura can be seen watching herself and Alec as they walk along the subway towards Number 4 platform. The sound of an express*

222

train roaring overhead becomes the sound of loud music. Fred's voice is heard.

Fred is calling out to Laura about the loudness of the music coming over the radio. Then the scene dissolves into the library —a long shot over Laura's shoulder, Laura in the same position as that of the dim outline in the preceding shot. The use of the simultaneous images of Laura—Laura in the subway and the dim outline of Laura in the foreground—is comparable to that in the reverse transition earlier in the film—from the frame to the subjective part, when the image of Laura in the library remains on the screen in the foreground for several seconds after the dissolve to Laura in the refreshment room is completed. The sound in the transition is natural, in that sounds imagined in dreams have realistic counterparts, and it is germane, in that the loudness of the music which induces Laura to imagine the sound of the train is that of the radio playing the Concerto.

Transition in which the means are integrated with content is, in fact, characteristic of *Brief Encounter*. When Laura looks out the window and imagines herself and Alec in glamorous settings, the imagined scenes are linked not merely by dissolves but also by the interpolated shots of the landscape outside, by Laura's voice, and by the interchanging of the sound of the train with that of music. When the camera tracks and pans forward, the car window becomes a motion-picture screen itself, on which the imagined scenes appear. After the last of these scenes the return to the compartment is effected not only by dissolves and a drawing back of the camera but by elements inherent in the content. Laura's voice on the sound track implies what is happening: "Then the palm trees changed into those pollarded willows by the canal just before the level crossing." The sound of the music fades again into the sound of the train and, before the camera pulls back, Laura's reflection is seen in the window.

In the inner monologue in which Laura imagines that she hears her voice and Alec's, sound is the principal means of transition. There is a close-up of Laura as she is sitting in the refreshment room. *"A train bell goes. She fumbles in her bag and*

223

finds a cigarette. She lights it. There is the sound of her train approaching." After the loudspeaker has announced the Ketchworth train and as the camera remains on Laura, the voices are heard on the sound track. And the camera remains on Laura after the voices are heard. These transitions are thus made in a single shot, the scene not changing from the refreshment room.

When Laura again comes out of her reverie, the return to reality is effected, not by a dissolve, but by a cut and a moving of the camera. Laura has just re-entered the refreshment room, having rushed out to the platform to throw herself under the train. She shuts the door and leans back against it—in a medium shot, from which there is a cut to a close-up of her. But because of the lighting in the close-up, the door, against which she is supposedly leaning, is indistinguishable. Then the camera pulls back, the light comes up, and Laura is seen, not leaning against the door in the refreshment room, but sitting in her chair in the library.

Brief Encounter is faithful to the realism of *Still Life*. As in the play, the principal characters are middle aged and middle class. They have the same commonplace names—Laura Jesson and Alec Harvey. There is no attempt to make them or their love affair more glamorous than in the play. Laura's clothes *"are not smart but obviously chosen with taste."* Laura's home is unpretentious, and the drab realism of the refreshment room in the station is accentuated by detail that would have satisfied von Stroheim. Laura and Alec go to the movies, go boating, take drives into the country, where they stop by a stone bridge over a little stream, meet clandestinely in a friend's flat—occasions which might imply a glamorous treatment. But the glamor is deliberately played down: the film they see at the Palladium so bad that it is a parody of bad films, the boating expedition on a wintry day and Alec's lack of oarsmanship resulting in minor disaster, the bleak scene at the bridge in the country, and the bare and cold flat with the smoldering fireplace. The lack of glamor makes Laura's reverie on the train all the more effective by contrast: Laura and Alec, a little younger than they are, "dancing a gay waltz . . . being together in a box at the Opera

The River
Written and Directed by Pare Lorentz
for the U. S. Farm Security Administration in 1937.

"The theme of this film is nature's retaliatory power and man's being forced to reckon with it."

Brief Encounter
Directed by David Lean and Produced by Noel Coward in 1946.

"The film's last scene, in the refreshment room of the railway station, is a re-enactment of the first scene. However, this second time the scene is presented, not from the former objective point of view, but from Laura's."

. . . drifting along the Grand Canal in a gondola . . . driving through beautiful countryside . . . leaning on the rail of a ship . . . standing on some tropical beach in the moonlight."

Brief Encounter makes the most of possibilities for realism inherent in a railway station. Whereas in the play the trains are represented only by off-stage noises, the film presents them directly and with a documentary-like quality. The train scenes, which were shot in the station at Carnforth in Lancashire, are reminiscent of *Night Mail*. The arrival and departure of the local trains and the roaring through of the expresses are made interesting, but not just for their own sake. Roger Manvell has pointed out that the express trains "gradually become symbolic of the lover's inability to fulfill their passion, confined as they were to catching the slow, necessary and useful locals." "The first awful feeling of danger swept over me," Laura is heard saying, and her statement is emphasized by a noise of escaping steam as a locomotive comes toward the foreground. In the scene in which Alec startles Laura by saying that he is going back to Stephen's flat, an express is heard approaching in the distance. As Laura and Alec look at each other, *"the noise of the express rises to a thundering crescendo out of which emerges the scream of the train whistle."* The scene cuts to the tunnel entrance. *"An express hurtles out of the tunnel."* The scene then cuts back to Laura and Alec: they are in each other's arms. This montage is comparable to the scene in *Greed* in which the express flashes past as McTeague embraces Trina.

This kind of "dramatized reality," as David Lean, the director of *Brief Encounter,* calls it, is evidenced even in the lighting. As the film opens, Albert Godby is clocking a train passing through the station. His face, beaming approval because the train is on time, is illuminated by flashes of light reflected from the windows of the passing coaches. Just before the end of the film, when Laura is also watching a train pass, similar flashes, together with the deafening noise, accentuate her distraught expression.

Some of the realistic touches in the film have ironic overtones. Whereas in *Still Life* the station attendants become aware of the couple's weekly meetings in the refreshment room, in *Brief Encounter* the ticket taker does not recognize Laura and Alec when they hand him their tickets. On the station platform, as Laura and Alec are discussing a momentous matter, three girls run giggling by. There is dramatic irony in the sequence in which Laura telephones Mary Norton. Although upset, Laura makes her voice sound natural, and thus Mary is unaware that "the most appalling domestic lie" in which Laura is asking her to back her up is not so appalling as the truth. The scene is intercut with a shot of Mary at her dressing table at the other end of the line. She is holding the telephone, over which Laura's voice is heard, but she shows no interest in what Laura is saying. Instead she is intent on her make-up as she leans forward to examine herself in the mirror.

Although *Brief Encounter* has been praised primarily for being about real people treated realistically, its chief contribution to the art of the motion pictures is something more. The critics called *Brief Encounter* adult. David Lean said, "We defied all the rules of box-office success. There were no big names. There was an unhappy ending to the main love story. The film was played in unglamorous surroundings. And the three leading characters were approaching middle age. A few years ago this would have been a recipe for box-office failure, but this wasn't the case with *Brief Encounter*." Because it was not a box-office failure and because it has been continually revived, it should encourage the making of other films like it. An exemplary adaptation of a one-act play to the screen, it is inherently cinematic.

Adaptation of a play to the screen implies, then, a translation of the dramatic into the cinematic. To present the play in its own terms is not to adapt it. It is this presentation that accounts for the failure of some of the films based on Shakespeare's plays. The weakness of Laurence Olivier's *Hamlet* is the extent to which the film depends on Shakespeare's dialogue. What makes Olivier's *Henry V* a better film is the extent to which it is adapted. It is the adaptation that accounts for the effectiveness of *Abe Lincoln in Illinois* and *Brief Encounter*. Without violating the purpose and the spirit of the play, each of these films tells the story as a film should tell it. In telling it in this way, it represents not just the motion-picture machine but motion-picture art.

13. From Novel to Film

Discussion of a film based on a novel or a play arrives sooner or later at a comparison of the film with its source. This kind of criticism may have its advantages. But somehow it leads to the mistaken conclusion that the excellence of the film depends on similarity to the novel or the play from which it is adapted.

It is relevant to observe that the method of the motion pictures is more like that of the novel than of the play. The way a novel tells a story—primarily by description and narration—is comparable to the way a film does—primarily by pictures—whereas the dramatic method is primarily dialogue. It is true of course that a more literal adaptation can be made of a play than of a novel. A film resembles a play in manner of presentation; that is, it can be seen and heard. A play might therefore be so recorded by camera and microphone as to be almost identical to the play produced on the stage. The more faithfully a film "follows the play," the more like the play it becomes—and the less cinematic. A novel, on the other hand, is faithfully adapted to the screen by a translation of the novelistic terms into cinematic ones and thus by being different. For these reasons a film adapted from a play is seldom better than, or even as good as, the original play, whereas a film adapted from a novel is frequently as good as the original novel, and occasionally better. With few exceptions, films made from novels are better than films made from plays. They are invariably better than films adapted from plays literally—and they are better because of the ways in which they are different.

Although a film made from a novel is sometimes praised for

"following" the book, literal likeness is of course impossible. Even von Stroheim failed to put *McTeague* "completely on the screen just as it was originally written." It is ironic, however, that frequently the conspicuous differences between a film and its source are due not to the cinematic way of storytelling, but to changes imposed arbitrarily. First of all, there is censorship, the screen unfortunately being denied the freedom permitted the printed word or even the stage. Then because the movies are Big Business and a film must therefore appeal to as wide an audience as possible, concessions are made in a work of literary merit to this mass audience, which, it has somehow been determined, has the capacity to understand equivalent to that of a child of fourteen. A comparison of a film with the novel from which it is adapted usually reveals that in the film certain incidents and characters are left out. These deletions are due less to the cinematic method of storytelling than to the convention of the trade that a film should be ninety minutes long.

The changes may be as minor, for example, as the one in *Great Expectations* (1946) in which the sound of the mice rattling behind a panel in Miss Havisham's dining room in Dickens' novel becomes, in the film, a mouse seen nibbling the wedding cake on the table. Or the changes may be as radical as the one in *The Informer* in which the motivation for Gypo's informing, that is, a half-realized need of money for a night's lodging, becomes in the film Gypo's wanting money for two steamship tickets to America. Although it might be argued that on the screen a mouse is more effective seen than heard or that the hero's wanting to take his girl to America is a more plausible motive than wanting shelter, such changes are for the most part not dictated by the necessities of the medium.

Considerably less arbitrary, however, is the matter of style. In the adaptation of a play, the playwright's style can be retained only in whatever dialogue is carried over verbatim into the film. However, the extent to which a film in this way retains the author's style implies the motion pictures only as a machine. What, though, if the adaptation be that of a novel? The film *Great Expectations* begins with a shot of a book being opened and the voice of John Mills, the actor who plays the older Pip, reading the first paragraph of *Great Expectations* as Dickens wrote it. This literal injection of the paragraph into the film, however, is hardly cinematic. A film adapted from a novel cannot naturally retain the author's style. In describing a scene in the estuary Dickens writes:

> . . . some ballast-lighters, shaped like a child's first rude imitation of a boat, lay low in the mud; and a little squat shoal-lighthouse on open piles, stood crippled in the mud on stilts and crutches; and slimy stakes stuck out of the mud, and slimy stones stuck out of the mud, and red landmarks and tidemarks stuck out of the mud, and an old landing-stage and an old roofless building slipped into the mud, and all about us was stagnation and mud.

But, for all the reality in which the scene in the estuary was shot, the film here cannot approximate the style in Dickens' description. On the other hand, if the passage were merely recited on the sound track, it would be as extrinsic as the recitation of Auden's poem in *Night Mail*.

Although it has become standard practice for films to be only about ninety minutes long, there are of course exceptions. But because a film like a play, implies an audience, its length is affected by the length of time an audience can be expected to sit still in a theatre. That time is about three hours. The running time of *Great Expectations* is two hours. Dickens' novel runs to about five hundred pages. On the assumption that one can read a page a minute, it might be estimated that the reading time of *Great Expectations* is eight hours, although one would not ordinarily read five hundred pages continuously at this rate. In one respect it may be said, then, that the film adaptation of *Great Expectations* is only a quarter as long as the novel. What accounts for the contraction?

Consider Dickens' description of Miss Havisham's dining room:

> I crossed the staircase landing, and entered the room she indicated. From that room, too, the daylight was completely excluded, and it had an airless smell that was oppressive. A fire

had been lately kindled in the damp old-fashioned grate, and it was more disposed to go out than to burn up, and the reluctant smoke which hung in the room seemed colder than the clearer air—like our own marsh mist. Certain wintry branches of candles on the high chimney-piece faintly lighted the chamber; or, it would be more expressive to say, faintly troubled its darkness. It was spacious, and I dare say had once been handsome, but every discernible thing in it was covered with dust and mould, and dropping to pieces. The most prominent object was a long table with a tablecloth spread on it, as if a feast had been in preparation when the house and the clocks all stopped together. An epergne or centre-piece of some kind was in the middle of this cloth; it was so heavily overhung with cobwebs that its form was quite indistinguishable.

A picture, according to the Chinese proverb, is worth a thousand words. Excepting the airless smell and the temperature, not to mention Dickens' style, the description of Miss Havisham's dining room can be represented on the screen—and in only a few seconds. Although it happens that in depicting this particular scene in the film the camera probes about the room for more than a few seconds, the time could be reduced to nothing. For whereas in a novel the action ceases whenever the novelist stops to describe, in a film the description can be effected while the action is progressing. For example, Dickens takes a page to describe Miss Havisham. In the film we *see* Miss Havisham while Pip is entering the room, and we continue to see her throughout most of the scene. Since a film takes less time to describe than a novel, it cannot be said that a film is shortened by a curtailing of description.

On the other hand, a film takes more time to narrate than a novel. Suppose, for example, the novelist writes that the hero went to London. The narration is effected as briefly as that. But if the hero's going to London were presented in a film, even if the action were reduced to a minimum, as for example, just the hero's departure and arrival, it would require more time than that for a reading of the statement. In *The Informer* O'Flaherty narrates McPhillip's death in hardly more than a hundred words:

At thirty-five minutes past seven Francis Joseph McPhillip shot himself dead while trying to escape from No. 44 Titt Street, his father's house. The house had been surrounded by Detective-Sergeant McCartney and ten men. Hanging by his left hand from the sill of the back-bedroom window on the second floor, McPhillip put two bullets into McCartney's left shoulder. While he was trying to fire again, his left hand slipped and lost its hold. The pistol muzzle struck the edge of the sill. The bullet shot upwards and entered McPhillip's brain through the right temple.

In the film this incident comprises a sequence lasting more than three minutes. "At thirty-five minutes past seven," the novel briefly states. The sequence opens with a scene representing the interior of the McPhillip kitchen. The camera shoots down at a clock on the wall by a door. The hands indicate sixteen minutes after six. In the immediately preceding scene another clock has also been made conspicuous—the clock on the wall of the police station. In this scene Gypo is sitting, his back to the camera, looking up at a clock, the hands of which indicate five minutes after six. There is an intervening shot, and then Gypo is again shown looking up at the clock. The hands now indicate six minutes after six. Then there is a lap dissolve to the clock in the McPhillip kitchen. In directing attention to the clocks the film links the sequences, but it also helps to expand the phrase "at thirty-five minutes past seven." The rest of the passage is correspondingly expanded. Thus although in the adaptation of a novel to the screen, description implies contraction, narration implies expansion.

But in terms of time the contraction by no means compensates for the expansion. Whereas description may be reduced in a film to no time at all, narration expands. Furthermore a novel comprises more narration than description. Thus even three hours would be too short a time in which to include all of the characters, incidents, scenes, details, etc. of an average-length novel. A film adapted from a novel therefore implies deletions.

When *Great Expectations* was adapted to the screen, Orlick, Joe's journeyman, was left out and therefore all of that part of

the plot which depends on him. Other characters were omitted—
Mr. Wopsle's great aunt, Trabb, Trabb's boy, the Avenger, Miss
Skiffins, and Clara—and the film is accordingly narrower in scope
than the novel. Episodes are abridged: Pumblechook's taking
Pip to Miss Havisham's, Pip's preparation for leaving home, Mrs.
Joe's death, and the return of Magwitch. In the novel Mr. Jaggers finds Pip and Joe at the Three Jolly Bargemen and then
accompanies them home, where Pip's great expectations are revealed. In the film, all of the scenes at the public house having
been deleted, the incident is compressed into a single scene at
the forge.

This kind of contraction tends to make a film like a play not
only in scope, for it results in fewer characters, scenes, incidents,
and plots than in a novel, but also in detail, for when a novel is
adapted to the screen, detail is elaborated as in a play. The brief
passage in *The Informer* narrating Frankie's death is expanded
in the film to present, in detail, Frankie's arriving home, his conversation with his mother and his sister, the police surrounding
the house, Frankie's attempt to escape, etc. Furthermore the film
presents the setting and the appearance of the characters in as
much detail as in a play produced on the stage.

In being adapted to the screen a novel, then, is both contracted and expanded. It is contracted in scope and expanded
in detail, according to Mortimer Adler's dictum. Whereas a
play in being adapted to the screen takes on certain aspects of a
novel, a novel in being adapted takes on certain aspects of a play.
However, because the cinematic way is more like the novelistic
than like the dramatic, a film is more like a novel than like a
play. It cannot of course be exactly like a novel. It is something
less than a novel. But it is also something more.

Although a film cannot "follow the book" in the matter of
style, it can remain true to it in other ways. The most impressive
parts of Dickens' *Great Expectations* are the descriptions of the
marshes and the effect of the marshes on Pip. These are the Cool-
ing Marshes in East Kent, where Dickens himself lived. He refers
to them again and again, not just for the sake of description but
for projection of character. Dickens was conscious of the effect

of the marshes on himself, and he has them similarly affect **Pip**. "Ours was the marsh country down by the river, within, as the river wound, twenty miles of the sea," Dickens writes in beginning his story. The scene of the impressive opening sequence of the film is the marshes, and the marshes and the river are the backgrounds for other scenes too. The scenes were shot in the actual marsh country, the British Royal Navy providing a tank landing craft for the purpose. The film is true to the novel in another way in which character is delineated. Dickens has a good enough memory to see his own unhappy childhood clearly, and in *Great Expectations* he describes the treatment of a child from a child's point of view. The film, like the novel, shows Pip ordered about, nagged at, regarded condescendingly and, above all, having his dignity imposed upon. Mrs. Joe's experience with Orlick is left out of the film, but not Mrs. Joe's treatment of Pip. The Christmas dinner, as in the novel, is made the occasion for the grown-ups to torment the boy. Joe is the only one of the company to respect Pip's feelings. The film is also true to the autobiographical in the novel in its reflection of Dickens' consciousness of his own poverty-stricken background. As though ashamed of his early life, Dickens went to extremes to show that he was a gentleman. He dressed ostentatiously, to the point of vulgarity. Pip goes to London to learn to be a gentleman and is ashamed of his sister because she is married to a blacksmith. He is even ashamed of Joe. This attitude of Pip's is emphasized in scene after scene.

The theme of the novel is ingratitude. As a child Pip is told to be grateful. Magwitch's gratitude for Pip's little kindness results in Pip's great expectations. Later Pip is bothered by his conscience, but not enough to keep him from becoming a snob. It is not until he has lost his money that he really repents and begs forgiveness for his ingratitude. Mainly as a result of contraction in scope the emphasis on theme is lessened in the adaptation. For example, whereas in the novel Pip becomes snobbish before he leaves the forge, in the film his snobbishness is not evident until Joe visits him in London. But the film is true to the theme and to the irony implicit in it.

One of the reasons that *Great Expectations* is a promising source for a film is that its characters are depicted not so much by complex psychological make-up as by physical appearance, mannerisms, dress, and other outward manifestations. They are interesting as individuals, but they are types. Pumblechook is a pompous nincompoop, Mrs. Joe is a termagant, Joe is a likable rustic, Estella is a spoiled child, Drummle is an adventurer, etc. By acting, costuming, and make-up these characters can be faithfully translated to the screen. They are theatric themselves. On the screen they look as Dickensian as the Cruikshank drawings.

Even the incredible Miss Havisham is no less believable than in the novel. Although a novel can be more fantastic than a film, a film, as Adler has pointed out, can be at once more fantastic and more realistic than a novel. Miss Havisham, together with her impossible surroundings, is as credible in the film as the more realistic Pip. Dickens would be satisfied with Martita Hunt's impersonation of his eccentric creation.

Dickens' novel is almost cinematic itself in its variety of striking and often spectacular scenes. And these David Lean has made the most of—Pip's meeting the convict in the graveyard and other scenes on the marshes, Pip's visit to Satis House, the surprise return of Magwitch, and particularly the running down of the skiffs by the packet boat. The stagecoach scenes are no less fascinating in the film than in the novel.

The construction of *Great Expectations* is particularly well suited to screen adaptation. Having more sense of form than most of Dickens' novels, *Great Expectations* is put together like a fan. Pip is the handle, and the sticks are linked by his first meeting with the convict. As a result of the contraction in scope in the adaptation, some of the sticks are left out, as for example, Orlick's beating Mrs. Joe and Pip's adventures with Orlick. The adapters did not find it necessary even to make radical changes in the order of events.

Watching the film, however, one has the continual impression of being rushed through Dickens' novel—of pauses, now for one scene or episode, now another, but of pages and pages being flipped by. It is disconcerting to a Dickens reader who would have the film literally "follow the book." But it is not so disconcerting if one appreciates the impossibility of literal duplication and the necessity of "contraction in the direction of dramatic magnitude," that is, if one accepts the film on its own terms. As a matter of fact, though, the film does not disregard all of the flipped-by pages. Consider, for example, the gap between the scene in which Pip tells Miss Havisham that he can no longer "come to play," because he is going to be apprenticed to Joe—itself a condensation of a corresponding scene in the novel—and that in which, five chapters later, Jaggers informs Pip of "great expectations." Bridging the gap is only the more difficult because in the former scene Pip is played by a young actor, and in the latter an older one. The gap is bridged by the voice of the older Pip heard on the sound track. It is also bridged cinematically. As the latter scene opens, Pip is not directly visible; instead, his shadow is cast on the wall of the forge. And before Pip himself is seen, he is heard answering Jaggers' question. The shadow and the voice help to bridge the gap and make the change from the younger to the older Pip less sudden and less startling than it would be otherwise. Again pages are flipped by, as it were, until Pip is seen presenting himself at Satis House to pay his respects before leaving for London. Here editing and movement of the camera effect the transition. From a shot of Pip in his blacksmith's apron just after he has heard of his "great expectations," the film dissolves to another shot of Pip. At the beginning of this second shot only his feet are visible. Then the camera tilts slowly up, revealing Pip, fashionably dressed, standing at Miss Havisham's gate. Still another method condenses much that Dickens writes about Pip's learning to become a gentleman. This time it is a montage of scenes in which Pip is taking dancing, fencing, and boxing lessons.

To the extent that the film reproduces the dialogue in Dickens' novel, the film may be said to "follow the book." Dickens, who had a flair for the dramatic, writes many of his scenes as though for the stage. The chapter in which Pip reproaches Miss Havisham for letting him suppose that she was his benefactor is like a scene from a play. It is composed largely of dialogue, which can be literally reproduced on the sound track. But to the extent to which it is so reproduced, the scene is dramatic rather than cinematic. It is no more cinematic than the comparatively static images of the actors permit. The ineffectiveness of this scene in the film is the extent to which it "follows the book."

There are in the novel, on the other hand, scenes which, although consisting primarily of dialogue, contain in the dialogue cues for cinematic treatment. There is, for example, the scene in which Herbert Pocket and Pip, having just met for the first time since childhood, are at dinner. Since in this scene Dickens has Herbert narrate antecedent action, the scene is talky. But Dickens interpolates Herbert's exposition with Herbert's criticism of Pip's table manners. In the novel Pip's manners are thus only implied. In the film they are visual as well, and camera and editing make the most of them.

The narrative passages in some of these scenes are themselves the cues for cinematic treatment. In the chapter in which Joe visits Pip and Herbert in London, Dickens includes, as it were, stage directions for the business with Joe's hat, which keeps falling off the mantlepiece. Similarly he writes cues for breaking up the dialogue between Pip and Wemmick at Wemmick's Castle—the exchange of exaggerated nods between Pip and the Aged Parent.

The visual elements in these scenes are as dramatic as they would be in a play, but because of editing they become cinematic as well. This distinction between the merely dramatic and the dramatic together with the cinematic is particularly evident in the way in which the film treats the scene of the Assembly Ball at Richmond. Dickens writes the scenes almost entirely in dialogue, the background merely mentioned. Although the film includes much of this dialogue, it presents it as accompaniment to a variety of shots, in which the background is the ballroom, the dancers, the music, etc. The scene is one of the most spectacular scenes in the film. Furthermore the dialogue is broken up by the announcing of the dances—the announcer seen as well as heard—and by such other visual images as the dancing of the Spanish polka, during which Pip and Estella are continually being separated.

These scenes are dramatic, but to the extent that they are edited they are also cinematic. And it is to the extent that they are cinematic that they are effective on the screen. The kind of detail and emphasis that editing can effect is illustrated by what is called the "reaction shot." For example, when Mrs. Joe starts whipping Pip, there is a cut to a medium shot of Joe. We hear the swishes of the whip outside the scene, but we see Joe wince with each swish. When Jaggers pours the gold pieces onto the table in the forge, there are reaction shots to show Pip's and Joe's amazement. When Herbert dashes into the room and suddenly sees the convict, the camera rushes at Herbert in a veritable zoom shot to catch his frightened expression. Particularly effective is the reaction shot in the scene of Jaggers' explaining to Pip why Magwitch is in danger of his life by returning to England. "Look out that window," Jaggers tells Pip. The scene cuts to the street below. Here has been erected a gallows, on which several prisoners are about to be hanged and around which is a crowd of people. The scene cuts back to a close-up of Pip watching the execution. Then while the camera remains on Pip, a roar goes up from the crowd, out of the scene, and Pip's face contorts in revulsion.

Sound helps to tell the story other than as a merely realistic accompaniment to the pictures. When Pip slowly opens the door to Miss Havisham's room and thus reveals the weird scene within, the background music swells to emphasize the startling effect. Music imitates the rocking motion of the stagecoach, and as the coach enters London the music is picked up by the ringing of the London church bells. In the scene in the estuary when Pip sees the pursuing boat, we hear the screaming of the gulls. We have seen and heard the gulls in a preceding shot. The sound is now at once realistic and symbolic. Sound also links shots in another way. The steersman in the pursuing boat is calling the stroke. The scene cuts to Pip's boat, and Pip and Pocket are rowing in time to the steersman's count. A combination of sounds is made

effective when Mrs. Joe, driving up to the forge with Pumblechook, opens her mouth to scream at Pip and is inarticulate because the sound of the wind drowns out what she is saying. It is
a cinematic metaphor: Mrs. Joe's words and the wind are one.
Absence of sound increases humor in the scene in which Pumblechook and Pip are driving to Miss Havisham's, the camera tracking along with them. Pumblechook is seen speaking to Pip, who
holds out his hands for inspection. Pumblechook fatuously nods
approval. The only sound is that of the spirited background
music in imitation of the brisk movement of the chaise.

The film may also be said to "follow the book" in that it
tells the story from the same point of view as the novel, that is,
in the first person, the narrator being the chief character. In
presenting the story from Pip's point of view, however, the adapters compromise. Pip is represented as telling part of the story
directly, that is, through John Mills' voice heard reading as
though from the novel. In this mechanical use of the microphone, the film is hardly cinematic. On the other hand, the subjective is effected in ways that *are* cinematic.

Consider, for example, the opening scene. Dickens begins
the narration of it as follows:

> Ours was the marsh country, down by the river, within, as
> the river wound, twenty miles of the sea. My first most vivid
> and broad impression of the identity of things, seems to me
> to have been gained on a memorable raw afternoon towards
> evening. At such a time I found out for certain, that this bleak
> place overgrown with nettles was the churchyard; and that
> Philip Pirrip, late of this parish, and also Georgiana wife of the
> above, were dead and buried; and that Alexander, Bartholo-
> mew, Abraham, Tobias, and Roger, infant children of the
> aforesaid, were also dead and buried; and that the dark flat
> wilderness beyond the churchyard, intersected with dykes and
> mounds and gates, with scattered cattle feeding on it, was the
> marshes; and that the low leaden line beyond was the river;
> and that the distant savage lair from which the wind was rush-
> ing, was the sea; and that the small bundle of shivers growing
> afraid of it all and beginning to cry, was Pip.

"Hold your noise!" cried a terrible voice, as a man started up from among the graves at the side of the church porch. "Keep still, you little devil, or I'll cut your throat!"

A fearful man, all in coarse grey, with a great iron on his leg. A man with no hat, and with broken shoes, and with an old rag tied round his head. A man who had been soaked in water, and smothered in mud, and lamed by stones, and cut by flints, and stung by nettles, and torn by briars; who limped, and shivered, and glared and growled; and whose teeth chattered in his head as he seized me by the chin.

The problem in the adaptation was to present the incident from the point of view of the small frightened boy. The film does it in this way:

1. Exterior Thames Estuary. Sunset. The wind is making a high-pitched, ghostly whistling noise. VLS of a small boy— Pip running left to right along the bank of the Estuary. Camera tracks and pans with Pip as he runs round a bend in the pathway and comes toward camera. A gibbet is built on the edge of the path, camera right, and Pip glances up at it as he passes— he continues running and moves out of picture camera right. *Dissolve to*:

2. Exterior Churchyard. Wind continues. MS Pip. He is carrying a bunch of holly in his right hand. He climbs over a broken stone wall and camera pans right with him as he walks past the tombstones and old graves in the churchyard. Camera continues panning as he makes his way towards one of the tombstones and kneels in front of it—he is now in MLS.

3. MS of Pip kneeling at the foot of the grave. Wind continues. Pip pulls up an old rose bush, which he throws aside, pats down the earth again and then places his bunch of holly at the head of the grave near the engraved tombstone. Crackling of branches.

4. MCS Pip kneeling near the tombstone. Wind gets louder. Pip looks round nervously towards camera.

5. LS from Pip's eyeline of the leafless branches of a tree. Wind and crackling of branches. The wind is blowing the branches, which look to Pip like bony hands clutching at him.

6. MCS Pip looks round as in 4.

7. MS of the trunk of an old tree from Pip's eyeline. The tree makes a creaking sound. The tree looks sinister to Pip, like a distorted human body.

8. MS Pip. He jumps up from the grave and runs away right to left towards the stone wall. Camera pans with him, then becomes static as he runs into the arms of a large, dirty, uncouth and horrible-looking man. From his clothes and shackles it is obvious that he is an escaped convict. Pip screams loudly.

9. CS Pip. His mouth is open as he screams, but a large, dirty hand is clapped over it, silencing him.

10. CS of the Convict. His face is dirty and scowling, his hair is closely cut. He leers down at Pip.

CONVICT: Keep still, you little devil, or I'll cut your throat.

The sudden appearance of the convict is made as frightening to us as to Pip, because the scene has been built up from Pip's point of view. Lean's method is similar to that in *The Informer* when the soldiers are photographed from the point of view of Frankie hiding in the archway. But the scene in *Great Expectations* is subtly subjective throughout. Pip's solitariness is indicated in the first shot—a very long shot of a small boy. The method is comparable to that in *Intolerance* when Griffith photographs the manager of the factory seated alone at the end of a room. The eeriness of the opening scene in *Great Expectations* is heightened by the lighting, the solitary marshes, the gibbet, the graveyard, the wind, etc. In the medium-close shot of Pip kneeling near the tombstone, the camera, at Pip's height, makes the tombstone loom larger than it really is. At the sound of the crackling branches Pip looks nervously around, and we see the branches *from Pip's eyeline.* The interpolated shots of the bare branches, which *look like bony hands clutching at him,* and of the gnarled tree, which *looks sinister to Pip, like a distorted human body,* are pictorial counterparts of the sounds. The sound track singles out the crackling of the branches and the creaking of the tree so that we not only see, but *hear,* from Pip's point of view.

The empathy is so well established that when Pip can stand the frightening atmosphere no longer and starts to run away, we run with him, as it were. And we run with him into something still more frightening—the convict. As Pip starts to scream, there is an instantaneous cut to the close-up of Pip and the convict's hand clamping over Pip's mouth. Jack Harris, who edited the film, explains how the point of view is effected here:

> The most difficult thing to get over by photography was the sudden appearance of the convict. The effect was finally obtained by panning with the boy until he runs straight into the stationary convict.
>
> The difficulty in the editing was to decide on the exact frame up to which to leave the panning shot on the screen and to cut to the boy screaming. The effect aimed at was to leave the shot on the screen sufficiently long to let the audience see that the boy had run into a man—and not a very nice man, at that— but not sufficiently long to get a good look and be able to decide that he was after all something recognisably human. As a matter of interest, there are fourteen frames from the time the convict appears to the close-up of Pip. The sound of Pip's scream starts four frames before the cut, at just the precise moment that the apparition is taken away from the audience's sight.

A subjective point of view is similarly effected in other parts of the film. For example, in the Christmas-dinner scene when Pip can stand the table talk no longer, he gets up and starts to run out of the room—and runs directly into a soldier standing in the doorway. Since we have not seen the soldier before, we are as startled as Pip. By dramatic irony the scene has built up Pip's apprehension that the theft of the pie will be discovered. Thus the apprehension is as intense for us as for Pip, and thus the sudden frustration of Pip's attempt to escape is vicariously ours. In the scene in which Magwitch visits Pip in London, subjectivity is effected in somewhat the same way. Magwitch's sudden appearance is prepared for, but it is not expected. The sequence opens with a view of the city at night—wind, mist, rain. Then Pip is seen in his lodgings, the sound of the wind and the rain continuing. When in response to a knock Pip opens the door, the camera is facing the black, muffled figure standing in the hall outside. We do not see Pip's expression of surprise. We see Magwitch—and are surprised ourselves.

The door opening to reveal Magwitch is comparable to an iris-in. But the use of the door for this purpose is more effective than an iris-in would be because the door is part of the scene itself. Similarly when Pip timidly opens the door to Miss Havisham's room, the room is gradually revealed to us. Conversely a door can be closed on a scene in the manner of an iris-out. When Pip leaves Jaggers' office, he closes the door behind him. Since the camera is on the passage, the closing door shuts off our view of the office. But the opening and closing of these doors are not merely for effect. They represent Pip's point of view.

Point of view is also effected by sound used creatively, as in *The Informer*. In the opening scene in the graveyard, Dickens has the convict threaten Pip:

> "You bring me, to-morrow early, that file and them wittles. You bring the lot to me, at that old Battery over yonder. You do it, and you never dare say a word or dare to make a sign concerning your having seen such a person as me, or any person sumever, and you shall be let to live. You fail, or you go from my words in any partickler, no matter how small it is, and your heart and your liver shall be tore out, roasted and ate. Now, I ain't alone, as you may think I am. There's a young man hid with me, in comparison with which young man I am a Angel. That young man hears the words I speak. That young man has a secret way pecooliar to himself, of getting at a boy, and at his heart, and at his liver. It is in wain for a boy to attempt to hide himself from that young man. A boy may lock his door, may be warm in bed, may tuck himself up, may draw the clothes over his head, may think himself comfortable and safe, but that young man will softly creep and creep his way to him and tear him open. I am keeping that young man from harming of you at the present moment, with great difficulty. I find it wery hard to hold that young man off of your inside. Now, what do you say?"

As a result Pip is in terror not only of the young man, but of himself, for having to rob Mrs. Joe of food to appease the convict:

If I slept at all that night, it was only to imagine myself drifting down the river on a strong spring-tide, to the Hulks; a ghostly pirate calling out to me through a speaking-trumpet, as I passed the gibbet-station, that I had better come ashore and be hanged at once, and not put it off. I was afraid to sleep, even if I had been inclined, for I knew that at the first faint dawn of morning I must rob the pantry. There was no doing it in the night, for there was no getting a light by easy friction then; to have got one, I must have struck it out of flint and steel, and have made a noise like the very pirate himself rattling his chains.

In the film the convict similarly threatens Pip, but it is part of the contraction in the adaptation that Pip's thoughts about the pirate, the necessity of robbing Mrs. Joe, and the difficulties concerning a light are left out. In their place a single image is substituted to represent Pip's fear. Although it would be possible to indicate cinematically all of Pip's thoughts as Dickens records them, to do so would mean an ineffective digression in the film. Instead the adapters chose an image which is not Dickens' but which is suggested by what Dickens has had the convict say to Pip. They have Pip imagine that he hears again the convict threatening him. The post-production script indicates how it is done:

> Interior Pip's Bedroom—Dawn. Medium Close Shot Pip lying in bed awake—Music starts. He pushes the clothes off and sits up in bed—he is fully clothed in his outdoor clothes—he crawls down the bed and looks out of the window.

> Exterior Joe Gargery's House—Dawn. Camera shooting on to Pip's bedroom window—Pip can be seen peering through one of the window-panes.

> Long Shot of the marshes and the estuary from Pip's eyeline— a mist hangs over the water; a leafless tree waves its branches in foreground.

> Interior Pip's Bedroom—Dawn. Medium Shot Pip quickly getting back into bed and pulling the clothes up tightly round his chin.

244

CONVICT'S VOICE (in Pip's thoughts): A boy may be warm in bed. (*Pip pulls the clothes right over his head.*) He may pull his clothes right over his head (*Camera tracks forward on to Close Shot of Pip's covered head*)—but that young man will softly creep his way to him and *Tear Him Open.* . . .

Pip throws back the bedclothes with a breathless 'No' and jumps out on to the floor.

The substitution of Pip's recollection of the convict's threat for Pip's imaginings about the pirate is proper cinematic treatment. The repetition of the convict's words, which are actually heard—whereas of course they could not be in a novel—makes the substitution particularly effective. The effectiveness depends on our having heard the words before. It depends particularly on the separation of the convict's voice from its natural counterpart, the convict, and the linking of the voice with another visual image—Pip. It is pure cinema in that it constitutes the creative use of sound.

Sound is also used creatively in other ways to effect an introspective point of view. As Pip goes downstairs to steal the food, he imagines, as Dickens expresses it, "every board and every crack in every board" calling after him, " 'Stop thief!' and 'Get up, Mrs. Joe!' " In reproducing this scene, the film is almost as near a literal version of the novel as the two mediums permit:

Interior Blacksmith's House Stairway—Dawn. Medium Shot of Pip's feet walking slowly down the stairs; the music in background is in an eerie theme. Camera pans down to the bottom of the stairs and then upwards to include Pip—he moves across the room towards the pantry door.

WHISPERED VOICE (as in Pip's mind): Wake up, Mrs. Joe. Wake up. Mrs. Joe, wake up.

Having obtained the provisions for the convict, Pip starts out across the marshes. Dickens' narration here is almost cinematic itself:

The mist was heavier yet when I got out upon the marshes, so that, instead of my running at everything, everything seemed to run at me. This was very disagreeable to a guilty mind. The gates and dykes and banks came bursting at me through the mist, as if they cried as plainly as could be, "A boy with Some-body-else's pork pie! Stop him!" The cattle came upon me with like suddenness, staring out of their eyes, and steaming out of their nostrils, "Holloa, young thief!" One black ox, with a white cravat on—who even had to my awakened conscience something of a clerical air—fixed me so obstinately with his eyes, and moved his blunt head round in such an accusatory manner as I moved round, that I blubbered out to him, "I couldn't help it, sir! It wasn't for myself I took it!" Upon which he put down his head, blew a cloud of smoke out of his nose, and vanished with a kick-up of his hind-legs and a flourish of his tail.

Recognizing that Dickens had written part of the scenario for them, the adapters took their cue accordingly:

> *Close Shot* Pip running through fog, looking from right to left, camera panning with him.
>
> *Medium Shot* cows looking towards Pip, out of picture. Mooing noise in background. *Camera panning* right to left from one cow to another.
>
>> First Cow: A boy with somebody else's brandy.
>> Second Cow: With somebody else's file.
>> Third Cow: With somebody else's pork pie.
>
> *Medium Shot* Pip running through fog, camera panning with him.
>> Third Cow (off): Stop him!
>> Pip stops and looks out of picture, *camera left.*
>
> *Close Shot* Black Ox.
>> Ox (to Pip): Halloa, young thief.
>
> *Medium Shot* Pip looking out of picture, *camera left.*
>> Pip (to Ox): I couldn't help it, sir.
>> He runs out of picture, *camera right. Music swells,* sounding like ox bellowing.

The purpose in *Great Expectations,* according to David Lean, who directed it, is to create the larger-than-life picture that is characteristic of Dickens. Lean points out that the scenes of Pip lying terrified in his bedroom, creeping downstairs, and stealing food for the convict are "something Dickens wrote as if he were right inside the boy himself," and that the film attempts "to make the audience share Pip's fear." If this had not been attempted, he says, the audience would have found the convicts merely funny. Accordingly everything in the film is made larger than life "as it is in a boy's imagination." The audience is made to "share Pip's own exaggerated experience." It is made to hear the voices which Pip imagines he hears. The convicts are made "figures of terror out of some childish nightmare."

Separation of sound from image effects introspection in the stagecoach scene when Pip is on his way from London to Rochester. His conscience bothers him because he is ashamed to stay at the forge. Accordingly as he is seen riding on the coach, voices are heard commenting on his going to the Blue Boar—Joe's, Biddy's, Estella's, and Miss Havisham's.

After Magwitch's death, Pip walks in a daze through the London streets. The street noises are distorted on the sound track. They sound to us as they do to Pip.

Particularly effective is the creative use of sound in the final sequence of the film—Pip's last visit to Satis House. The adapters wish to show that Pip is thinking of his visits to the house as a child. Accordingly on the sound track lines are heard from previous scenes there. The speakers are recognized only by their voices—Estella and Pip as children, Pumblechook, Miss Havisham, and Mr. Jaggers. We see Pip enter the gate where Pumblechook, years ago, turned him over to Estella, and we hear again:

> "What name?"
> "Pumblechook."
> "Quite right."

In the courtyard Pip looks up at the clock tower and hears Miss Havisham's voice: "I know nothing of days of the week, nothing of weeks of the year."

As Pip makes his way into the house, we hear Estella's voice: "Don't loiter, boy. . . . Come along, boy. . . . Take your hat off."

On the stairs Pip remembers his first encounter with Mr. Jaggers:

"Whom have we here?"

"A boy."

"A boy of the neighborhood, eh?"

And he hears once more Miss Havisham's cruel aside to Estella: "You can break his heart."

The method is that of *Brief Encounter* when Laura imagines that she hears again a conversation she has had with Alec.

In ways like these a film adapted from a novel can represent the novel on the screen. Here and there it can almost reproduce the novel. More often it compensates for what cannot be reproduced. If the adaptation is faithful to the intent of the novel, to its theme, and to its characters, it may be said that it "follows the book."

14. From Short Story to Film

The short story lends itself readily to motion-picture adaptation. Whereas a novel adapted to the screen must be contracted in scope and a play must be expanded, a short story may be adapted with only slight change in scope, if any at all. Given the usual short story, that is, one dependent largely on narration, an adapter has for the most part only to translate epic terms into cinematic ones. It is not surprising that short stories were popular sources of early films. Many a short story was ready-made for representation in one or two reels.

Although films are now longer, short stories continue to be drawn on as source material. But the increased length of films has resulted in a different treatment. A short story made into a feature-length film must be expanded, although not in the same way as in the adaptation of a novel. For whereas a novel adapted to the screen is expanded in detail and contracted in scope, a short story is made into a feature-length film by an expansion of both scope and detail. A short story so adapted to the screen therefore implies a film more different from the story than a film adapted from a novel is different from the novel. But although this additional difference implies a correspondingly greater freedom in adaptation, the resulting film, if it is to be faithful to its source, must not distort subject, theme, characterizations, etc.

The greater freedom not only allowed but demanded in the adaptation of short stories has resulted in a variety of treatments. Ernest Hemingway's short story "The Killers," which tells about two gunmen waiting to kill a Swede called Ole Andreson and Andreson's doing nothing to escape, was made into a film which begins by presenting Hemingway's story faithfully and then, after answering a question Hemingway purposely does not answer, that is, as to what happens next, answers in a flashback, which constitutes most of the film, other questions Hemingway also purposely leaves unanswered—who Andreson is, who the gunmen are, what Andreson has done, and why anyone should want him killed. The original story is thus represented as only a brief introduction to the film. F. Scott Fitzgerald's short story "Babylon Revisited" presents, like Hemingway's story, only the results of a long untold narrative except that, whereas Hemingway is not concerned with answers to questions, Fitzgerald implies the answers while he presents the result. In *The Last Time I Saw Paris,* adapted from "Babylon Revisited," the expansion constitutes the first part of the film, to which the original story is made the climax. A different treatment is represented in the adaptation of another Hemingway story, "The Snows of Kilimanjaro," about a writer dying of gangrene in a camp on the African veld and recollecting his lost opportunities. The film version expands the scope by a direct presentation of the stricken man's recollections, including not only those in Hemingway's story but others created by Casey Robinson, the author of the screen play.

Another kind of treatment is represented by *All That Money Can Buy,* a film based on Stephen Vincent Benét's short story "The Devil and Daniel Webster." Benét's story is about Daniel Webster's defense of a New Hampshire farmer, Jabez Stone, whose opponent in an unearthly court trial is the devil, or Scratch, as he calls himself. Because Jabez had been having bad luck in farming, he sold his soul to Scratch in return for seven years of prosperity. Before payment was due, Jabez obtained a three-year extension and then to anticipate foreclosure got Daniel to defend him. In writing the film play Benét and Dan Totheroh retain most of the original story and expand the scope primarily by presenting what happens to Jabez after he makes the compact with Scratch.

What happens is the degeneration of Jabez's character. To show the changes in Jabez the film shows Jabez in his relation to, and his treatment of, other people. Thus it is that characters only referred to in the original story are presented directly and in detail. And the chief characters in the story are presented at even greater length in the film. Furthermore additional characters are created. The most important of these is Belle Dee, the mysterious woman from "over the mountain." Belle not only symbolizes but aggravates Jabez' degeneration.

All That Money Can Buy represents not only expansion in scope but expansion in detail, which naturally results in the adaptation of a short story or a novel to the screen. In the adaptation of "The Devil and Daniel Webster" some of this kind of expansion involves details which have been substituted for those in the original story. In narrating in "The Devil and Daniel Webster" the immediate cause for Jabez' selling his soul, Benét writes:

> He'd been plowing that morning and he'd just broke the plowshare on a rock that he could have sworn hadn't been there yesterday. And, as he stood looking at the plowshare, the off horse began to cough—that ropy kind of cough that means sickness and horse doctors. There were two children down with the measles, his wife was ailing, and he had a whitlow on his thumb. It was about the last straw for Jabez Stone. "I vow," he said, and he looked around him kind of desperate, "I vow it's enough to make a man want to sell his soul to the devil! And I would, too, for two cents!"

It would be possible to represent these details on the screen— the broken plowshare, the coughing horse, the sick children, the ailing wife, even the whitlow on Jabez' thumb—but the adapters chose other details and expanded them instead because they would be more effective pictorially. Thus they show Jabez chasing the pig and falling in the mud in his Sunday clothes, the pig's breaking a leg, the sheriff's warning Jabez that he must pay Miser Stevens, Mary's falling off the wagon, and the seed's bursting the sack and running into a puddle of dirty water. The substitution of these details for those in the short story is made for the same reason as that for the change, in the adaptation of *The*

Informer, in Gypo's motivation for informing. Furthermore the changed details in *All That Money Can Buy* also introduce the characters and establish relationships and the situation from which the story is to proceed.

There are also changes in detail to represent Jabez' prosperity. According to the short story, Jabez' "cows got fat and his horses sleek, his crops were the envy of the neighborhood, and lightning might strike all over the valley, but it wouldn't strike his barn." In the film Jabez' uncanny prosperity is presented directly. Kicking loose a board in the barn floor, Scratch shows Jabez a pot of Hessian gold. Jabez accordingly pays off his mortgage to Miser Stevens and makes extensive purchases at the village store. A series of scenes show Jabez' fields in blossom, the barley and corn ripe and golden. An August hail storm levels the fields of the neighbors but leaves Jabez' fields untouched, and the camera sights along the boundary line to show the marked and astonishing contrast. The neighbors are hired to help Jabez harvest his crops, hauling them by the wagonload into Jabez' big new barn. Jabez builds himself a mansion. These are details that lend themselves to pictorial representation. It would be possible to represent in the film, for example, the lightning striking other barns than Jabez', but, like the substitution in the adaptation of *Great Expectations,* of the mice nibbling the cake on the table for the mice rattling behind the panel in the dining room, the shot of the contrasting fields is more effective for the purpose.

Such changes, which do not distort the theme or spirit of the original, are justifiable. But in the course of the adaptation of "The Devil and Daniel Webster" there are other changes too.

Back of the original story is Benét's recurring theme—the importance of freedom. In "The Devil and Daniel Webster" the kind of freedom Benét is writing about is personal freedom. The crisis is Daniel's realization that it is not only for Jabez Stone that the unearthly jury has come but for him. If he should fight them with his own weapons, he'd fall into their power. So he bases his appeal on the meaning of freedom and the sorrows of slavery. And he wins his case. Although in the film Daniel's

252

speech to the jury is represented directly and specifically, its relation to the crisis is not established. In fact the crisis is changed too, for the subject of the film is not so much the conflict between the devil and Daniel Webster as the degeneration of the character of Jabez Stone. The trial is kept in the adaptation, is, in fact, expanded, but Daniel becomes primarily a *deus ex machina* who rescues the hero from perdition. The change in the title accords with the change in theme—from "The Devil and Daniel Webster" to *All That Money Can Buy*.

The film also represents a change in the spirit, or mood, of the original story. If Daniel Webster has become an American legend, it is because Benét has created folk tales about him. In "The Devil and Daniel Webster" Benét adapts the Faust legend to American characters in an American setting. Like the Faust legend "The Devil and Daniel Webster" shows that the most precious thing in the world—the soul—can be bought. The story is a fantasy, and the fantasy is effective because of Benét's artful simplicity and simple indirectness. The devil, who is called that only in the title and, by reference, in the frame in which Benét tells the story, is "a soft-spoken, dark-dressed stranger." He introduces himself to Daniel only as Scratch. Jabez "didn't like the looks of the stranger nor the way he smiled with his teeth. They were white teeth, and plentiful—some say they were filed to a point, but, "says Benét, heightening the indirectness, "I wouldn't vouch for that." Jabez never liked the looks of the stranger's boots either, "particularly the toes," nor did he like it "when the dog took one look at the stranger and ran away howling, with his tail between his legs." What Jabez saw fluttering out of the stranger's black pocketbook was "something that looked like a moth, but it wasn't a moth." When the stranger poured himself a drink from the jug, "the liquor was cold in the jug, but it came steaming into the glass."

This kind of indirectness cannot be expressed so well on the screen. A film can be fanciful, but not so naturally as a novel or a short story. Now and then in *All That Money Can Buy* the fanciful is attempted, but in direct terms of pictures and sound. When Scratch first appears in the film, he is represented by his shadow on the wall. Later he materializes out of a bright light. Similarly a bright light blurs Belle when she asks Miser Stevens to dance. Whereas in the story Benét tells what Daniel's speech to the jury is about, in the film the speech is literal; one hears Edward Arnold speak it. And whereas Benét only suggests what the jury is like, in the film the jury is represented by twelve actors. The jury is seen through a haze to suggest unearthliness, but the haze does not make the jury so unearthly as Benét's indirectness. Scratch sweeps his finger across the bark of a tree, and suddenly there is the date upon it: "April 7, 1847." But these are theatric devices, not essentially different from Méliès' abracadabra in *A Trip to the Moon*. They are no less real for being tricks. They are not comparable to Benét's indirectness, an approach to which is effected in the film in a different way when in the final scene Scratch points directly at the camera. It is the method of the final scene of *The Great Train Robbery* when the bandit fires point blank at the audience.

All That Money Can Buy might present the New England background more faithfully than it does. "It's a story they tell in the border country," Benét begins, "where Massachusetts joins New Hampshire and Vermont." Jabez' farm is at Cross Corners, New Hampshire. It's a New England farm, boulders and all. Jabez is a genuine New Hampshireman. Daniel is a New Hampshireman too, although he now lives in Massachusetts. Daniel and Jabez wait for Scratch in the farmhouse kitchen, not in the front parlor, because Daniel knows front parlors. When the trial is over, Daniel expresses the hope that they'll be pie for breakfast. The adaptation of a novel or a short story is not expected to retain the author's style or the kind of fantasy which it is the province of words alone to create, but the allusions to New England in "The Devil and Daniel Webster" are cues for a background more authentic than most of the prettified and artificial scenes in *All That Money Can Buy*.

With a minor exception the background music for *All That Money Can Buy* is more appropriate than the sets. The singing of the harvest hymn incongruously accompanies the scene in which the neighbors help to fill Jabez' barn with crops made bountiful by the devil. Otherwise the score, composed by Bernard Hermann, evokes the mood of the story. Based on the folk song "Springfield Mountain," the score is not only evocative of nineteenth-century New England but, as Lawrence Morton has pointed out, "powerful because in its creativity it goes beyond the mere evocation of time and place."

Pictures, however, cannot connote in the way that music or words can. In "The Devil and Daniel Webster" Benét creates fantasy through the connotative quality of language itself. Connotation effected through the editing of pictures is of a different kind. If a film is to attempt the fanciful, it should do so in cinematic terms or, indirectly, through realism. For the most part *All That Money Can Buy* is presented realistically, including even scenes involving Scratch. It is only now and then, as though a reminder that the story is not real, that theatric tricks are resorted to. On the surface Benét's story is represented by realistic images. These might have been translated intact and consistently into pictures and sound.

Whereas "The Devil and Daniel Webster," like "The Killers," "The Snows of Kilimanjaro," and "Babylon Revisited," is adapted to the screen by an expansion of scope as well as of detail, the film *Quartet* represents a different treatment.

Although *Quartet* is, as the title implies, a four-part film, it has unifying elements. The stories from which it is adapted are by one author, Somerset Maugham, and one author, R. C. Sherriff, wrote the film plays. Although each of the films which compose *Quartet* is the work of a different director, they were produced as a unit by one staff. Mr. Maugham appears on the screen and speaks a prologue to the whole film, and a narrator introduces each of the parts by reading the opening sentence or so of the story while an insert of the page is seen on the screen. Nevertheless each of the films in *Quartet* is complete in itself.

The films are, however, similarly adapted. Sheriff implies in the Foreword to the published text of *Quartet,* which includes both the stories and the film plays, that each of the plays is "allowed to run its natural course" with the result that each film, he says, "ends when the story is finished." In defending his method Sherriff declares that "it stands to reason that no story can be good if it appears on the screen stretched out beyond its natural length." He refers to "the padding and cutting that generally has to happen" in the process of adaptation. He admits, however, that "when the *Quartet* screenplays are compared with their originals . . . it may be said that we have defeated our purpose by leaving out parts of certain stories and adding scenes to others." A comparison of Sherriff's film plays with Maugham's short stories reveals, however, that the scope of the added "scenes" hardly compensates for that of "parts" left out. Furthermore, in the adaptation of the film plays to the screen, the scope is even narrower than Sherriff indicates in the script. And since detail is expanded in accordance with the difference in medium, the adaptation of these four stories is comparable to that of a novel. Although scope is not contracted to the extent that it is in the adaptation of a novel, the method is more nearly that of a novel than of a short story adapted in the manner of "The Devil and Daniel Webster."

In Maugham's story "The Facts of Life" irony is more important than characterization. The characters in "The Facts of Life" are hardly more than types. Henry Garnet is a clubman. His son Nicky is a callow youth. The girl—Maugham does not even give her a name—is an adventuress. The chief irony is that Nicky is successful by deliberately doing the three things his father warns him against. And the story ends ironically in the advice which the lawyer gives Henry. Maugham tells the story in a frame, which not only makes Nicky's adventure in Monte Carlo more than just a story but creates suspense. But the primary advantage of the frame is that it establishes a basis for the irony, which becomes dramatic as, step by step, Nicky is observed disregarding his father's advice and being successful.

The adaptation of "The Facts of Life" is true to the structure of the story and thus to the irony. The motion pictures lend themselves readily to the "frame" method of narration as illustrated by many films from *The Cabinet of Dr. Caligari* to *Brief Encounter*, and in Maugham's short story Sherriff had the structure ready-made. He had only to adapt it as literally as possible.

But the "cutting" to which Sherriff takes exception is nevertheless evident in the adaptation of this story as in that of the other three in *Quartet*. For example, whereas Maugham begins "The Facts of Life" with a page of exposition about Henry Garnet, the film adaptation begins abruptly with the particular afternoon on which Henry tells the story about his own son Nicky. And the film almost completely disregards Maugham's even longer exposition about Nicky. Maugham describes the baccara dealer in the casino at Monte Carlo, tells who he is, and narrates the effect on Nicky of the baccara game. He describes Monte Carlo in the early morning as Nicky walks through the deserted streets. But these and other "parts" of the story are presented only slightly in the film, if at all. On the other hand, if the scope were not so contracted in all four of the stories, the film would be unwieldy in length.

Detail is correspondingly expanded. Whereas, for example, Maugham writes, "Another rubber was begun and in the second game Henry denied a suit," the film presents the bridge game directly, including the concomitant dialogue. Maugham devotes less than a page to the scene at the night club; in the film the scene is of five minutes' duration. In these and other ways detail is expanded. The expansion is similar to that in the adaptation of a novel.

On the other hand, some of the changes Sherriff makes in Maugham's stories are arbitrary; that is, they are not implicit in the cinematic method but are made for reasons of effectiveness or simplicity. They are comparable to changes made in the adaptations of *The Informer, Great Expectations,* and "The Devil and Daniel Webster."

Whereas in "The Facts of Life" Maugham has a Colonel Brabazon, one of Henry Garnet's tennis friends, suggest to Henry at a City dinner that Nicky enter the tournament at Monte Carlo, in the film Colonel Brabazon becomes Professor Branksome of Cambridge, and the City dinner a tennis match at Wimbledon. There is nothing in the cinematic method to prevent the adaptation to the screen of the former instead of the latter. But, a film being visual, a tennis match provides a more effective setting than a dinner. Sherriff indicates how the scene is to be staged:

> 2. Exterior Wimbledon Centre Court (*Stock*). Day. This should be the best possible stock shot of Wimbledon during a match on the centre court—and if possible one which *pans over* to the crowd in the stands, or at least shows the crowd to some advantage.
>
> 3. Exterior Wimbledon Centre Court (*Stock*). Day. *Another stock shot,* this time of the crowd in the stand watching the play, with their heads moving to and fro in unison, as they follow the flight of the ball. (NOTE: There are *several excellent stock shots* of this available.)
>
> 4. Exterior Wimbledon Centre Court (Studio). Day. A section of stand to match up to SCENE 3, with about twenty people following the play. We *move in* to concentrate on Henry. He is sitting with his wife on one side of him and a distinguished looking man of fifty or sixty on the other side. This is PROFESSOR BRANKSOME.[1]

The substitution also makes for simplicity. In his Foreword Sherriff points out that an adaptation of a story to the screen makes the proper allowance for the different perspective of the reader lounging in his armchair and the people sitting upright in a cinema. "The reader, as it were," Sherriff says, "can see the story from a distance, with all its side shoots and wandering tendrils: there is nothing to distract him. Subconsciously the man in the cinema puts on blinkers to help him concentrate: his perspective is narrowed while vision sharpens his conception, so you have to prune the story to the main stem to save him getting lost among the side shoots." In changing the City dinner to a tennis match at Wimbledon and Colonel Brabazon to Professor Branksome, Sherriff makes the proper allowance for the different perspective of the reader and the people at the cinema. A City dinner and a Colonel Brabazon would be side shoots. Nicky

---

[1] "Facts of Life" appears in *Quartet,* stories by W. Somerset Maugham and screen plays by R. C. Sherriff. The story is copyright 1939 by W. Somerset Maugham, and the screen play is copyright 1948 by R. C. Sherriff. Excerpts reprinted by permission of the publishers, Doubleday & Company, Inc.

plays tennis; a tennis scene is to the point. Nicky is at Cambridge; Professor Branksome is, as Henry says, "the Poo Bah of tennis" there.

The substitution of the tennis scene for the dinner scene makes not only for simplicity and effectiveness but even for humor. Whereas Maugham narrates at considerable length and in detail what happens to make Henry change his mind about letting Nicky play in the tournament at Monte Carlo, Sherriff represents this action in one short scene. But in the final adaptation, the scope was further contracted: Sherriff's scene was deleted entirely. The deletion is appropriate, because to narrate how Henry is made to change his mind would involve another digression. The film instead merely implies how he is made to change his mind. Mrs. Garnet is not present at the City dinner in the story, but she is at the tennis match in the film, and after Professor Branksome leaves, she urges Henry to let Nicky play in the tournament at Monte Carlo. The scene ends as Henry declares flatly, "No, I've made up my mind and I'm not going to change it." There is a cut to the airport as Nicky is saying to Henry, "It's awfully decent of you to let me go, Dad."

Because of expansion of detail and the presentational method of narration, characters become specific in a film. In a novel or a short story they may be only vaguely represented. Whereas in "The Facts of Life" there are only four specifically named characters, in the film adaptation there are nine. In the story Nicky meets an acquaintance at the casino. In the film the acquaintance is Nicky's friend John. Sherriff uses John to avoid a subjective treatment. Maugham says that Nicky reflected that he hadn't promised his father not to gamble, he'd promised him not to forget his advice. It would of course be possible to present Nicky's thoughts on the screen. But Sherriff, who is a playwright, chooses a dramatic rather than a cinematic method, and thus a dialogue:

JOHN: Wotcha Nicky! Doing any good?
NICKY: I haven't been playing.
JOHN: You ought to have one little flutter before you go.
NICKY: I suppose so—but my father wasn't any too keen on

my coming at all, and one of the things he particularly warned me against was gambling.

JOHN: It isn't gambling if you know when to stop. I had a go with a hundred francs and lost it, and that's that. You're crazy if you leave Monte Carlo without trying your luck once. Surely your father wouldn't mind you losing a hundred francs!

NICKY (*weakening*): I don't suppose he would, really. After all, I didn't promise him not to gamble—I only promised not to forget his advice.

By means of the specific character John the film similarly dramatizes the anticlimax, which in the story is presented subjectively. Maugham has Nicky, riding in the car from Monte Carlo to the aerodrome, think about the twenty thousand francs:

He thought he would like to have a look at them. He had so nearly lost them that they had a double value for him. He took them out of his hip-pocket into which for safety's sake he had stuffed them when he put on the suit he was travelling in, and counted them one by one. Something very strange had happened to them. Instead of there being twenty notes as there should have been there were twenty-six. He couldn't understand it at all. He counted them twice more. There was no doubt about it; somehow or other he had twenty-six thousand francs instead of the twenty he should have had. He couldn't make it out. He asked himself if it was possible that he had won more at the Sporting Club than he had realized. But no, that was out of the question, he distinctly remembered the man at the desk laying the notes out in four rows of five, and he had counted them himself. Suddenly the explanation occurred to him; when he had put his hand into the flower-pot, after taking out the cineraria, he had grabbed everything he felt there. The flower-pot was the little hussy's money-box and he had taken out not only his own money, but her savings as well. Nicky leant back in the car and burst into a roar of laughter. It was the funniest thing he had ever heard in his life.

Here again the film could present Nicky's thoughts, but Sherriff substitutes a dialogue between Nicky and John on the plane taking them back to England:

Great Expectations
Directed by David Lean and Produced by Ronald Neame
for Cineguild in 1946.

"In the novel Pip's table manners are only implied. In the film they are visual, and camera and editing make the most of them."

Great Expectations
Directed by David Lean and Produced by Ronald Neame
for Cineguild in 1946.

"The door opening to reveal Magwitch is comparable to an iris-in."

JOHN: You don't say! You know she took *me* in when *I* saw her. I guessed she was a gambler—but she was decently dressed and not made up. I never thought she was just a rotten little thief.

NICKY: She took me in, too—at first.

JOHN: I bet she does that every night to some mug or another.

NICKY: She didn't get a mug last night, anyway.

They laugh. Nicky is feeling very proud of himself.

JOHN: How much was it?

NICKY: Twenty thousand francs.

JOHN: I say!

NICKY: Enough for that motor bike.

JOHN: Is it all there?

NICKY: It must be.

JOHN: She might have taken some for safety and put it somewhere else.

NICKY: I don't think she'd have had time. . . .

But he looks worried at this. He fumbles in his pocket, and pulls out the wad of notes. He counts the notes quickly in fives.

NICKY: Five thousand . . . ten thousand . . . fifteen . . . hey! there's more than twenty here. Twenty . . . twenty-five . . . thirty . . . (*Nicky has counted to thirty but there are still several notes untouched.*) Well—I'll be damned!

JOHN: You know what? That flower pot was her money-box. You've got all her loot as well . . . nearly enough to buy a car.

They burst out laughing.

Other arbitrary changes are made for various reasons, not all of them obvious. Maugham says that Nicky is eighteen; in the film he is a year older. In the story Nicky wagers a hundred francs and wins twenty thousand; in the film these amounts are increased tenfold. In accordance with Maugham's story, Sherriff indicates that Jeanne and Nicky take a taxi to the hotel. In the film the taxi is a barouche, and the hotel "a quiet little place." And Jeanne's room becomes a suite, whereby the sleeping arrangements can satisfy the censors. In the story Nicky is in a car on his way to the aerodrome when he discovers the additional franc notes; in the film the discovery takes place in an airplane.

261

These and other variations, however, are minor, and the film remains essentially faithful to its source.

The longest of the four stories as Maugham wrote them is "The Alien Corn," more than twice as long as "The Facts of Life." Yet whereas on the screen "The Facts of Life" runs for twenty-two minutes, "The Alien Corn" is only four minutes longer. Obviously, then, in the adaptation of "The Alien Corn" scope is contracted even further than in that of "The Facts of Life." In "The Alien Corn" Maugham is concerned primarily with members of a wealthy Jewish family ashamed of their race. Intolerant of art, they are unhappy when the eldest son wants to make music his career. The scope is contracted largely by deletion of this character study; the film concentrates instead on George's failure to become a concert pianist. Maugham tells the story in the first person, represented as a friend of the family. Although this point of view could be effected cinematically, as it is, for example, in the adaptation of *Great Expectations,* the storyteller is among the characters deleted in the contraction in scope. Maugham has the storyteller visit George in Munich; in the film the visitor is a girl, Paula, created to introduce a love interest. The only suggestion of the subjective point of view is in the scene in which George plays for Lea Makart. While he plays, Paula's thoughts are represented by shots of Paula and George in previous dialogues, the shots superimposed on a close-up of Paula and the music fading so that the voices can be heard above it. But the subjective is not introduced so much to suggest the substitution of Paula for the first-person storyteller as to give the impression of extended time. *"As it is obvious that George's playing could not be fairly judged under at least twenty minutes,"* Sherriff notes in the script, *"some device will have to be used here to give an artistic impression of time-lapse."*

The other two stories, "The Kite" and "The Colonel's Lady," are adapted more in the manner of "The Facts of Life" than of "The Alien Corn" in that they undergo comparatively little contraction in scope. Each is expanded by a denouement for the sake of "a happy ending." Whereas Maugham implies in "The Kite" that the hero's love of freedom is so strong that, ironically, he prefers staying in jail to returning to his wife, in the film the wife is reconciled to the kite, and the husband to the wife. And whereas "The Colonel's Lady" has an enigmatic ending, Sheriff appends a sentimental denouement identifying the lover. As in "The Facts of Life" and "The Alien Corn," there are a few arbitrary changes.

With the exceptions noted, however, each of these films is as faithful to its source as "The Facts of Life." Staging, casting, acting, etc. are in keeping with the intention and essence of the original stories. Here and there in the adaptation an incident is broadened or a subtle point is lost, but for the most part Maugham's satire of British manners, morals, and mores is as effective on the screen as on the printed page.

A short story, then, can be more faithfully adapted to the screen than a play or a novel. Whereas a film adapted from a play represents something more than the play, and a film adapted from a novel something less than the novel, a film adapted from a short story may be comparatively similar. It is not to be inferred, however, that the excellence of a film depends on similarity to source. A film must be judged on its own merits. *The Devil and Daniel Webster* might have been better if it had not expanded the scope of Benét's story. On the other hand, it might have been better if it had expanded the scope differently. The fact, however, remains that because the cinematic way of storytelling resembles that of the novel and the short story more than it does that of the play, and because the scope of a film is more nearly that of a short story than of a novel, the short story is promising material for adaptation to the screen.

15. Television

The motion pictures, it has been shown, are both an art and a machine. May a comparable distinction be made for television? And if television is an art, is it different from the art of the motion pictures?

As a machine, television implies not only the box-like contraption with the glassy front—somehow called a "set"—from which the pictures and sound emerge but also the cameras and microphones together with the electronic devices whereby the pictures and sound are transmitted. The television machine has three main uses. The first of these uses is the recording and projecting—called "telecasting"—of news events. This use includes not only the telecasting of athletic contests, conventions, parades, the goings and comings of public officials, catastrophes, etc.—that is, happenings not staged for television but at which the television camera is only, as it were, a spectator—but also speeches, news reports, interviews, etc. made expressly for television and at which the camera is, as it were, the only spectator. The second use of the television machine is the telecasting of motion-picture films. And the third use is the telecasting of plays, variety shows, advertising, etc.

An understanding of the difference between art and the machine in the motion pictures makes it at once obvious that the first of these three uses implies only the machine in television. The telecasting of news is comparable to the motion-picture newsreel—with an important difference to be discussed in connection with the third use. And it is also obvious that television is only a machine when it is used to telecast motion-picture films.

Those who contend that television is an art which is comparable to the motion pictures but different have in mind the third use. The contention is valid if it can be shown that, for example, a television play is essentially different from a film—if, in other words, the arrangement which characterizes television is different from that of the arrangement of shots in the motion pictures.

In the telecasting of a play, arrangement is effected by the use of several cameras. Instead of waiting until the pictures have been printed before arranging them in separate shots, the director of a television play cuts during the telecast itself by switching from one camera to another. Although the means of effecting the arrangement is different from that in the motion pictures, the arrangement is essentially the same.

But only essentially. Arrangement in television admits of less flexibility than that in the motion pictures. Take, for example, the filming of two actors in a dialogue. In the motion pictures the camera can photograph the scene first from one side and then, after an interval in which the position of the camera is changed, from the opposite side. In telecasting, this kind of cutting would be difficult if not impossible because there would have to be a camera on each of the two sides with the result that the cameras would photograph each other. Thus a television play tends to be viewed from only one side. Furthermore, whereas in television, editing is limited by the number of cameras, in the motion pictures there is no comparable limitation. The motion-picture director can break his film down into as many shots as he chooses. Imagine attempting to make a television performance of *The Battleship Potemkin.*

Television is limited in another way. Because television pictures are viewed on a small screen and because the images are not as clear as those on a motion-picture screen, scenes in television pictures are photographed comparatively close to the camera. The resulting limitation in spatial scope, together with the previously mentioned limitations, makes a television play more like a play on the stage than a motion picture is. In fact, even the adaptation of a novel to television is called a "television play."

There are other limitations which, although they affect the content of television plays, are not inherent. There is, for example, the tendency to fit the plays into prescribed lengths of time because of the schedules of the television studios. Furthermore television plays are subject to interruption by commercials. Then, whereas a motion-picture director has in mind an audience which will view his film comparatively free of distractions, the television director knows that his audience consists of many small and diverse audiences subject to innumerable distractions.

These and other differences, however, are relevant here only in that they represent limitations of television. There is nothing in the arrangement of shots in television that cannot be similarly effected by the motion pictures. If television is an art, it is the art of the motion pictures.

There is, however, a characteristic of television that the motion pictures do not possess—immediacy. Whereas in the motion pictures, time must elapse between filming and screening, in television the recording and projection can be simultaneous. This kind of reality is, of course, an advantage in the telecasting of news, and some directors contend that it is also an advantage in the telecasting of a play because, they say, it gives the acting spontaneity. On the other hand, tape is being increasingly used to record television plays for telecasting later. Taping a performance enables the director to do a scene over and over until it is satisfactory. It has other advantages, as for example, enabling a gathering together of actors who might have other commitments at the time scheduled for the telecast. Taping a performance is of course comparable to making a film. Be that as it may, whether a television play is live or taped, its arrangement is similar to that of the motion pictures. The reality that a live telecast makes possible has to do only with the content of the shots. Although creating the illusion of reality is within the province of the art of the motion pictures, reality itself is of the machine.

There are, in fact, advantages in a lack of reality. Von Stroheim's interpolation of the funeral procession in the wedding

266

scene in *Greed* was intended to compensate for the lack of sound at the time. If the persistent noise of sawing heard, according to Norris's novel, could be heard in the film, the film would be more real. But von Stroheim's substitution is more effective. The absence of color may also be artistically advantageous. Laurence Olivier chose what he calls "the beautiful medium of black and white" in making his film *Hamlet* although he could have made it, as he had made his film *Henry V,* in color.

A third dimension in the motion pictures increases reality, but a film in only two dimensions may have artistic advantages in its very lack of reality. Rudolf Arnheim points out that in a two-dimensional film a locomotive coming toward the foreground actually becomes larger on the screen but that an observer of a real locomotive would not receive the same impression and that the reason for the difference is what the psychologists call the constancy of size. Although the image cast on the retina, as on the photographic plate, diminishes in proportion to the square of the distance, the size seems to the observer to remain constant. Because the constancy of size depends on three dimensions, it obtains in a three-dimensional film. Conversely, it cannot obtain in a two-dimensional film. In the scene in "The Alien Corn" (in *Quartet)* in which George plays the piano as a test of his promise as a musician, the effectiveness of one of the shots depends on the film's being in only two dimensions. The scene is a large drawing room, and the shot is that in which the piano keyboard extends across the bottom of the frame. The keyboard, the symbol of George's aspiration and of the crisis of the film, dwarfs everything else in the room. If the film were in three dimensions, the effect would be nullified by the constancy in size.

It is the same, as Arnheim points out, with the constancy of shape. In a photograph of a rectangular table the end nearer the camera is larger than the other end. But looking at a real table, one is not conscious of this difference. The constancy of shape makes the table seem rectangular although the image on the retina is trapezoidal. In the scene in *Great Expectations* in which Pip pulls the cloth off the table in Miss Havisham's dining room, one end of the table is wider than the other, and the table thus appears longer than it is. The effect is possible because the film is in only two dimensions.

That reality in the motion pictures and in television is of the machine does not, however, imply that it is unimportant. On the contrary, it is the kind of reality which is possible in the motion pictures but which has not yet been duplicated in television that has kept the television machine from making the motion-picture machine obsolete. Although in its immediacy, television is more real than the motion pictures, the motion pictures are more real than television in several other ways. In the first place, the motion pictures are more real in the size of the images on the screen. By comparison, the television screen is reminiscent of the slot through which one peered to see the pictures in the kinetosope. In fact, all of the ways in which the motion pictures are more real than television are comparable to the ways in which the motion pictures are more real than they used to be. For example, images on the motion-picture screen are consistently clearer than those on television. They are more real as to sound and color. Furthermore, whereas the motion-pictures can effect three dimensions, television is limited to two. On the whole, then, the motion pictures are, at present, more real than television.

Already the difference in reality between television and the motion pictures has begun to decrease. Improvements or elaborations in the television machine make television increasingly real. As the reality continues to increase, as for example, in the size of the screen, in the color of the images, in the reproduction of sound, and even in an additional dimension, the television machine will supplant the motion-picture machine as the means of transmitting pictures. Economic pressure can retard these improvements, as it retarded improvements in the motion-picture machine by confining the pictures to the peep-show box, by limiting the length of a film to one reel, by resisting the introduction of sound, and by delaying the use of color. But eventually the machine will win.

16. Art and the Machine

Originating as a machine, the motion pictures happened to take on resemblances to the already established arts of narration—the drama and the epic. A film is like a play because it is representational. It is like a novel because its method is description and narration. Because of description and narration it can tell a story from the various points of view that a novel can. Nevertheless the motion pictures tend to narrate from the single point of view that is characteristic of the drama.

At a play one sees as though into a room from which a wall has been removed. But one does not see into the characters' minds, that is, except in the old plays, in which thoughts were presented in asides and soliloquies, and in modern plays incorporating the expressionistic device of distortion of reality. Although these exceptions are important, the usual method of the drama limits the point of view in a play to that of an outsider looking in, and looking in only so far as the action and speech of the characters permit. A novel, on the other hand, can narrate from a third-person point of view or from an omniscient one. It can also narrate in the first person. Whereas the presentational nature of a play limits the playwright to an external, or objective, point of view, description and narration enable the novelist to write from a subjective point of view.

It is because the motion pictures are presentational that they tend to narrate objectively, like plays, rather than subjectively, like novels. A film, however, need not be so limited. It can narrate not only from as many points of view as a novel but in a way that neither the novel nor the drama can. Although the possibilities in this combination are peculiar to the motion pictures, it is remarkable how little they have been exploited. On the other hand, from the time that Edwin S. Porter incorporated a dream balloon in his little film *The Life of an American Fireman* to give "the impression," as the 1903 Edison Catalogue states, that the fire chief "dreams of his wife and child," the motion pictures have been groping toward a principle governing these possibilities.

Point of view is sometimes implied in the presentation of dialogue in a film. For example, when the voice of one of the characters in a dialogue is matched with the image of the character on the screen, the point of view may be that of another character listening. Conversely, when the voice is separated from the image, that is, when one only sees the listener and only hears the speaker, the point of view may be that of the character speaking. Here are possible four different situations: (a) the first character simultaneously seen and heard, (b) the second character simultaneously seen and heard, (c) the first character seen while the second character is heard, and (d) the second character seen while the first character is heard. It would be awkward, however, if a film attempted to narrate throughout from the point of view of only (a) and (c) or of only (b) and (d), because one of the characters would never be seen on the screen at all. Nevertheless this kind of narration was attempted in a film called *Lady in the Lake,* in which all of the scenes were photographed as though the camera and the eyes of the main character were identical. But the attempt was unsuccessful because, as Joseph P. Brinton, III has pointed out, the camera and the human eye do not record reality alike, and to pretend that they do only calls attention to the difference. But even if this difficulty were overcome, the film would be just a tour de force, for it would negate the cinematic method, which is, paradoxically, like the drama, presentational. "Every time I play tennis," Robert Frost has said, "I don't try to change the tennis court."

A subjective point of view, however, can be presented cinematically. When the outlaw in *The Great Train Robbery* fires directly at the camera, the audience is given the point of view of the posse. In including this shot in his film, Porter was not trying to present a point of view. He was only adding an exciting scene, which, the Edison Catalogue states, "can be used to begin or end the picture." Even included at the end, where it would follow the scene in which the outlaws battle the posse, the close-up of Barnes would represent the point of view of the posse only vaguely, for in the preceding shot the outlaw has been killed. But in including this scene, Porter was groping toward the presentation of a point of view through editing.

As in the example of dialogue cited, point of view is implied when the film cuts from a character to what the character sees or hears. Griffith showed how a subjective point of view could thus be effected. In *The Birth of a Nation* when Elsie Stoneman notices John Wilkes Booth moving along the galley in Ford's Theatre, Griffith cuts from a shot of Elsie pointing in the direction of the gallery to a masked shot of Booth. In *Tol'able David,* a film markedly influenced by Griffith, vignettes are used to associate a character with the object of the character's attention, a shot of the latter being in vignette.

But directors found that full-frame images could effect the same purpose as masks and vignettes. Here and there in *Greed* von Stroheim presents an incident from the point of view of this or that character. "His dream was gone," reads the title after Trina and Marcus leave McTeague's dental parlors. The next shot is of the street as seen through McTeague's window. Trina and Marcus are getting on a streetcar. Then to emphasize that the action is being presented from McTeague's point of view, von Stroheim cuts back and forth between the street and McTeague: a medium-close shot of McTeague looking out the window; a long shot of the street as the streetcar moves out of the scene; a shot of McTeague, the camera this time pointing down to include the moving streetcar; another angle shot of the street, now empty; and finally a close-up of McTeague. In the sequence in which Trina gets out her gold coins while McTeague is away, von Stroheim wants to show that Trina suddenly hides the coins because she hears McTeague coming. But in *Greed* von Stroheim does not have the advantage of a sound

271

track. So he cuts from a shot of Trina occupied with the coins to a close shot of McTeague's feet as McTeague approaches along the hall and then back to Trina as she suddenly puts the coins away. The use of the visual image here is comparable to von Stroheim's substitution of the funeral procession, in the wedding scene, for Norris' noise of sawing. But in cutting from Trina to McTeague, von Stroheim is also narrating from Trina's point of view. In the sequence in which McTeague appears outside Trina's window at night, von Stroheim has McTeague photographed from inside the room, as though seen through the window by the frightened Trina. In the flight-and-pursuit sequence, shots are interpolated to represent Death Valley from McTeague's point of view, as for example, the close shots of the rattlesnake and of the gila monsters.

This way of presenting point of view is a refinement of Porter's having Barnes fire at the audience in *The Great Train Robbery*. In *The Informer* when Bartley shoots Gypo, Bartley is shown, like Barnes, firing in the direction of the camera. The spectator is for the moment in Gypo's place, and he is there not only because of the position of the camera but because the shot of Bartley is preceded by a shot of Gypo. David Lean uses the same method in several of the scenes in *Great Expectations* when, for example, we see and hear the creaking tree and the rattling branches from Pip's point of view or, again, when we are in Pip's place in the skiff and see the packet boat bearing down on us.

Point of view can also be effected without editing. Thus even in so theatric a film as *Queen Elizabeth* there is an implication of point of view in one of the scenes. As Elizabeth watches Essex being led in procession to the tower, the camera includes Sarah Bernhardt as well as the procession passing in the background. In *Intolerance* Griffith suggests point of view by following the title "The High Priest looks down on the city he seeks to betray to Cyrus" with a shot of Babylon framed by an opening beside which the High Priest is standing. In *The Informer* when Frankie runs into the archway to hide, the camera is in the archway too; when the soldiers flash their lights into the archway, they flash them into the camera. When Frankie is shot, the camera, behind him, looks down into the muzzle of the machine gun. Or the camera itself may move. For example, in *Great Expectations* when Pip runs into the convict, the camera pans with him so that the audience has the impression of running into the convict too. Lean uses this method again and again in *Great Expectations,* as pointed out in Chapter XIII.

A subjective point of view may be more effective than an objective one. Two scenes in the film *Picnic* illustrate this difference. The opening scene is a spectacular one of a train approaching the camera. Then the film presents the hero exploring the town into which the train has brought him. But now, as he crosses a backyard and approaches a house, the camera is behind him, and the spectator, made to approach the house from the hero's point of view, shares the hero's hesitancy and apprehension. What makes the commonplace back-yard scene more exciting than the spectacular scene of the train is the subjective point of view. The effectiveness of point of view is illustrated in a negative way, in a sequence in *The Man Who Never Was.* The transfer of an all-important tube from a ship to a submarine is photographed from the point of view of an intelligence officer, whose concern for the safe transfer of the tube the spectator thus shares. But then, as the submarine starts moving away, there is a cut to a shot of the submarine from a different angle. The spectator is thereby abruptly wrenched away from the concern he has been sharing with the officer, and the shift from the subjective point of view is disconcerting.

Presenting a scene from the point of view of this or that character is not, of course, tantamount to presenting the character's thoughts. Griffith used to say that you can photograph thought. But when Margaret Cameron, in *The Birth of a Nation,* is represented as remembering her brother's death on the battlefield, the flash back only *approximates* thought, since Margaret was not a witness to the scene she seems to be remembering.

On the other hand, point of view is concomitant to the presentation of thought. In *Intolerance* a flash back not only shows why the girl on the ledge shoots the Musketeer but photographs what the girl remembers. An introspective point of view is not, however, characteristic of Griffith's films. For all their cinematic qualities, they narrate for the most part objectively. But the flash back represents the motion pictures groping toward narration from a point of view other than that of a play.

Only three years after the production of *Intolerance* Robert Wiene adapted the Caligari story to the screen by putting the story into a frame and thus representing it as the experience of a narrator. *The Cabinet of Dr. Caligari*, it will be remembered, opens as the narrator, Francis, and a companion are conversing. "In Holstenwall, where I was born," Francis begins, and the scene becomes Holstenwall. At the conclusion of Francis' story the scene returns to that of the frame. What is framed —and constitutes most of the film—is an extended flash back, which is the means of presenting the framed story from a subjective point of view.

In *The Informer* an introspective point of view is effected primarily by visual images. An exception is the singing heard when the scene of Frankie and Gypo singing at the bar is superimposed on the reward poster that Gypo is looking at. Another is Frankie's voice when Gypo imagines that Frankie is speaking to him. We *see* Gypo but we *hear* Frankie. In both of these scenes thought, as Griffith would say, is photographed. In fact, both are variations of Griffith's flash back. But most of the introspection in *The Informer* is effected visually, as in the superimposition on the ship model of the scene of Katie and Gypo on shipboard and in the various superimpositions of the posters.

Although introspection in *Abe Lincoln in Illinois* is slight, it is the means whereby the crisis is presented. The image of Ann Rutledge superimposed on the trees at the edge of the clearing at New Salem and the voice of Sarah Lincoln on the sound track present Abe's recollections of earlier scenes and motivate Abe's return to Springfield and to Mary Todd.

In *Great Expectations* introspection is effected by a separation of sound from image. When Pip wanders in a daze through the London streets, the street noises are distorted. When he remembers the convict's threat, one hears the convict's voice. The sound track also simulates the voices Pip imagines he hears when he steals the food for the convict and when he encounters the cattle on the marshes. On the Rochester coach Pip imagines Joe, Estella, and others commenting on his staying at the Blue Boar. When Pip returns to Satis House for the last time and remembers his visits there as a child, one hears voices speaking out of those early scenes. Furthermore Pip's thoughts are now and then directly presented by the narrator's voice on the sound track. Separation of sound from image is the cinematic counterpart of introspection in Dickens' novel.

The fantasy in *All That Money Can Buy* consists largely of trick photography and bizarre lighting—a means of implying an introspective point of view in a film—but *All That Money Can Buy* is predominantly objective. An exception is the scene in which Daniel Webster is writing his speech. Scratch's shadow appears on the wall of Daniel's study while Scratch's voice is heard in a whisper on the sound track, the shadow and the voice representing Daniel's thoughts. They are an extension of the device of the dream balloon which presents the fire chief's dream in *The Life of an American Fireman*. The last scene of *All That Money Can Buy* is also an exception, for when Scratch points his finger at the camera, the audience is brought into the film in the same way as in the close-up of Barnes in *The Great Train Robbery*.

Of the films constituting *Quartet*, two represent stories told in frames—"The Facts of Life" and "The Kite." But the frame device does not make either of these films any more introspective than *The Cabinet of Dr. Caligari*. A first-person point of view is, however, effected briefly in "The Alien Corn" in the scene in which the hero's ability as a pianist is tested. The point of view here, though, is not essential; it is not even the hero's. It is introduced, Sherriff says, because *"some device will have to be used here to give an artistic impression of time lapse."* Accordingly dialogue out of a preceding scene is heard on the sound track to represent Paula's thoughts while George is playing. And in "The Colonel's Lady," in a brief scene in the compartment of the railway car, the Colonel's thoughts are presented: *"We hear what is running through his mind—the shop assistant's and*

Daphne's voices repeating some of the phrases they used in their descriptions of the book."

Whereas an introspective point of view can be made continuous in a novel because the medium of the novel is words, the presentational nature of the motion pictures makes continuousness a problem. At the beginning of the film *Tea and Sympathy* an alumnus returns to his school for a reunion, goes up to his old room, and recalls his school days. An extended flash back then presents the action of the play from which the film is adapted. But the scenes in the flash back are not presented introspectively; they are not even consistently presented from the alumnus' point of view. In *The Snows of Kilimanjaro,* a film expanded from Hemingway's short story, the recollections of the hero are presented in five flash backs, but, with a minor exception, the scenes in the flash back are as objectively presented as the single flash back in *Tea and Sympathy.* In parts of these scenes the hero is not even present. Nor is the narrator-voice device a solution. This device introduces the film *Rebecca,* in which the narrator appears as a character in most of the scenes, but the spectator soon forgets this affinity. And even though the narrator's voice is interpolated frequently in *Jane Eyre,* it does not give the film the continuously subjective point of view possible in a novel. The device by itself is not really a cinematic one. It is comparable to the voice of the "lecturer" who sometimes spoke from behind the screen in the days before the screen talked; it is like the spoken commentary in a newsreel.

An introspective point of view is effected in the modern drama by expressionism. *The Cabinet of Dr. Caligari* shows the influence of expressionistic drama, which was reaching its height in Germany at the time Wiene made his film there. It shows it in a way comparable to that of some American plays written in the 1920's, as for example, Eugene O'Neill's *The Emperor Jones,* George Kaufman and Marc Connelly's *Beggar on Horseback,* and Connelly's *The Green Pastures,* which incorporate expressionistic devices to make the point of view introspective. Like *The Cabinet of Dr. Caligari,* each of these plays presents, within a realistic frame, the thoughts of a character or characters. Since

276

thoughts are a distortion of reality, expressionistic distortion is appropriate to the purpose. It is particularly appropriate since in the film, as in the plays, the part within the frame—the flash back, as it were—represents a point of view that in itself implies distortion: in *The Emperor Jones,* that of a fear-crazed fugitive; in *The Cabinet of Dr. Caligari,* that of a madman; in *Beggar on Horseback,* of a distraught young pianist; and in *The Green Pastures,* of Sunday school children equating supernatural phenomena with their own experience.

In each of these plays, as well as in Wiene's film, the relationship of the realistic frame to the "thoughts" within it is similar. First there is a realistic scene: in *The Emperor Jones,* a throne room; in *Beggar on Horseback,* an artist's apartment; in *The Green Pastures,* a corner in a church; in *The Cabinet of Dr. Caligari,* a garden. The realistic introductory scene introduces the character or characters whose thoughts are to be presented. In each of the plays a lowering and raising of the curtain or of lights makes the transition from the frame to the part within the frame; in the film an iris-out followed by an iris-in accomplishes the same purpose. The relationships between frame and content are similar in another way. In *The Emperor Jones,* Brutus Jones remains realistic in the expressionistic scenes. In *Beggar on Horseback* Neil's piano and easy chair, representing the realism of the frame, remain on the stage throughout the play. In *The Green Pastures* voices of the Sunday school class are heard in the darkness between some of the expressionistic scenes. And in *The Cabinet of Dr. Caligari* cuts back to the realistic scene of the storyteller in the garden interrupt the first part of the expressionistically presented action in Holstenwall. Furthermore in the film and, with the exception of *The Green Pastures,* in the plays, there is a return to the reality of the frame at the end.

In these plays, as in *The Cabinet of Dr. Caligari,* the expressionistic parts are represented by distortion of the media of the drama and the stage: dialogue, acting, costumes, make-up, scenery, stage properties, and lighting. Although the expressionistic parts are intended to present particularly introspective points of view, the method of presentation all but defeats the purpose. The expressionistic scenes are at best only symbols of the thoughts of the main characters. Watching these scenes, the spectator forgets what they are intended to symbolize. Although there are reminders of the realistic frames—Jones in his increasingly bedraggled uniform, the piano and the easy chair, the voices in the darkness, the garden—these intrusions of reality, these extensions of the frames, somehow are as much separated from the introspective parts as the frames themselves. The frames are so subordinate to the stories within them that the stories would be hardly less effective if the frames were forgotten. In fact, in *The Green Pastures* there is no return to the frame at the end of the play. Instead the curtain comes down on the last of the expressionistic scenes. The point of view no longer matters. As for *Beggar on Horseback,* one has the impression that the realistic frame is only an excuse for the spectacularly expressionistic scenes that it encloses. It is worth remembering that the original scenario for *The Cabinet of Dr. Caligari* had no frame at all. As written by Hans Janowitz and Carl Mayer, the scenario indicated a unified story showing the madness of authoritarianism. But wanting to glorify authoritarianism, Wiene reversed the meaning by putting the story into a frame. The expressionistic parts in the plays and in the film are, in a way, complete in themselves.

Be that as it may, the frame method of narration to present this or that point of view can be almost literally transferred to the screen, as evidenced by the screen versions of these very plays. Although *The Cabinet of Dr. Caligari* did not originate as a play, it is playlike not only in its frame method but in its entirety. With only the slightest of concessions to the difference in media, it could be presented on a stage. In particular it could similarly present the story within the frame as a tale told by a madman. For the point of view is effected by distortion of one or another of the media of the drama. To this extent it represents the motion pictures only as a machine. Herein lies the weakness of *The Cabinet of Dr. Caligari* as a film and in the film versions of *The Emperor Jones, Beggar on Horseback,* and *The Green Pastures.* For whereas introspection can be shown on the screen in the same way as on the stage, it can be done in ways in which it cannot on the stage. That is, it can be done cinematically.

Since the twenties, playwrights have been experimenting with introspection in the drama. For example, Thornton Wilder's *Our Town,* of the thirties, Tennessee Williams' *The Glass Menagerie,* of the forties, and, more recently, Arthur Miller's *A View from the Bridge* present, like *The Emperor Jones, Beggar on Horseback,* and *The Green Pastures,* stories told in frames which establish a first-person point of view. In these later plays, however, the frames are not realistic. In each the frame is represented by a narrator who takes his place downstage and directly addresses the audience. The device is comparable to the expressionistic use of the aside and the soliloquy. The story which the narrator tells becomes a monologue acted out. It becomes monodrama, another expressionistic manifestation.

In modern plays introspection is effected by distortion of the media of the drama. Because the motion pictures like the drama, are presentational, point of view in a film must be effected presentationally. But the means of presentation should not be those of the drama.

No other film so successfully effects an introspective point of view as *Brief Encounter.* Most of the story in *Brief Encounter* is told by flash backs intended to present previous action according to the heroine's recollection of it. And the difference between actuality and the recollection of it is illustrated by the presentation, in *Brief Encounter,* of the action of the last scene of *Still Life,* first from an objective point of view and then from an introspective one.

Although *Brief Encounter* employs the familiar narrator-voice device, there is a difference. The voice is not that of the narrator merely addressing the audience but of Laura addressing her thoughts to her husband, Fred, who is seated opposite her in the living room. The problem of continousness of the introspective point of view is partly solved by the use of the Rachmaninoff Concerto, which is heard intermittently throughout the flash back. The flaw of the use of familiar music as background music becomes a virtue, for the music emphasizes the point of view.

It is not to be inferred that *Brief Encounter* is completely exemplary of the motion-picture way of narrating introspectively. At least once during the film a close-up of Laura, almost immobile, remains awkwardly long on the screen while her voice is heard on the sound track. At other times the spectator may forget whose point of view the introspective part represents. Even the point of view itself is not consistent throughout, the presentation of Laura's recollections including action that Laura could not have witnessed. But no other film so extensively and so cinematically illustrates the possibilities of introspective narration on the screen.

Point of view in a film, as in a novel, should be determined by subject and purpose. *The Birth of a Nation, Intolerance, Nanook of the North, The Covered Wagon, The Battleship Potemkin, The Grapes of Wrath, The Bicycle Thief,* and other films which have helped to establish the motion pictures as the only new art of the twentieth century narrate primarily from an objective point of view. In them the point of view is appropriate. On the other hand, subject and purpose may call for introspection, as for example, in a film in which the character of an individual predominates. For all its cinematic qualities, *Citizen Kane* does not satisfactorily answer the question it conspicuously poses: What is the explanation for the character of Kane? Instead it resorts to a symbol, which, like the film, is completely objective. The possibilities of the introspective point of view might well be exploited in the adaptation to the screen of stories by writers not primarily concerned with externals. For although the motion pictures cannot narrate introspectively in the manner of the novel, they can, because they are presentational, narrate introspectively in ways that the novel cannot. And although they are presentational, they can narrate introspectively in ways that the drama cannot. By exploitation of these ways something essential might be added to the art of the motion pictures. But if anything essential is to be added, it will not be so much by elaboration of the machine as by that kind of selection that is essentially cinematic.

Notes on Sources

CHAPTER I: *The Machine*

THE PERSISTENCE OF VISION AND THE ILLUSION OF MOTION: Terry Ramsaye, *A Million and One Nights: A History of the Motion Pictures* (2 vols., New York, 1926), I, 170–75; Gilbert Seldes, *An Hour with the Movies and the Talkies* (Philadelphia and London, 1929), 9–14.

EARLY DEVICES TO DEPICT MOTION: Martin Quigley, Jr., *Magic Shadows: The Story of the Motion Pictures* (Washington, 1948), 9–129; Ramsaye, *A Million and One Nights*, I, 1–64; Georges Sadoul, *Histoire Générale du Cinéma* (3 vols., Paris, 1948–52), I, 7–172.

THE KINETOSCOPE AND MACHINES BASED ON IT: W. K. L. Dickson and Antonia Dickson, *The Life and Inventions of Thomas Alva Edison* (London, 1894), 300–19; Thomas A. Edison, *The Diary and Sundry Observations of Thomas Alva Edison*, ed. by Dagobert D. Runes (New York, 1948), 68–79; Quigley, *Magic Shadows*, 130–61; Ramsaye, *A Million and One Nights*, I, 65–245.

ANNOUNCEMENT OF THE VITASCOPE: *New York Times*, April 14, 1896.

FIRST SHOWING OF THE VITASCOPE: *New York Times*, April 24 and 26, 1896.

HOWARD B. HACKETT'S PREDICTION ABOUT THE MOTION PICTURES: New York *World*, quoted by Ramsaye, *A Million and One Nights*, I, 134.

CHARLES FROHMAN'S OPINION OF THE VITASCOPE: *New York Times*, April 26, 1896, p. 10.

CHAPTER II: *"Arranged Scenes"*

LIFE AND WORK OF MELIES: Maurice Bardèche and Robert Brasillach, *History of the film*, ed. and trans. by Iris Barry (London,

1938), 7–16, 33–35; Maurice Bessy and Lo Duca, *Georges Méliès, Mage; et "Mes Mémoires" par Méliès* (Paris, 1945); Lewis Jacobs, *The Rise of the American Film: A Critical History* (New York, 1939), 22–32; Georges Méliès, *Complete Catalogue of Genuine and Original "Star" Films (Moving Pictures) Manufactured by Geo. Méliès of Paris* (Paris and New York, 1905); Sadoul, *Histoire Générale du Cinéma*, II, 42–70, 154–66, 221–37.

MELIES' ADVERTISEMENTS OF SEPTEMBER, 1897: Sadoul, *Histoire Générale du Cinéma*, II, 42.

MELIES' COMPARISON OF STAGE WITH SCREEN: Sadoul, *Histoire Générale du Cinéma*, II, 156, 158, 160–61.

ACTORS IN *A Trip to the Moon*: Letter from Méliès to Jean Le-Roy, 1930—in possession of the Museum of Modern Art Film Library.

CHAPTER III: *Arranged Shots*

EXPLOITATION OF THE MOTION-PICTURE MACHINE, 1896–1903: Jacobs, *The Rise of the American Film*, 3–21; Ramsaye, *A Million and One Nights*, I, 246–89, II, 425–33.

LIFE AND WORK OF PORTER: *Edison Catalogues* (New York, 1903 and 1904); Theodore Huff, "Sadoul and Film Research," *Hollywood Quarterly*, Vol. II, No. 2 (January, 1947), 203–206; Jacobs, *The Rise of the American Film*, 35–51; John Howard Lawson, *Theory and Technique of Playwriting and Screenwriting* (New York, 1949), 313; *National Cyclopaedia of American Biography* (42 vols., New York, 1893–1958), XXX, 407; Ramsaye, *A Million and One Nights*, I, 341–52, II, 414–24; Sadoul, "Early Film Production in England," *Hollywood Quarterly*, Vol. I, No. 3 (April, 1946), 256; Sadoul, "English Influences on the Work of Edwin S. Porter," *Hollywood Quarterly*, Vol. III, No. 1 (Fall, 1947), 41–50.

CHAPTER IV: *"Famous Players in Famous Plays"*

PORTER'S LATER FILMS: Jacobs, *The Rise of the American Film*, 46–51.

FILM EXCHANGES, THE NICKELODEON, MOTION-PICTURE PRODUCTION, THE MOTION-PICTURE PATENTS COMPANY: Jacobs, *The Rise* of the American Film, 52–66, 81–86; Ramsaye, A Million and One Nights, II, 401–403, 426–33, 440–98.

SARAH BERNHARDT AND THE FILMING OF Queen Elizabeth: May Agate, Madame Sarah (London, 1945); Sadoul, Histoire Général du Cinéma, III, Part I, 26–27; Louis Verneuil, The Fabulous Life of Sarah Bernhardt, trans. by Ernest Boyd (New York and London, 1942).

THE STAR SYSTEM: Jacobs, The Rise of the American Film, 86–90; Ramsaye, A Million and One Nights, II, 523.

THE FAMOUS PLAYERS COMPANY: William Henry Irwin, The House That Shadows Built (Garden City, 1928), 154–94; Jacobs, The Rise of the American Film, 49–50, 90–92; Ramsaye, A Million and One Nights, II, 594–99.

CHAPTER V: Editing

LIFE AND WORK OF GRIFFITH: Iris Barry, "A Corner in Wheat," Program Notes, Series 1, Program 2, the Museum of Modern Art Film Library; Lillian Gish, "The Birth of an Era," Stage, Vol. XIV (January, 1937), 100–102, and "D. W. Griffith—A Great American," Harper's Bazaar, Vol. LXXIV (October, 1940), 74–75, 106; Mrs. D. W. Griffith (Linda Arvidson), When the Movies Were Young (New York, 1925); Otis L. Guernsey, Jr., Interview, New York Herald Tribune, October 4, 1942; Jacobs, The Rise of the American Film, 95–119, 171–201; Julian Johnson, "The Shadow Stage," Photoplay, Vol. XI (December, 1916), 77–81; Lawson, Theory and Technique of Playwriting and Screenwriting, 391; Ramsaye, A Million and One Nights, II, 453–58, 508–18; 635–44, 755–60; David Robinson, "Spectacle," Sight and Sound, Vol. XXV (Summer, 1955), 26; Seymour Stern, "The Birth of a Nation," Special Supplement to Sight and Sound, Index Series No. 4 (July, 1945), "D. W. Griffith: An Appreciation," Sight and Sound, Vol. XVII (Autumn, 1948), 109–10, and "An Index to the Creative Work of David Wark Griffith," Special Supplement to Sight and Sound, Index Series No. 8, Part II (September, 1946).

DIXON'S CURTAIN SPEECH AT THE Première of The Birth of a Nation: New York Times, March 4, 1915.

SCRIPT FOR The Birth of a Nation: Prepared by Theodore Huff

—in possession of the Museum of Modern Art Film Library, New York City.

RENE CLAIR'S EVALUATION OF GRIFFITH: *Time,* Vol. LII (August 2, 1948), 72.

CHAPTER VI: *Expressionism*

Excursion: Bardèche and Brasillach, *History of the Film,* 7–8.

The Cabinet of Dr. Caligari: Jacobs, *The Rise of the American Film,* 303–305; Siegfried Kracauer, *From Caligari to Hitler: A Psychological History of the German Film* (Princeton, 1947); Erich Pommer, "The Origin of Dr. Caligari," *Art in Cinema: A Symposium on the Avantgarde Film together with Program Notes and References for Series One of Art in Cinema,* ed. by Frank Stauffacher (San Francisco, 1947), 35–37.

CHAPTER VII: *Naturalism*

LIFE AND WORK OF VON STROHEIM: Rodney Ackland, "Greed: A Personal Note," in the Appendix to Peter Noble's *Hollywood Scapegoat: The Biography of Erich von Stroheim* (London, 1950), 221–23; A. R. Fulton, "Stroheim's 'Greed,' " *Films in Review,* Vol. VI (June–July, 1955), 263–68; Jacobs, *The Rise of the American Film,* 343–54; Gavin Lambert, "Stroheim Revisited: The Missing Third in the American Cinema," *Sight and Sound,* Vol. XXII (April–June, 1953), 165–71, 204; Noble, *Hollywood Scapegoat* and "The Return of the Master," *Theatre,* No. 8 (Winter, 1947), 15–17; Herman G. Weinberg, "An Index to the Creative Work of Erich von Stroheim," Special Supplement to *Sight and Sound,* Index Series No. 1 (June, 1943).

SOURCE OF *Greed:* Frank Norris, *McTeague: A Story of San Francisco* (New York, 1899).

ORIGINAL LENGTH OF *Greed:* Jacobs, *The Rise of the American Film,* 349; Seldes, *An Hour with the Movies and the Talkies,* 90; Weinberg, "An Index to the Creative Work of Erich von Stroheim," Special Supplement to *Sight and Sound,* Index Series No. 1 (June, 1943), 4.

BARRIE'S DISTINCTION BETWEEN A NOVEL AND A PLAY: *The Plays of J. M. Barrie* (New York, 1945), 249.

DICTUM FOR THE ADAPTATION OF A NOVEL TO THE SCREEN: Mortimer Adler, *Art and Prudence: A Study in Practical Philosophy* (New York, 1937), 511.

CHAPTER VIII: *Montage*

LIFE AND WORK OF EISENSTEIN: Boris Ingster, "Serge Eisenstein," *Hollywood Quarterly*, Vol. V (Summer, 1951), 380–88; Marie Seton, *Sergei M. Eisenstein: A Biography* (New York, 1952).

BY EISENSTEIN: *Film Form: Essays in Film Theory*, ed. and trans. by Jay Leyda (New York, 1949); *The Film Sense*, ed. and trans. by Jay Leyda (New York, 1947); "The Twelve Apostles," *The Cinema 1952*, ed. by Roger Manvell (Harmondsworth, 1952), 158–73.

MEISEL'S MUSICAL SCORE FOR *Potemkin*: Kurt London, *Film Music: A Summary of the Characteristic Features of Its History, Aesthetics, Technique, and Possible Developments* (London, 1936), 73–74, 93.

WILLA CATHER ON THE NOVEL: *Not Under Forty* (New York, 1936), 40.

CHAPTER IX: *Sound*

RIVALRY OF THE MOTION PICTURES AND THE DRAMA: Brander Matthews, "Are the Movies a Menace to the Drama?" *North American Review*, Vol. CCV (March, 1917), 447–54.

EDISON'S ORIGINAL IDEA OF THE MOTION PICTURES AS A DEVICE WHEREBY "MOTION AND SOUND COULD BE RECORDED SIMULTANEOUSLY": Dickson and Dickson, *The Life and Inventions of Thomas Alva Edison*, 300.

INTRODUCTION OF SOUND: Jacobs, *The Rise of the American Film*, 297–301, 433–44; Frederic M. Thrasher (ed.), *Okay for Sound: How the Screen Found Its Voice* (New York, 1946).

DICTUM FOR THE ADAPTATION OF A PLAY TO THE SCREEN: Adler, *Art and Prudence*, 511.

SOURCE OF *Anna Christie*: Eugene O'Neill, *Anna Christie: A Play in Four Acts* (New York, 1922).

Anna Christie AS TRAGEDY: Ludwig Lewisohn, "Drama: Eugene O'Neill," *Nation*, Vol. CXIII (November 30, 1921), 626.

GARBO'S VOICE ON THE SOUND TRACK: Mordaunt Hall, Review of *Anna Christie, New York Times,* March 15, 1930.

GARBO'S PREPARATION FOR THE FILMING OF *Anna Christie:* Donald Henderson Clarke, "Greta Garbo Talks," *New York Times,* January 26, 1930.

CHAPTER X: *The Creative Use of Sound*

LIFE AND WORK OF FORD: *Current Biography* (New York, 1941), 296–98; William Patrick Wooten, "An Index to the Films of John Ford," Special Supplement to *Sight and Sound,* Index Series No. 13 February, 1948).

SOURCE OF *The Informer:* Liam O'Flaherty, *The Informer* (New York, 1925).

The Informer: "Cutting Continuity of *The Informer,*" *Modern British Dramas,* ed. by Harlan Hatcher (New York, 1941), 301–67; Jacobs, *The Rise of the American Film,* 480–83; Dudley Nichols, "The Writer and the Film," *Twenty Best Film Plays* (New York, 1943), *xxxi–xl.*

CHAPTER XI: *Documentary Film*

DEFINITION OF "DOCUMENTARY": Forsyth Hardy (ed.), *Grierson on Documentary* (London, 1946); Paul Rotha, in collaboration with Sinclair Road and Richard Griffith, *Documentary Film: The Use of the Film Medium to Interpret Creatively and in Social Terms the Life of the People as It Exists in Reality* (London, 1936); Raymond Spottiswoode, *A Grammar of the Film: An Analysis of Film Technique* (London, 1933), 87–93, 276–96.

FLAHERTY AND *Nanook of the North:* Robert Flaherty, "Robert Flaherty Talking," *The Cinema 1950,* ed. by Roger Manvell (Harmondsworth, 1950), 11–29; Hugh Gray, "Robert Flaherty and the Naturalistic Documentary," *Hollywood Quarterly,* Vol. V (Fall, 1950), 41–48; Richard Griffith, *The World of Robert Flaherty* (New York, 1953); Rotha, *Documentary Film,* 82–86, 106–108, 319–21; Robert Lewis Taylor, "Moviemaker," *New Yorker,* Vol. XXV (June 11, 1949), 30–41, (June 18, 1949), 28–38, (June 25, 1949), 28–43.

Night Mail: Ernest Lindgren, *The Art of the Film: An Introduction to Film Appreciation* (London, 1948), 150–52; Karel Reisz,

The Technique of Film Editing, 3rd ed. (London and New York, 1955), 166–70.

LORENTZ AND *The River*: Lindgren, *The Art of the Film*, 153; Pare Lorentz, *The River* (New York, 1938); W. L. White, "Pare Lorentz," *Scribner's*, Vol. CV (January, 1939), 7–11, 42.

CHAPTER XII: *From Play to Film*

SOURCE OF *Abe Lincoln in Illinois*: Robert Emmet Sherwood, *Abe Lincoln in Illinois* (New York, 1939).

SCOPE OF A PLAY: St. John Hankin, "A Note on Happy Endings," *The Dramatic Works of St. John Hankin* (3 vols., New York, 1912), III, 120–21.

ADAPTATION OF A PLAY TO THE SCREEN: Adler, *Art and Prudence*.

SOURCE OF *Brief Encounter*: Noel Coward, "Still Life: A Play in Five Scenes," *Tonight at 8:30* (New York, 1935), 221–59.

SCREEN PLAY OF *Brief Encounter*: "Brief Encounter," *Three British Screen Plays*, ed. by Roger Manvell (London, 1950), 1–82.

Brief Encounter: David Lean, "Brief Encounter," *Penguin Film Review*, No. 4 (London and New York, 1947), 27–35; Roger Manvell, "Britain's Self-Portraiture in Feature Films," *Geographical Magazine*, Vol. XXVI (August, 1953), 222–34.

CHAPTER XIII: *From Novel to Film*

ADAPTATION OF A NOVEL TO THE SCREEN: Adler, *Art and Prudence*; A. R. Fulton, "It's Exactly Like the Play," *Theatre Arts*, Vol. XXXVII (March, 1953), 78–83.

SOURCE OF *Great Expectations*: Charles Dickens, *Great Expectations*, first published in *All the Year Round* from December 1, 1860 to August 3, 1861.

NARRATION IN *The Informer*: O'Flaherty, *The Informer*, 35.

Great Expectations: David Lean, "David Lean Talks to Roger Manvell, *The Cinema, 1952*, 19–20; Reisz, *The Technique of Film Editing*, 237–41.

THE SCRIPT OF *Great Expectations:* David Lean, "Extract from the Post-Production Script of *Great Expectations:* Pip Steals the Food," *The Cinema 1952,* 21–29; Reisz, *The Technique of Film Editing,* 237–38.

JACK HARRIS' NOTES ON THE SCRIPT OF *Great Expectations:* Reisz, *The Technique of Film Editing,* 238–39.

CHAPTER XIV: *From Short Story to Film*

SOURCE OF *All That Money Can Buy:* Stephen Vincent Benét, "The Devil and Daniel Webster," *The Selected Works of Stephen Vincent Benét* (New York, 1937).

All That Money Can Buy: Lawrence Morton, "Film Music of the Quarter, *Hollywood Quarterly,* Vol. V (Fall, 1950), 51–52.

SOURCE OF *Quartet:* W. Somerset Maugham and R. C. Sherriff, *Quartet* (Garden City, 1950).

CHAPTER XV: *Television*

THE FILM *Hamlet:* Laurence Olivier, "An Essay in Hamlet," *The Film Hamlet: A Record of Its Production,* ed. by Brenda Cross (London, 1948), 11–15.

CONSTANCIES OF SIZE AND FORM: Rudolf Arnheim, *Film As Art* (Berkeley and Los Angeles, 1957), 58–65.

CHAPTER XVI: *Art and the Machine*

Lady in the Lake: Joseph P. Brinton III, "Subjective Camera or Subjective Audience," *Hollywood Quarterly,* Vol. II (July, 1947), 359–66.

Credit Titles

Released by RKO Radio Pictures, 1940
Directed by John Cromwell
Produced by Max Gordon for the Plays and Pictures Corporation
Based on the Play by Robert E. Sherwood.
Screen Play by Mr. Sherwood
Adaptation by Grover Jones
Assistant Director: Dewey Starkey
Director of Photography: James Wong Howe
Musical Score by Roy Webb
Musical Effects by Vernon L. Walker
Art Director: Van Nest Polglase
Associate Art Director: Carroll Clark
Set Decorations by Casey Roberts
Wardrobe by Walter Plunkett
Dance Director: David Robel
Montage by Douglas Travers
Recorded by Hugh McDowell, Jr.
Edited by George Hively

Cast

Abe Lincoln	Raymond Massey
Stephen Douglas	Gene Lockhart
Mary Todd Lincoln	Ruth Gordon
Ann Rutledge	Mary Howard
Elizabeth Edwards	Dorothy Tree
Ninian Edwards	Harvey Stephens
Joshua Speed	Minor Watson
Billy Herndon	Alan Baxter
Jack Armstrong	Howard da Silva

John McNeill	Maurice Murphy
Ben Battling	Clem Bevans
Seth Gale	Herbert Rudley
Mr. Crimmin	Roger Imhoff
Mr. Rutledge	Edmund Elton
Dr. Chandler	George Rosener
John Hanks	Trevor Bardette
Sarah Lincoln	Elizabeth Risdon
Gobey	Napoleon Simpson
Judge Bowling Green	Aldrich Bowker
Mentor Graham	Louis Jean Heydt
Denton Offut	Harlan Briggs
Stage driver	Andy Clyde
Mrs. Rutledge	Leona Roberts
Mrs. Bowling Green	Florence Roberts
Mrs. Seth Gale	Fay Helm
John Johnston	Syd Saylor
Tom Lincoln	Charles Middleton
Trum Cogdall	Alec Craig

ALL THAT MONEY CAN BUY

Released by RKO Radio Pictures, 1941
Produced and Directed by William Dieterle
Associate Producer: Charles L. Glett
Assistant Director: Argyle Nelson
Based on Stephen Vincent Benét's Short Story "The Devil and Daniel Webster"
Screen Play by Dan Totheroh and Mr. Benét
Director of Photography: Joseph August
Music Composed and Conducted by Bernard Herrmann
Art Director: Van Nest Polglase
Special Effects by Vernon L. Walker
Costumes by Edward Stevenson
Set Decorations by Darrell Silvera
Dialogue Director: Peter Berneis
Recorded by Hugh McDowell, Jr., and James G. Stewart
Edited by Robert Wise

Cast

Daniel Webster	Edward Arnold

Mr. Scratch	Walter Huston
Ma Stone	Jane Darwell
Belle	Simone Simon
Squire Slossum	Gene Lockhart
Miser Stevens	John Qualen
Justice Hawthorne	H. B. Warner
Jabez Stone	James Craig
Mary Stone	Anne Shirley
Sheriff	Frank Conlan
Daniel Stone	Lindy Wade
Cy Bibber	George Cleveland

ANNA CHRISTIE

Produced by Metro-Goldwyn-Mayer, 1930
Directed by Clarence Brown
Adapted by Frances Marion from the Play by Eugene O'Neill
Recording Director: Douglas Shearer
Film Editor: Hugh Wynn
Art Director: Cedric Gibbons
Photography by William Daniels
Gowns by Adrian

Cast

Anna	Greta Garbo
Mat	Charles Bickford
Chris	George F. Marion
Marthy	Marie Dressler
Johnny the Harp	James T. Mack
Larry	Lee Phelps

THE BATTLESHIP POTEMKIN

Produced by the First Studio of Goskino, Moscow, 1925
Directed by Sergei Eisenstein
Scenario by Eisenstein, from an Outline by Nina Agadzhanova-
   Shutko
Photography by Edward Tisse
Assistant Director: Grigori Alexandrov
Assistants: A. Antonov, Mikhail Gomarov, A. Levshin, and Maxim
   Shtraukh

Supervisor: Yakov Bliokh
Subtitles by Nikolai Aseyev

Cast

Vakulinchuk	A. Antonov
Chief Officer Giliarovsky	Grigori Alexandrov
Captain Golikov	Vladimir Barsky
Petty Officer	A. Levshin
A Sailor	Mikhail Gomarov
Other Officers, Crew, Citizens of Odessa, etc.	Sailors of the Red Navy, Citizens of Odessa, and Members of the Prolet-kult Theatre

THE BIRTH OF A NATION

Produced by the Epoch Producing Corporation, 1915
Directed by D. W. Griffith
Based on *The Clansman* and *The Leopard's Spots,* by
    Thomas Dixon
Adaptation by D. W. Griffith and Frank Woods
Photography by G. W. Bitzer
Music Composed by Joseph Carl Briel and D. W. Griffith

Cast

Benjamin Cameron (the "Little Colonel")	Henry B. Walthall
Flora Cameron, as a Child	Violet Wilkey
Flora, the Younger Sister	Mae Marsh
Margaret Cameron, the Older Sister	Miriam Cooper
Mrs. Cameron	Josephine Crowell
Dr. Cameron	Spottiswoode Aitken
Wade Cameron, the Second Son	Andre Beranger
Duke Cameron, the Youngest Son	Maxfield Stanley
Elsie Stoneman	Lillian Gish
The Hon. Austin Stoneman, Her Father	Ralph Lewis

Her Brother Phil	Elmer Clifton
Her Younger Brother, Tod	Robert Harron
Lydia Brown, Stoneman's	
Mulatto Housekeeper	Mary Alden
Silas Lynch, Leader	
of the Blacks	George Siegmann
Gus, the Negro Renegade	Walter Long
"White-Arm" Joe, Owner	
of the Gin Mill	Elmo Lincoln
Jeff, the Blacksmith	Wallace Reid
Abraham Lincoln	Joseph Henaberry
Gen. U. S. Grant	Donald Crisp
Gen. Robert E. Lee	Howard Gaye
Sen. Charles Sumner	Sam de Grasse
John Wilkes Booth	Raoul Walsh
Laura Keene	Olga Grey
Slave Auctioneer	Elmo Lincoln
Stoneman's Negro Servant	Tom Wilson
Union Soldier	Eugene Pallette
Piedmont Girl	Bessie Love
Jake, a Servant of the	
Camerons	William de Vaull
Cyndy (Mammy), Another	
Cameron Servant	Jennie Lee

BRIEF ENCOUNTER

Released by Universal Pictures Company, 1946
Directed by David Lean
Produced by Noel Coward
Presented by J. Arthur Rank
In Charge of Production: Anthony Havelock-Allan and
    Ronald Neame
Adapted by Noel Coward from His One-Act Play *Still Life*
Director of Photography: Robert Krasker
Art Director: L. P. Williams
Film Editor: Jack Harris
Art Supervisor to Noel Coward: G. E. Calthrop
Associate Editor: Margery Saunders
Sound Editor: Harry Miller

Sound Recordists: Stanley Lambourne and Desmond Dew
Production Manager: E. Holding
Assistant Director: George Pollock
Camera Operator: B. Francke
Continuity: Margaret Sibley
Rachmaninov Piano Concerto No. 2 Played by Eileen Joyce with
the National Symphony Orchestra, Conducted by
Muir Mathieson

Cast

Laura Jesson	Celia Johnson
Alec Harvey	Trevor Howard
Albert Godby	Stanley Holloway
Myrtle Bagot	Joyce Carey
Fred Jesson	Cyril Raymond
Dolly Messiter	Everley Gregg
Beryl Waters	Margaret Barton
Stanley	Dennis Harkin
Stephen Lynn	Valentine Dyall
Mary Norton	Marjorie Mars
Mrs. Rolandson	Nuna Davey
Woman Organist	Irene Handl
Bill	Edward Hodge
Johnnie	Sydney Bromley
Policeman	Wilfred Babbage
Waitress	Avis Scutt
Margaret	Henrietta Vincent
Bobbie	Richard Thomas
Clergyman	George V. Sheldon
Doctor	Wally Bosco
Boatman	Jack Man

THE CABINET OF DR. CALIGARI

Produced by Decla-Bioscop, 1919
Directed by Robert Wiene
Scenario by Carl Mayer and Hans Janowitz
Design by Hermann Warm, Walter Röhrig, and Walter Reimann
Photography by Willy Hameister

Cast

Dr. Caligari	Werner Krauss
Cesare	Conrad Veidt
Francis	Friedrich Feher
Jane	Lil Dagover
Alan	Hans von Twardowski
Dr. Olsen	Rudolf Lettinger
A Criminal	Rudolf Klein-Rogge

GREAT EXPECTATIONS

Produced by Ronald Neame for Cineguild, 1946
Directed by David Lean
Adapted for the Screen by David Lean, Ronald Neame, Anthony
    Havelock-Allan, Kay Walsh, and Cecil McGivern—from the
    Novel by Charles Dickens
Executive Producer: Anthony Havelock-Allan
Photographed by Guy Green
Production Designed by John Bryan
Film Editor: Jack Harris
Art Director: Wilfred Shingleton
Costumes Designed by Sophia Harris of Motley—Assisted by
    Margaret Furse
Assistant Director: George Pollock
Production Manager: Norman Spencer
Sound Recordists: Stanley Lambourne and Gordon K. McCallum
Sound Editor: Winston Ryder
Camera Operator: Nigel Huke
Continuity: Margaret Sibley
Dances Arranged by Suria Magite
Musical Score Composed and Conducted by Walter Goehr—with
    the National Symphony Orchestra

Cast

Pip	John Mills
Young Pip	Anthony Wager
Estella	Valerie Hobson
Young Estella	Jean Simmons
Joe Gargery	Bernard Miles

Mr. Jaggers	Francis L. Sullivan
Magwitch	Finlay Currie
Miss Havisham	Martita Hunt
Herbert Pocket	Alec Guinness
Mr. Wemmick	Ivor Bernard
Mrs. Joe	Freda Jackson
Biddy	Eileen Erskine
Convict	George Hayes
Uncle Pumblechook	Hay Petrie
The Pale Young Gentleman	John Forrest
Bentley Drummle	Torin Thatcher
The Aged Parent	O. B. Clarence
Mr. Wopsle	John Burch
The Sergeant	Richard George
Mrs. Wopsle	Grace Denbigh-Russell
Sarah Pocket	Everley Gregg
Relation	Anne Holland
Mike	Frank Atkinson
Night Porter	Gordon Begg
Mrs. Whimple	Eddie Martin
The Dancing Master	Walford Hyden
Galley Steersman	Roy Arthur

THE GREAT TRAIN ROBBERY

Produced by the Edison Company, 1903
Directed by Edwin S. Porter
Scenario by Edwin S. Porter
Photographed by Edwin S. Porter

Cast

George Barnes, Max (Bronco Billy) Anderson, A. C. Abadie, Frank Hunaway, Marie Murray, Employees of the Edison Company, and Others

GREED

Produced by the Goldwyn Company, 1923
Directed by Erich von Stroheim
Released by Metro-Goldwyn-Mayer

Based on Frank Norris' Novel *McTeague*
Adapted by Erich von Stroheim
Abridged by June Mathis
Photography by Ben E. Reynolds, William H. Daniels, and
    Ernest Schoedsack

Cast

Trina	Zazu Pitts
McTeague	Gibson Gowland
Marcus	Jean Hersholt
Maria	Dale Fuller
Mother McTeague	Tempe Pigott
Papa Sieppe	Chester Conklin
Mama Sieppe	Sylvia Ashton
Selina	Joan Standing
August Sieppe	Austin Jewell
The Sieppe twins	Oscar Gottel and Otto Gottel
Others	Max Tyron
	Frank Hayes
	Fanny Midgley
	Cesare Gravina
	Hughie Mack
	Tiny Jones
	J. Aldrich Libbey
	Rita Revela
	Lon Poff
	William Barlow
	Edward Gaffney
	S. S. Simons

THE INFORMER

Produced by John Ford for RKO Radio Pictures, 1935
Directed by John Ford
Associate Producer: Cliff Reid
Screenplay by Dudley Nichols—from the Novel by Liam O'Flaherty
Photography by Joseph H. August
Musical Score by Max Steiner
Art Director: Van Nest Polglase

Associate Art Director: Charles Kirk
Costumes by Walter Plunkett
Recorded by Hugh McDowell, Jr.
Edited by George Hively

Cast

Gypo Nolan	Victor McLaglen
Mary McPhillip	Heather Angel
Dan Gallagher	Preston Foster
Katie Madden	Margot Grahame
Frankie McPhillip	Wallace Ford
Mrs. McPhillip	Una O'Connor
Terry	J. M. Kerrigan
Bartley Mulholland	Joseph Sawyer
Tommy Connor	Neil Fitzgerald
Rat Mulligan	Donald Meek
Blind Man	D'Arcy Corrigan
Donahue	Leo McCabe
Daly	Gaylord Pendelton
Flynn	Francis Ford
Aunt Betty	May Boley
Lady	Grizelda Harvey
Street Singer	Dennis O'Dea
Man at Wake	Jack Mulhall
Young Soldier	Bob Parrish

INTOLERANCE

Produced by the Wark Producing Corporation (D. W. Griffith), 1916
Directed by D. W. Griffith
Scenario by Griffith
Scenario of "The Modern Story" (Originally *The Mother and the Law*). Adapted by Griffith, in part, from a Report of a Federal Industrial Commission and, in Part, from the Records of the Stielow Murder Case
Settings Supervised by Griffith
Costume Designs Supervised by Griffith
Photographic Style and Technique Supervised by Griffith
Research Supervised by Griffith
Research on "The Judean Story": Rabbi L. Myers

Architectural Conceptions of the City of Babylon (Motifs Suggested by the Sun Buildings and the Causeway of the Panama-Pacific Exposition at San Francisco, 1915): Griffith
Construction Supervisor and Chief Engineer on the Babylonian Sets: Frank Wortman
Photography: G. W. Bitzer and Karl Brown
Assistant Directors: George Siegmann, W. S. Van Dyke, Joseph Hennaberry, Erich von Stroheim, Edward Dillon, and Tod Browning
Chief Second Assistant Directors: Ted Duncan and Mike Siebert
Editing: Griffith
Cutters: James and Rose Smith
Musical Score by Joseph Carl Briel and Griffith

The Principal Characters

OF ALL AGES

The Woman Who Rocks the Cradle	Lillian Gish

OF THE MODERN STORY (A.D. 1914)

The Dear One	Mae Marsh
Her Father, a Mill Worker	Fred Turner
The Boy	Robert Harron
Jenkins, Mill Magnate	Sam de Grasse
Mary T. Jenkins, His Sister	Vera Lewis
Self-styled Uplifters and Professional Meddlers	Mary Alden
	Eleanor Washington
	Pearl Elmore
	Lucile Brown
	Mrs. Arther Mackley
The Friendless One	Miriam Cooper
The Musketeer of the Slums	Walter Long
The Kindly Policeman	Tom Wilson
The Governor	Ralph Lewis
The Judge	Lloyd Ingraham
Father Farley, the Boy's Confessor	The Rev. A. W. McClure
The Friendly Neighbor	Dore Davidson

Strike Leader	Monte Blue
Debutante	Marguerite Marsh
A Crook	Tod Browning
Another Crook	Edward Dillon

OF THE JUDEAN STORY (A.D. 27)

The Nazarene	Howard Gaye
Mary, the Mother	Lillian Langdon
Mary Magdalene	Olga Grey
First Pharisee	Gunther von Ritzau
Second Pharisee	Erich von Stroheim
Bride of Cana	Bessie Love
The Bride's Father	William Brown
Bridegroom	George Walsh

OF THE MEDIEVAL FRENCH STORY (A.D. 1572)

Brown Eyes, Daughter of a Huguenot Family	Margery Wilson
Prosper Latour, Her Sweetheart	Eugene Pallette
Her Father	Spottiswoode Aitken
Her Mother	Ruth Handforth
The Mercenary (of the Swiss Soldiery)	A. D. Sears
Charles IX, King of France	Frank Bennett
Duc D'Anjou, Brother to the King and Heir to the Throne	Maxfield Stanley
Catherine de Médici	Josephine Crowell
Marguerite de Valois, Sister of Charles IX	Constance Talmadge
Henry of Navarre	W. E. Lawrence
Admiral Coligny	Joseph Henaberry
A Page	Chandler House

OF THE BABYLONIAN STORY (539 B.C.)

The Mountain Girl	Constance Talmadge
The Rhapsode, Her Suitor and Secret Agent of the High	

300

Priest of Bel	Elmer Clifton
The Prince Belshazzar	Alfred Paget
The Princess Beloved	Seena Owen
The King Nabonidus	Carl Stockdale
The High Priest of Bel	Tully Marshall
Cyrus, Emperor and War Lord of the Persians	George Siegmann
Gobyras, the Mighty Man of Valour, Belshazzar's Bodyguard	Elmo Lincoln
Captain of the Great Gate of Imgur-Bel	Ted Duncan
The Runner, Messenger to the Princess Beloved	Guino Corrado (Lisserani)
Princess Beloved's Bodyguards	Ted Duncan Felix Modjeska
Babylonian Judges	George Fawcett Robert Lawlor
Old Woman of Babylon	Kate Bruce
Solo Dancer	Ruth St. Denis
Slave Girls, Dancers, Hand-Maidens from Ishtar's Temple of Laughter and Love; Virgins of the Sacred Fires of Life; Entertainers at Belshazzar's Feast, etc.	Alma Rubens Carmel Myers Pauline Starke Mildred Harris Chaplin (Mrs. Charles Chaplin) Eve Southern Winifred Westover Jewel Carmen Colleen Moore Natalie Talmadge Carol Dempster Ethel Terry Daisy Robinson Anna Mae Walthall The Denishawn dancers

Also playing Bit Parts or Extra Roles: Douglas Fairbanks, Sir Herbert Beerbohm Tree, De Wolf Hopper, Frank Campeau, Donald Crisp, Nigel de Brullier, Wilfred Lucas, Owen Moore, Andre Beranger, Tammany Young, and Francis Carpenter

NANOOK OF THE NORTH

Produced by Robert Flaherty for Revillon Frères, 1922
Directed and Photographed by Robert Flaherty

Cast

Nanook and other Eskimos

NIGHT MAIL

Produced by John Grierson for the General Post Office Film
    Unit, 1936
Direction and Scenario by Basil Wright and Harry Watt
Camera Work by H. E. Fowle and Jonah Jones
Sound by Alberto Cavalcanti
Music by Benjamin Britten
Edited by R. Q. MacNaughton
Commentary in Verse by W. H. Auden

Cast

Workers of the Traveling Post Office and the L. M. S. Railway

QUARTET

Produced by Antony Darnborough for Gainsborough Pictures, 1948
Presented by J. Arthur Rank
Released through General Film Distributors, Ltd.
In Charge of Production: Sydney Box
Screen Play by R. C. Sherriff
Adapted from Four Short Stories by Somerset Maugham
Music Composed by John Greenwood and Played by the
    Philharmonic Orchestra of London
Music Director: Muir Mathieson
Schubert Impromptu Played by Eileen Joyce

Production Controller: Arthur Alcott
Directors of Photoplay: Ray Elton and Alec Wyer
Supervising Editor: A. Charles Knott
Editor: Jean Barker
Supervising Art Director: George Provis
Art Director: Cedric Dawe
Production Manager: Billy Boyle
Camera Operator: Bernard Lewis
Assistant Director: Bob Attwooll
Special Effects: P. Guiddbaldi
Make-Up: W. T. Partelton
Dress Designer: Julie Harris
Director of Sound: Brian C. Sewell
Recording: L. Hammond and W. S. Salter

"THE FACTS OF LIFE"

Directed by Ralph Smart

Cast

Henry Garnet	Basil Radford
Leslie	Naunton Wayne
Jeanne	Mai Zetterling
Mrs. Garnet	Angela Baddeley
John	Nigel Buchanan
Professor Branksome	James Robertson-Justice
Nicky	Jack Watling
Thomas	Jack Raine
Ralph	Ian Flyming
Cabaret Artist	Jean Cavall

"THE ALIEN CORN"

Directed by Harold French

Cast

George Bland	Dirk Bogarde
Lea Makart	Francoise Rosay
Lady Bland	Irene Browne
Sir Frederick	Raymond Lovell

Uncle John	George Thorpe
Paula	Honor Blackman
Aunt Maud	Mary Hinton
Coroner	Maurice Denham
Foreman of Jury	James Hayter
Butler	Henry Morrell
Frenchman	Marcel Poncin

"THE KITE"

Directed by Arthur Crabtree

Cast

Samuel Sunbury	Mervyn Johns
Mrs. Sunbury	Hermione Baddeley
Betty Baker	Susan Shaw
Herbert Sunbury	George Cole
Herbert Sunbury, as a Boy	David Cole
Prison Governor	Frederick Leister
Prison Officer	George Merritt
Man from *Advertiser*	Cyril Chamberlain
Ned Preston	Bernard Lee

"THE COLONEL'S LADY"

Directed by Kenn Annakin

Cast

Railway Passenger	Cyril Raymond
Henry Dashwood	Ernest Thesiger
Henry Blane	Clive Morton
Blane's Clerk	Ernest Butcher
Martin	Felix Alymer
Second Woman	Yvonne Owen
Third Woman	Margaret Thorburn
George Peregrine	Cecil Parker
Evie Peregrine	Nora Swinburne
Daphne	Linden Travers
Assistant in Bookshop	Bill Owen

| Bannock | Lyn Evans |
| John Colman | John Salew |

QUEEN ELIZABETH

Produced by the Histrionic Film Company, 1912
Directed by Louis Mercanton
Adapted from the Play by Émile Moreau
Dresses, Armor, and Furniture from the Sarah Bernhardt
    Theatre, Paris

Cast

Queen Elizabeth	Sarah Bernhardt
The Earl of Essex	Lou Tellegen
The Countess of Nottingham	Mlle Romain
The Earl of Nottingham	M. Maxudian
and Other Members of Sarah Bernhardt's Company	

THE RIVER

Produced by the U. S. Farm Security Administration, 1937
Written and Directed by Pare Lorentz
Photography by Stacy Woodward, Floyd Crosby, and Willard
    van Dyke
Film Editors: Leo Zochling and Lloyd Nosler
Research Editor: A. A. Mercy
Musical Score by Virgil Thomson—Played by Members of the
    New York Philharmonic Society
Commentary Narrated by Thomas Chalmers

A TRIP TO THE MOON

Produced by Georges Méliès, 1902
Directed by Georges Méliès
Scenario by Georges Méliès
Sets and Costumes by Georges Méliès
Photographed by Lucien Tainguy

Cast

| President of the Scientific Congress | Georges Méliès |

Members of the Scientific Congress	Victor André Delpierre Farjaux-Kelm-Brunnet and Others
The Girl in the Crescent	Bluette Bernon
The Girls in the Stars	Ballerinas of the Théâtre du Châtelet
The Sélénites	Acrobats of the Folies-Bergère

Glossary of Motion-Picture Terms

Angle Shot: shot resulting from the camera's being placed at other than a right angle to its object; also, a shot made from a different angle than that of a preceding shot in the same scene.

Author's title: see *credit title.*

Back lighting: lighting effected by extra illumination behind the object photographed.

Back projection: incorporation, into a shot, of a scene or scenes previously photographed and thus made the subject of a second camera, as, for example, background seen through the window of a train to give the effect of a moving train; also called *process shot, rear projection,* and *back,* or *background projection.* In *background projection,* the images are thrown onto a translucent screen by a projector behind the screen.

Bridging title: continuity title.

Cast list: see *Credit title.*

Close shot: shot for which the camera is brought near the object to emphasize a particular detail.[1]

Close-up: shot including not more than an actor's head and shoulders, filling or almost filling the screen.[1]

Composite shot: simultaneous projection of more than one shot; also called *split screen.*

Continuity title: printed matter projected on the screen—usually between sequences—to aid in the telling of the story; also called *bridging title.*

Crane shot: shot obtained by the camera moving on a crane, as, for example, in an overhead view.

Credit title: list—usually projected on the screen at the beginning of a film—which includes the title of the film, the names of the production staff, the cast, etc.; sometimes differentiated by *main title* (the title of the film), *director's title, author's title, cast list,* etc.

Creeping title: title that moves over the screen, usually from bottom to top.

Crosscut: cut from one scene to another to present simultaneous action and, usually, to prolong suspense; also called *cutback, switchback, intercut,* and *Griffith last-minute rescue.*

Cut: instantaneous end of a shot or instantaneous transference from one shot to another. A *cut* indicates continuous or simultaneous action.

Cutback: crosscut.

Cut-in: still of an object—such as a poster, a letter, or a page of a newspaper—which interrupts continuity; also called *insert.*

Director's title: see *credit title.*

Dissolve: blurring of images as one shot appears to melt into another, the first shot becoming increasingly indistinct and the second increasingly distinct; also called *lap dissolve, mix,* and *oil dissolve.*

Distance shot: shot in which the object is represented as at a great distance from the camera to show a wide sweep of action or immensity of background.[1]

Documentary: nonfiction film taking for its subject the real world but, unlike a newsreel or travelogue, having a theme and dramatic implication.

Dolly Shot: shot—from *dolly,* a small-wheeled truck—made as the camera moves up to, with, or away from the actors or along an object—such as the side of a building; also called *follow shot, tracking shot,* and *trucking shot.*

Double exposure: superimposition of one shot on another.

Dream balloon: double exposure in which a shot representing the thoughts of a character occupies part of the screen.

Edit: to arrange shots. In a sound film, editing includes combining the shots with the sound track.

Establishing shot: long shot, usually of an exterior, to establish the setting of a scene or the relationship of details to be shown subsequently in a closer shot or shots.

Fade-in: gradual disclosure of a scene as the screen becomes light.

Fade-out: gradual disappearance of the scene as the screen becomes dark.

Fast motion: action appearing faster than normal as a result of the film's having been moved through the camera more slowly than normal.

Flash back: scene interrupting the story to show past action.

Follow shot: dolly shot.

Frame: single photographic impression on the film. In each foot of 35 mm. film, there are 16 frames. This film passes through the motion-picture machine at the rate of 90 feet per minute, or 24 frames per second.

Full shot: medium shot.

Griffith last-minute rescue: crosscut.

Insert:cut-in.

Intercut: *Crosscut*

Iris: *mask.* See also *Iris-in* and *Iris-out.*

Iris-in: gradual appearance of the scene through an expanding circle.

Iris-out: gradual disappearance of the scene through a contracting circle.

Lap dissolve: dissolve in which the two sections of negative are overlapped, the end of the first fading out and the beginning of the second fading in.

Long shot: shot in which the camera is remote enough to take in, for example, fifteen or twenty people with room enough for them to move about and with space in the foreground.[1]

Low shot: shot in which the object is photographed from below.

Main title: see *Credit title.*

Mask: shot framed by a mask shaped, for example, like a keyhole or the lenses of binoculars—made by a cutout placed in front of the camera lens; sometimes called *iris.*

Medium-close shot: shot in which an actor standing would be cut off at about the waist.[1]

Medium shot: shot in which the camera is nearer to objects than in a long shot—near enough, for example, so that an actor standing would be cut off at the knees or below; also called *full shot* and *middle shot.*[1]

Middle shot: medium shot.

Mix: dissolve.

Montage: arrangement of shots to suggest a concept other than the sum of the concepts suggested in these shots. In one sense, *montage* means editing of the film. The popular, or Hollywood, conception of the term implies montage effects, as, for example, the tearing off of calendar leaves or a succession of shots of the same landscape in different seasons to represent the passage of time and shots of a train to represent a journey or a change of place.

Moving title: title that expands, contracts, or otherwise moves on the screen.

Oil dissolve: dissolve.

Out-of-focus shot: shot in which the outlines of objects are slightly indistinct.

Pan focus: focus which makes objects in both foreground and background appear in sharp relief.

Pan shots (from *panorama*): shot obtained by a vertical turning of the camera on its axis—hence the verb *pan.*

Photoplay: almost exact transference of a play to the screen, the camera remaining stationary as though representing the position of a spectator in a center orchestra seat.

Process shot: back projection.

Pull-back: shot in which the camera is pulled back from a close-up, close shot, etc. to reveal a wider angle; a form of tracking.

Reaction shot: shot to show the effect, on one or more characters, of something seen, heard, or otherwise realized.

Rear projection: back projection.

Reel: spool on which film is wound; also, amount of film on the spool—formerly about 1000 feet, now usually 2000 feet.

Scenario: plan for a film, including dialogue.

Scene: shot or series of shots unifying time and place.

Sequence: combination of shots or scenes to build up a particular effect.

Shot: episode or scene without a break in time or space, photographed without actual or apparent interruption.

Slow motion: action appearing slower than normal as a result of the film's having been moved through the camera faster than normal.

Soft focus: softening of the sharpness of line in varying degrees from a hardly perceptible difference to mistiness; an effect obtained by a gauze or a greased glass placed in front of the camera lens or by out-of-focus photography.

Spatial length: length of a shot in reference to the distance of the camera from the object photographed, as distinguished from *temporal length.*

Split screen: composite shot.

Split title: continuity title broken—usually within a sentence—by an intervening shot or shots.

Spoken title: subtitle.

Stereoscopic film: film giving a three-dimensional effect on the screen.

Still: photograph made from one frame; also, a series of similar frames casting a motionless picture onto the screen.

Strip title: printed matter superimposed on a shot, usually to translate dialogue into another language.

Subtitle: title in a silent film to print speech, to explain or narrate action, or to indicate locale. *Subtitle* is sometimes used to mean only speech, as distinct from *title,* which is more inclusive.

Superimposition: dissolve in which the light intensity of the overlapping scenes does not vary.

Switchback: crosscut.

Temporal length: length of a shot in reference to its duration on the screen, as distinguished from *spatial length.*

Tilting: perpendicular movement of the camera on its axis.

Title: printed matter projected on screen, apart from that in an insert or in a scene. See *Credit title, Moving title,* and *Subtitle.*

Tracking shot: dolly shot.

Trolley shot: shot in which the camera moves on a trolley.

Trucking shot: dolly shot.

Two-shot: close-up of two objects, as, for example, the faces of two actors.

Vignette: shot which does not occupy the whole screen but fades off around the edges.

Wipe: shift from one scene to another whereby the first scene appears to peel off, or to be similarly removed along a visible line, to reveal the second.

Zoom shot: shot in which the camera moves, or seems to move, quickly up to an object.

---

1 The terms *close shot, close-up, distance shot, long shot, medium-close shot,* and *medium shot* are relative.

Index